LARRY

TOMPKINS

www.**HERO**BOOKS.digital

BELIEVE

LARRY
TOMPKINS

WITH DENIS HURLEY

HEROBOOKS

PUBLISHED BY HERO BOOKS
1 WOODVILLE GREEN
LUCAN
CO. DUBLIN
IRELAND

Hero Books is an imprint of Umbrella Publishing

First Published 2020

A CIP record for this book is available from the British Library

ISBN 9781910827123

Cover design and formatting: jessica@viitaladesign.com
Ebook formatting: www.ebooklaunch.com
Photographs: Inpho and the Tompkins family collection

DEDICATION

To my wife, Orla
My daughter, Kate
And my son, Jack.
This is for you…

CONTENTS

ACKNOWLEDGEMENTS

GROWING UP IN the countryside, it was a simple life. Neighbours would head up to a farmer's field and kick football until dark. This, without me knowing it at the time, was the perfect foundation for the life that lay ahead of me.

To my late mother, Nancy and father, Martin; my brothers, Thomas, Joe, John and Martin, and my sisters, Jean and Mary, from the bottom of my heart thank you so much for being there every step of the way.

As the youngest of seven, I was told that I got the silver spoon in our family, but it didn't seem that way when we were playing against one another. My siblings tried their best to kill me.

Liam Hayes was always tormenting me on and off the field. He has been a good friend, and many times he asked me to think about writing my memoir. Many thanks, Liam. I have thoroughly enjoyed looking back on so many great moments.

To all the teams I have been played on – there have been quite a few!

A special thanks to the unsung heroes who devote their whole lives to training underage teams, and have touched my life in some way. I admire you greatly.

It has been 14 months now since Denis Hurley and myself first sat down and started talking. I did not realise there was so much to be done. Denis' knowledge and detail is incredible, but what else would you expect from a man from west Cork. A thorough professional. Sincere thanks Denis.

To all of the men and teams I have played with and against. It has been a great honour to have been on the field with so many outstanding footballers who have been coached by such dedicated and passionate people.

My days in the Big Apple brought me to a different level, as a footballer, and also as a man, and this is primarily due to all of the great men and women who make Donegal such a wonderful club, and especially to my outstanding friend and mentor, Donal Gallagher.

Donal's in-put to my life can never be fully repaid. I owe so much to this man.

Donal, thank you for everything.

The trouble with acknowledgements is that I realise that so many people who deserve my thanks might be overlooked. But I sincerely wish to thank everyone who has offered me their support and friendship down through the years. It is hugely appreciated, and always was, but especially I must mention JC Daly, Dave Carey and Tony Leen and his outstanding team at the *Irish Examiner* newspaper for their help on this book.

Finally, I would like to thank George Hatchell for supplying me with some precious photographs for this book, and also the following friends who gave of their time to be interviewed: Christy Collins, Francis Collins, Anthony Collins, Martin O'Mahoney, Mike Maguire, Niall Cahalane, John Cleary, Dr Con Murphy, Pádraig Dunne, Sean Sargeant, Mick Fitz, Ger Kavanagh, Dave Kavanagh and John Behan.

FINALLY, AND MOST important of all!

I would like to thank my wife, Orla for being my rock, and always being there for me in the good times and bad. Every step of the way, you have been an inspiration to me and our family.

To my daughter, Kate and my son, Jack, it's a real honour to be your dad. I am so proud of you both.

You both mean the world to me.

Larry Tompkins
August, 2020

I COULD NOT have been more fortunate in developing a real interest in sport in 1990.

My father, Jim had brought me to Kilbrittain's defeat to Valley Rovers in the Cork intermediate hurling final in 1989, carrying the flag my mother, Gretta had made - a yellow blanket married to black corduroy, but I didn't take a lot in and I don't recall much of the Cork City-Shamrock Rovers FAI Cup tie in March, 1990 either.

However, that summer brought the... Big Bang. The Republic of Ireland won the World Cup – well, West Germany took the trophy but Ireland might as well have won, for the fervour it inspired here – and Cork set off on their way to an historic double. I was there in Croke Park with my father (see us both below) for both victories, unable to appreciate at the time what a privilege it was but grateful with each passing year that doesn't bring a Rebel double.

For favourite players, I tended to gravitate towards captains. I had a No. 4 on the back of my Ireland shirt in honour of Mick McCarthy. I drew pictures of Tomás Mulcahy lifting the Liam MacCarthy Cup and it was a similar story with regard to the 1990 football captain, the man who had come from Kildare via New York to make Cork the best.

My father had nurtured the love of sport and my mother's influence turned me into a voracious reader. If I was unable to create a career as a sportsman – though I haven't ruled out making it as a professional golfer just yet – then becoming a sports journalist was a close second. I will be forever grateful to John McHale of the *Evening Echo* for giving me a shot in 2007 and even more grateful for allowing me the latitude to ghost-write Larry Tompkins' column in the paper in the spring of the following year.

Back then, we communicated over the telephone, with neither thinking that we would collaborate on a book like this one. The common factor in bringing this to fruition was Liam Hayes, publisher at Hero Books and, again, it is humbling for me to be entrusted with telling the story of a true footballing legend.

There was a period where Larry Tompkins was the best, most hard-working footballer in Ireland. I can't say the same about my qualities as a writer but I was more than happy to give it my best. The most valuable piece of advice I have been given is that, when you have a story, not to get in the way of it and ghost-writing is the same:

the tale is Larry's and so, hopefully, is the voice.

Those Monday mornings above the pub on Lavitt's Quay were something to get the week off to a good start and I can't thank Larry enough for the way he invested himself in the project. He arranged meetings with others who helped to add to the story and I am indebted to Jim Murphy, Dave Kavanagh, Gerry Kavanagh, Mick Fitzpatrick, Seán Sargent, Larry's brothers Tommy and Martin, John Cleary, Niall Cahalane, Martin O'Mahony and especially JC Daly for the assistance they provided.

Feedback came from valued friends, whose kindness I will try to repay. Fintan O'Toole, Paul Dollery, Mary White, Eoghan Cormican, Lisa Lawlor and Kieran McCarthy provided in-put which was welcomed and I must also express my thanks to Tracey Kennedy of Cork County Board.

Of course, I could not have managed any of this without the invaluable support of my wife, Jessica, who assumed the bulk of the parenting of our son, Johnny as I finished things off during the Covid-19 lockdown. To my own family, my parents and siblings, Susan, Lorna and James, and Jessica's family, Peter, Frances, Conor and Katie, thanks for everything.

I hope the finished product does all of my efforts, and all of yours, justice.

Denis Hurley
August, 2020

INTRODUCTION

I FIRST ENCOUNTERED Larry Tompkins 41 years ago.

We were young bucks in Croke Park, just 17 years-old, both of us consumed by the magic of a Croke Park which we did not see as an old, dilapidated stadium, which was well due to be smashed by a giant fist; an event that was just 20 years around the corner. No, running onto Croke Park from the dressing-rooms (dressing-rooms that were built 70 or 80 yards apart, allowing both teams a private 'chute' to take them onto the field) beneath the old Cusack Stand, was indeed magical. Neither did either of us notice much, I suppose, that the field of our dreams was lumpy and bumpy in places.

Larry was in the white of Kildare. I was in the green and gold of Meath. He was centre-forward in that Leinster minor championship game in the early summer of 1979 that we won. I was full-forward at the other end of the field, so we did not get to bump into one another. The following year we were both back out on that field in the Leinster minor final. Again, Meath won.

We won by three points, in the end. Larry hit the crossbar close to the finish and nearly pulled the game from the fire for his team. I was now in the middle of the field for Meath, so we did get to formally meet and introduce ourselves to one another with a shove or a shoulder, or a slap even, I suspect.

In building this book with Larry these last 12 months or so, and being honoured to be his publisher, I found out that he had totally forgotten that in that same game I missed not one penalty for Meath... but two. The first hit the butt of the right hand post down by the Canal End. The second was taken into the Hill 16 end, and the ball did indeed soar high and wide and land in the arms of the Dublin fans who were awaiting the meeting of Dublin and Offaly in the senior final.

We were still young bucks, teenagers. We were still immersed in the magic of the old home of the GAA, and no doubt each of us felt swamped by the images of the brilliant footballers we had watched out on that same field as us, on television sets and in person, down through those 18 years of our lives. We were experiencing the magic… and the mystery?

What would await us?

Next? And after that, and after that again?

OUR FOOTBALL LIVES moved on. And we became men. Larry still in white, me in green and gold still. But through the 80s we never got to meet in Croke Park again. We met elsewhere, in Newbridge and in Navan, and in other small towns around the country. But Croke Park still awaited our return.

When we did run back onto the same field, it was 1987, the entrance onto the field was a little wider, and we both appeared from the corner of the Canal End and the Hogan Stand, where the dressing-rooms were now situated. It was the afternoon of an All-Ireland final. Me in green and gold. Larry now in red and white.

Meath would beat Cork in two All-Ireland finals. Cork would beat Meath in one All-Ireland final, though Larry had already won his first All-Ireland medal by then. One final between Meath and Cork would also be drawn. Two All-Ireland wins each. It was a pretty fair return for both of us, all things considered.

How I got there, back to Croke Park for those All-Ireland finals against Cork in 1987, '88 and '90 was a journey without too much incident or drama. But, Larry?

How he managed it makes *his story* one of the greatest football stories ever told in the long, trampled history of the GAA.

And makes Larry Tompkins, the undisputed, the most formidable individual ever to play either of our great games. In my opinion, at any rate. How he got to Croke Park on the afternoon of an All-Ireland final… what he did to get there, yes, it took bravery and absolute belief.

It is not by accident that I asked Larry to consider the title 'Believe' for this memoir. Has anyone in Gaelic football or hurling ever believed in himself as thoroughly as Larry Tompkins?

I think not.

TWO YEARS BEFORE we got to battle in an All-Ireland final, I met with Larry in New York. It was late September in 1985. He was standing in the arrivals area in JFK airport, though he was not waiting for me.

I had travelled out to play for Monaghan on the Sunday in Gaelic Park, deep in the Bronx, where Larry was now considered a giant amongst Gaelic footballers. They talked about him being the... King of Gaelic Park.

That did not impress me greatly, though it was an achievement nonetheless becoming the No. 1 footballer in the city. Gaelic Park may have been a distant planet in the GAA's world, and one populated by a mixture of very fine footballers and mercenaries (like me arriving in on a jet plane for a couple of days' pay), average footballers and old footballers, but to win championships with the Donegal club took guts. It took self-belief.

Larry had clearly shown in New York – even though his Kildare career had ended prematurely; foolishly cut short by the blindness of the county board – that he was prepared to make himself the best of the best.

He still believed!

We spoke for 10 or 15 minutes that afternoon in the packed arrivals area in JFK airport. He was waiting to pick up a footballer, a young Kerry lad who had scored an important goal the Sunday before in helping Kerry defeat Dublin in the 1985 All-Ireland final. The Donegal club had brought him out to New York for a game.

Larry Tompkins was both this young man's reception committee and chauffeur. Larry was picking up a player who was of far lesser ability than himself, and someone who was going to be feted somewhat. And he was happy to do so.

Larry's life was in New York. He had made up his mind to remain through the rest of his young adult life in the embrace of possibly the soundest and most decent community of GAA people anybody could find, anywhere.

He never expected to ever play in an All-Ireland final himself. He had no idea whatsoever that two years later he would do so, and would play in a handful more after that. Neither had I any idea (after been trounced by 10 points in the Leinster semi-final that summer by Laois) that I would be so lucky, either.

I said my good-bye to him, and left him waiting.

And, I thought to myself... *He was a good one... Maybe the best footballer I had ever seen... Definitely the best I had ever played against!*

I ALSO THOUGHT he had settled for a life in a remote outpost. That I would possibly never see him play football again.

That, for Larry Tompkins, it was effectively over.

I would not see him on the field again, I thought, and neither would anyone else in Ireland, not in any game of any importance.

I had no idea what was living inside the man.

No idea whatsoever that he believed in himself more than any footballer I knew or had ever watched, and that given half a chance, given an inch, he would be more prepared than any footballer *I knew or had ever watched*, to prove himself one of the greatest athletes the GAA has ever possessed.

Such belief.

To first believe himself worthy of his Eadestown jersey. Then believe he had a right to slip a Wicklow jersey over his head.

To believe that he could do justice to a Kildare jersey.

To believe he would wear the Donegal NY jersey with rare distinction. And still not doubt himself when he came back to Ireland.

To believe he was the right man to accept a Castlehaven jersey.

And, to believe still, that the majestic red jersey of Cork should be his, and that he should be the man in that jersey to lift the Sam Maguire Cup.

Liam Hayes
Hero Books
August, 2020

PROLOGUE

New York, January, 1987

THE SUMMERS IN New York were so hot that you'd start work at 6am and, in the cramped dressing-rooms of Gaelic Park, you'd wait until just heading out on to the pitch to put on your jersey. The flip side of that was that the winters were cold and snow was a common sight, like on this particular night.

The snow didn't mean I gave myself a break from training, though.

After going to Jack Lalanne's gym on 231st St in the Bronx, I ran the hill in the nearby Ewen Park. Some nights, JC Daly from west Cork was with me but this time I was on my own, pounding up and down, over and over, just as I used to at Punchestown racecourse back in Kildare. I had helped Donegal to win the last two New York championships and we were gunning for three in-a-row.

I didn't go home for Christmas and I hadn't seen my parents for a while. You get a bit lonely when you are so far from home and Christmas and January magnify that. The letters from home were the only comfort I had.

New York was great, but there was a sense that I was missing something by not being at home.

I felt that I was playing the football of my life, however, and that I was in the shape of my life. I had become friendly with a gang of lads from Cork and all they ever talked about was football and Castlehaven. What had started out as slagging about joining them had grown more serious.

The snow kept coming but I kept going.

When I was done, I remember running into a shop to get a bit of shelter. I watched the traffic creep by and it was still pelting down. As I stood there, I decided that it was time. I needed to go home.

If I don't go back this time... I'll never go back.

I jogged back to the apartment, located at 3135 Godwin Terrace and, without a second thought, I knocked on 4F, Martin Connolly's door.

'Where's that bloody transfer form?' I was exhausted and soaked to the skin. Melting snow was running down my face,.

'I'll go back and have a cut off it,' I told Martin.

He stood at the door and he couldn't believe what I was saying.

But he had the form... and I signed it.

WHAT PEOPLE DON'T realise is that I wasn't coming back to play for Cork – all I had in my mind was Castlehaven. As well as Martin Connolly, there was Anthony and Vincie Collins, and Martin O'Mahony, all flying the blue and white flag high in New York.

The way they talked about it, it was the centre of the universe but as far as I was concerned it might as well have been Bangladesh. I had heard of Skibbereen and Clonakilty, but Castlehaven? I hadn't a clue.

After we won the New York championship in 1986, they had been saying I should join them, only as a bit of messing, but the thought of playing for them grew in my head. Once they saw I might be a interested, they chipped away.

It was a team with some serious players and as they reeled off all the lads they had – Niall Cahalane, John Cleary, Mick Burns, Michael Maguire – I was thinking they couldn't be half-bad.

Once I had made my decision, I left the rest to the lads in Cork.

Donegal would be travelling over to Ireland in May for a mini-tour and the plan was that I would stay on in Castlehaven after that. Francis and Christy Collins, brothers of Anthony and Vincie, were on the case and they had enlisted the help of the Cork county board secretary, Frank Murphy, who suggested that an inter-county transfer would be the most straightforward course of action.

▲▼▲▼▲

I ARRIVED IN Cork, and the Haven lads had set me up with a place to stay, and a job working with Christy Collins on Sherkin Island for the summer. But I was there to play football with Castlehaven. And that wasn't possible, as the Kildare county board had delayed signing my transfer form.

I had come home to play football.

Every day, I would pound the field, shoulder the goalposts, and push myself as hard as I could. The days turned to weeks, but there was still no sign of the signed transfer form coming back from Kildare. Every evening, I would walk down to the phone box near me, and ring my mother.

I was so frustrated. *What have I done,* I asked myself more than once. I was so close to jacking it all in. My bags were packed, ready to go home... home to New York.

My patience had worn thin.

ON FRIDAY, JUNE 12, the day before my birthday, the phone rang... it was Frank Murphy, looking to speak to me. He was a selector on the football team and they were playing Dublin in a challenge match in Parnell Park. He asked if I'd travel.

'Bring your gear... come up and it'll look good,' he said. 'The transfer will be gone through tomorrow.'

I said I'd do it, if that's what was needed.

I drove up to Kent Station on the Saturday, my 24th birthday. Apart from the Haven lads and Billy Morgan, I didn't know anyone else on the Cork panel but who was the first person I met on the train only Shea Fahy, my fellow Kildareman, who was stationed at Collins' Barracks.

That helped to break some of the ice. We arrived at Parnell Park, and Frank arrived into the dressing-room. He came over and shook my hand.

'Welcome to Cork...

'Your transfer went through an hour ago.'

PART 1

MADE IN KILDARE

CHAPTER 1

A YEAR AND a half later, the move to Cork could be classified as a qualified success.

I had helped Cork to win two Munster titles – the first time since 1974 that they had gone back-to-back in the province – and been honoured with two All Star awards, but we had lost two All-Ireland finals to Meath. With Castlehaven, the aim of winning a county championship remained a pipe-dream; since transferring in 1987 I had played two championship matches for the club, losing both.

Thankfully, everything would change for the better in 1989.

I would achieve what I been striving for; some of those aspirations relatively recent, others dating back to my childhood in Kildare.

▲▼▲▼▲

JUNE 13, 1963 SAW the Tompkins family of Greenmount, Rathmore, just outside Naas, welcome their seventh child, Laurence Christopher Bernard. How's that for a mouthful?

My mother and father probably thought they had had enough with six; Tommy, Jean, Mary, Joe, John and Martin, but then I came along. I was born in Holles Street in Dublin.

My mother, God rest her soul, was christened Ann, but people called her Nancy. Her maiden name was Wright. She was from a place called Castlemitchell, bordering Athy towards the Laois border. The Wrights were a fairly big name in Kildare;

her uncle, Paddy Wright played for Kildare and there was also a family link to the Donnelly clan, nine brothers who were all serious players.

She moved to Kildare and she was working as a cleaner just outside Naas. My father, Martin Sr came from Clonmore on the Wicklow-Carlow border, near Hacketstown and Tinahely. He would have played a small bit of football and there were 13 or 14 in that family. The farm couldn't take everybody, so my father moved away to get work. He moved to Naas and worked with a few local companies doing sand and gravel.

When my parents married, they lived in a place just outside Naas called 'The walls of Furness'. They had a little council house; there were probably four or five of the children born there before they moved. We were in the parish of Crosschapel and went to Mass there on Sundays, but while that was Blessington and in Wicklow, the home address was Kildare. It was the heart of the countryside.

Nowadays, you'd be into Dublin city centre in 40 minutes but my parents had no transport; neither of them ever drove.

Our mother and father were great workers.

He was in Roadstone for a long number of years. My mother had seven of us but she went out to work too, in a place called Telectron in Tallaght. She used to cycle two miles before she got a bus. My sisters would look after the younger boys. My mother had an old bike and she'd leave it behind the church at Crosschapel and get the number 65 bus from there.

She had to be in work for 8am so she'd be up at 5am, making lunches and preparing dinner. It was just non-stop, but my parents never complained and there were millions of people like that.

In later years, my mother told me how heartbroken she was that she didn't get to know me, as well as the others. I was only five years-old when she started work full-time.

My mother instilled in every one of us the ability to look after ourselves and to be able to cook. She was a fantastic cook and my brother, Martin became an incredible person in the kitchen. We had a bit of a garden at the back and we grew a lot of vegetables and had potatoes in a pit, covered in straw to preserve them for months.

We'd come in for the dinner, the big pot of potatoes would be put in front of the nine of us and if you didn't dive in early, you got nothing! My mother had the philosophy that if you get off on the right foot with food, it'll never leave you. To this day, my kids would want Chinese or whatever, but for me you can't beat the roast.

MY NATIONAL SCHOOL was Rathmore NS, which was in Kildare.

It took maybe 45 or 50 minutes to walk there in the morning; each of us just put the bags on our backs and we went.

When I was younger, my older brothers and sisters would have carried me some of the way. We had a neighbour down the road, Mick Molloy and he had lovely apple trees. If he saw us trying to rob any apples, he'd be out with the stick and he'd hammer us to get us off the trees!

We got electricity in the early 1970s and we thought it was unreal. We had to put in a septic tank and we didn't have the room, but the Sargents owned the field beside us and they had no problem with it going in there.

Everybody just helped one another out and the neighbourhood became very close. My kids hardly believe me now when I tell them we didn't have a television, electricity or running water, but you don't miss what you don't have. What we did have was a huge sense of community, with fantastic neighbours like the Sargents and the Fitzpatricks.

With so many kids of varying ages, we were always able to get a game of football going in the different fields we used.

I've captained four 'counties' – Kildare and Cork obviously, Wicklow vocational schools and Donegal GFC in New York – but the one least associated with football deserves some credit for my development too. The field we used most often was across the road and owned by the Finnegans, Bartle and his son, Batt.

They were originally from Kilkenny and big into hurling and GAA in general. They were the first to have a radio, a big old brown yoke, and on a Sunday we'd congregate there to listen to the matches.

There was a sizeable plot out the back, a good bit of land, and that's where we started playing. You could have 10 or 12 from the neighbourhood coming into Finnegans'. There was no mercy – my brothers used to mangle me and then tell me to get up! That became a massive foundation in terms of mental approach and sometimes a person forgets that.

If you look at a lot of people who've gone far in life, a lot of it comes back to those foundations. The attitude was... 'No mercy, toughen up and get on with it'. That's the way it was.

AS PART OF writing this book, I travelled back there to walk the road with Seán Sargent and Mick Fitzpatrick and the memories were still just as fresh.

Seán recalled a snowfall in the late 70s when his mother looked out the kitchen window and saw a shape running up and down the slope outside. It was me at 16 years of age – it wasn't just in New York that I trained in that kind of weather.

Kildare football was quite good at the time.

They had won the under-21 All-Ireland in 1965 and there were some great individual players but for whatever reason they didn't knit well together. They played in six Leinster finals between 1966 and '78, losing to Offaly, Meath and Dublin. Still, we took extreme pride in Kildare, and players like Tommy Carew and Pa Connolly.

My father took me in on the bus to some of those games and we often went to hurling matches too. I can remember when I was about six, watching Tony McTeague of Offaly, a genius of a footballer and a magnificent free-taker. And Tony Doran who was a giant at full-forward on the Wexford hurling team. Those fellas were like gods to me.

My first introduction to playing properly was under-11 with Eadestown. Naturally, I would have known a lot of the lads from Rathmore school and the playing in the field definitely stood to us. We didn't realise it then, but it was great practice.

The team was doing great but at that time we used to go on a small bit of a holiday once a year down to Galway, hiring a caravan. My mother's sister, Sid lived in Loughrea; her husband, Tom Kelly worked in the mines.

Tom was involved with the Galway football board and in 1973 I used to go along to training in Tuam to watch all these greats – Tommy Joe Gilmore, Jimmy Duggan, Johnny Tobin, John Dillon, Liam Sammon, Willie Joyce!

You'd spend an hour and a half just kicking the ball out to them but it was great. They got to the All-Ireland final that year, losing to Cork, as it happened.

Eadestown got to the under-11 final that year too, but I couldn't play in the game because I had to go to Galway. It broke my heart and they won the game without me, and that broke my heart even more. I was never a person that would be jealous of anyone and I love to see people winning or having things go right for them. I'd never knock anybody else's achievements but, all the same, that day hurt me.

I just couldn't get over it but it kind of drove me on even further.

I couldn't wait to get home, get back out on the field and kick the lard out of everyone. The matches on a Sunday helped to build that ambition too, conjuring images as we listened to that brown radio.

I'd be listening to Micheál O'Hehir saying the names of these stars and thinking... *Some day...I'm going to be in that radio too.*

On my Confirmation Day, and in need of a good haircut (top) and with my beloved mother, Ann. All the family together in Eadestown with the Sam Maguire and Liam MacCarthy Cups in Christmas 1990 (back, from left) Joe, John, me, Martin and Thomas and (front) Mary, my mother, my father Martin and Jean.

CHAPTER 2

IN CORK, WE were hurting in the winter of 1988 after losing two All-Ireland finals to Meath, but the hope was that a team holiday would recharge the batteries and help us to go again. Back then, everyone went to The Canaries.

There was no other place mentioned, so it probably wasn't a surprise in hindsight that it was where Meath went as well. There was a week or 10 days of an overlap.

I had gone straight back out to America to work following the All Stars and was heading from there to the Canaries, but back in Cork, the lads were on a war footing. Relations with Meath were not good and, apparently, it was said at a meeting that under no circumstances were we going to talk to them.

When I got out there, I said to Billy Morgan that I had known the Meath lads since I was 16 and whatever had happened in the games, so be it. 'I don't want to be going behind your back, but I'm going to talk to them,' I said.

It was tense, definitely.

We were staying in the same complex, both teams! Tensions were high between the two groups. No one spoke. I felt increasingly uncomfortable, as I had grown up with half of the Meath lads. I had enough of it, and finally I decided it was time to mix with both teams, which I did, beginning one afternoon on the beach when I left my group of Cork footballers and their wives and partners and went over and sat down with a few of the Meath boys.

The All-Ireland was over, in my book. We just had to get down to winning one ourselves.

Following the trip, I went back to America again and Cork were going well enough in the league, reaching the semi-final against Kerry. The winners of the league would get to go to New York for a special two-legged final in May to celebrate the 75th anniversary of the New York Board.

There had been talk that New York wanted special dispensation for me to play for them in the final, but Billy had other ideas and asked me to come back for the league semi-final against Kerry in April.

I was home on the Tuesday, and we were playing Kerry on the Sunday.

I didn't start the game; Shea Fahy and Barry Coffey were at midfield, but I was brought on after about 20 minutes and we won well in the end. Dublin were next up in the final. I was staying around for that. My older brother, Tommy had often said that we should go into business together in a bar or something. So, I used this time to see what was available on the market.

The Western Star was for sale along with a place down the Lower Glanmire Road across from the train station, Handlebars, a guest house and bar.

I was always the kind of person who felt that, if you didn't take a chance on something, you'd never know how it might have turned out.

Handlebars was on the front page of the property supplement; nine rooms. Back then, there were no parking restrictions at the train station and I was thinking that that would be a good thing in its favour.

I had a good bit saved and inside three or four days, I had it bought.

Tommy had been out in America with me for two years. He came back in 1989 and he was working in England. He was tied up on a job for another nine or 10 months; he'd see that out and come over then.

Nowadays, the banks would examine you left, right and centre, but we got finance handy enough, especially with a good down payment. My roots were going to be in Cork.

I was happy for that to be the case. I was enjoying it and I had built up great friendships with real, genuine people who were so supportive of that team. They were so enthusiastic about Cork football, which had been down for so long.

▲▼▲▼▲

AT UNDERAGE LEVEL, Eadestown amalgamated with Ballymore Eustace and Two Mile House to form St Oliver Plunkett's. There'd be a meeting point for games; you might have to walk to Rathmore to be picked up by Ned Hubbard or Jack Harold. The Mini was the popular car at the time; there could be 11 or 12 inside in it; you'd be hanging out the windows but that was just normal practice back then.

When I was 12, I played twice for Kildare under-14s. Tony Keogh was the man responsible for putting my name in circulation. He was the kind of fella who'd be at every match and know all that was going on. It was a special feeling to put on the white jersey.

This was the start of my journey.

Tony was with a club called Athgarvan, near The Curragh camp. He was a referee and took a big interest in Eadestown as he worked with the county council and came across a lot of the lads. He was so enthusiastic and it was easy to become friends with him – he was always there.

He never married and, after his mother died, he used to call up to our house. He'd call for a half-hour but we'd end up chatting for four or five hours and he loved my mother's homemade brown bread and scones. He took great interest in our family; he really liked Joe's style because he was such a no-nonsense player, and when I got on the Kildare teams, that connection became stronger.

I would have been deemed to have been a shy, laid-back individual in school, but I just loved sport and when you were one of the youngest out on the field, you had to fight for everything. My dream was to be the best footballer in Kildare. I wanted to be *in that radio.*

The Sargents' field next door to us was probably the flattest bit of land on the road, and we built goalposts with branches of trees and used chicken wire for the net. The chicken wire was also put to good use for a makeshift tennis court alongside the 'pitch' – anyone who wasn't playing tennis would be over playing football and vice-versa.

I fancied myself as a bit of a Bjorn Borg in the making, but football was always going to be the main focus. For example, people often ask me about my free-taking but simply that was something I practised every day from the start. I used to have competitions with the brothers because they were stronger than me but even at a young age I was kicking the ball as far as they were.

At that time, everything had to be kicked from the ground. When I was practising so much every evening, I was strengthening the right muscles. I was kicking with the old heavy laced football that got even heavier in the rain. As regards technique, people ask did I copy anybody and I would honestly say I had my own technique. I think if you try to copy someone, it's not natural.

I just prided myself on being the best at it.

Primary school passed, which was the best thing you could say about it. My brothers and sisters said I had the easiest of it, that the teachers had calmed down when I got there – I didn't always think they were calm!

One evening, my brother, Martin was being kept in but he made a run for it, out across the yard and hopped the wall and slid down a telegraph pole and away. What did the teacher do? She got into her car, drove after him, caught him by the head of hair and dragged him back into the car. Being the youngest, I was the one who got home first. First home had to pick the spuds from the pit and the other veg from the garden, and start the dinner for the nine of us. We all mucked in.

We attended St Mark's in Blessington, in Wicklow for secondary school, simply because it was two miles away and Naas was five. A minibus used to pick us up and drop us there

I liked metalwork and using my hands but I dropped French and Irish quickly enough. Of course, my favourite 'subject' was football. There was just one school team and no first-year had ever been picked on it but I was chosen.

There were great men involved. Paddy Hendrick, my woodwork teacher, really got the best out of players – he nurtured so many – but sadly he died young. Gerry McIntyre was my metalwork teacher but there'd be more talk about football than anything else in the classes. The deputy principal was Bill Hendrick, another great man, who took great pride in the school being successful.

Wicklow had won the All-Ireland vocational schools title in 1974. My older brother, Joe was on that team and the aim was to emulate him. When I was in third year, we won Leinster with my brother, John full-back, Martin at centre-back and me at centre-forward and I even got a call-up for the Wicklow schools hurling team.

Wicklow vocational teams definitely outperformed Wicklow county sides. We were lucky that there were so many good people, like Jim Murphy to give one example, who were really driving it.

IT BECAME MY life.

'What about the books?' my mother would ask.

I did the homework but, as soon as it was done, I rushed out the door. It was in my mind that I needed to get the best out of myself. Being in third year was a defining thing; the exams were coming up but I think it was around this time I realised that I was nearly the best in the school and the club.

It was always in me to work harder and that was the time to drive on. There were days when things mightn't go right for me but I'd dust myself down and move on. I would be the first to go back out the next day and spend six hours in the field practicing over and over, so I could get it right the next time.

I was 16 when I got the call-up to the Kildare minor panel.

Back then, it was a case of the panel being printed in the *Leinster Leader*, with the players to meet at a certain point. Kildare wasn't a county to go out of its way to make sure you were well prepared, but I just got on with it. This was the first time I met Shea Fahy.

Meath beat us in the Leinster minor championship quarter-final in Croke Park in 1979 and headquarters was an unhappy hunting ground the following spring too, while wearing the Wicklow colours. Blessington had won the Wicklow championship in 1978-79 and I was Wicklow captain as we beat Offaly in the Leinster vocational schools final and then I got my first win over Kerry in the All-Ireland semi-final in Cashel.

We were playing into a gale in the second-half and came from two points down with 15 minutes left to win by 0-11 to 0-9.

Unfortunately, we conceded 1-2 to Derry in the first six minutes of the All-Ireland final at Croke Park and lost by 2-8 to 0-6. I was marking the Derry captain, Damien Barton that day and it was a ferocious duel. Thirteen years later, he would win an All-Ireland senior medal for Derry against Cork, with me as a frustrated spectator.

IN 1980 THE KILDARE minor team made it through to the Leinster final, with Meath again in the opposite corner; a theme was forming, one that would last for what seemed like my whole career. Liam Hayes and Colm Coyle were on that Meath minor team in 1979 and '80; and I would see more of those two lads in the All-Ireland finals in 1987, '88 and '90.

It was a hell of a game in 1980, close all through. Near the end I soloed through and went for a goal but the ball hit the underside of the bar and came out.

Meath went up the field and got a goal, winning by three in the end.

I kicked seven points altogether and word came through soon after that I was wanted by the Kildare under-21s, who had drawn with Dublin in the Leinster final in Parnell Park and were awaiting a replay in Newbridge. I was named as a sub and was brought on shortly before half-time.

I kicked three points from play but we lost by 0-10 to 0-8, with Ciarán Duff and Barney Rock starring for Dublin. Then, that autumn, a petrol tanker drivers' strike would allow me to complete the treble of playing for Kildare minors, under-21s and seniors in the one year.

THE ARMY HAD been called in to deliver fuel during the strike and Kildare had a number of soldiers on the county team, including Tom Shaw, the free-taker. So it was at the start of October that I got a call from Kildare manager, Eamon O'Donoghue who was one of the nicest men I've come across.

His plea amounted to... 'I know you're very young but we've no free-taker'.

Kildare were away to Roscommon, who had lost to Kerry in the All-Ireland final the previous month. It was a bit surreal; here was I drafted on to this team, playing at Dr Hyde Park against the likes of Gerry Connellan, Pat Lindsay and Harry Keegan.

Roscommon gave us a big beating, 3-14 to 0-8, and I scored three points, one from a free. Connellan was a tough, hard marker. He was like a bulldozer coming out and I was like a piece of paper. Coming off the field that day I'll always remember Dermot Earley came up to me and put his hand on my shoulder.

'You're very young,' he said. 'You're going to be some player, but don't rush it too early.' He said that if I ever wanted help, he was down in The Curragh camp, only over the road.

I was in good spirits coming back, and Jimmy Magee was covering the game for RTÉ Radio. He said he had witnessed one of the youngest players to play senior county football.

'We'll be seeing more of him,' Jimmy told his listeners.

Now I was *in the radio* too, like all of the other famous names.

It was a big boost, to be a little fella on the bus with these giants from Kildare and to be mentioned by Jimmy.

SOON AFTER THAT, against Armagh, I was brought back to earth. I missed a penalty and we were beaten by a point in front of 13,000 people in Newbridge. That tore shreds out of me as I had practised morning, noon and night on these things.

I thought I hit it well, down low, but Brian McAlinden got down and put it around the post.

The only answer was to work even harder and that paid off just before Christmas when Eugene McGee, the manager of the Leinster team, called me in for Railway Cup trials. The competition was still a big deal back then and there was training twice a week, down in Tullamore.

Eugene was very intense; sometimes he'd hardly say hello to you, but I became very friendly with the Offaly players.

I was coming into contact with all of these big names and trying not to be overawed, but that was hard at times, like when Kildare lost to Kerry in the league in Tralee in March, 1981. They were still the best around and they beat us by 2-14 to 0-5. Before we headed back on the train, we went upstairs in Austin Stack Park for refreshments.

Eamon O'Donoghue was very friendly with Ogie Moran and Eamonn introduced me to him. Naturally, I was thrilled to meet someone like this and I asked him what he would do if he were me.

He started.

'I'd get myself into a gym... build myself up... do some more longer-distance running, up and down hills.

'That would bring you on a pile,' he promised me. I knew what I had to do.

I couldn't wait to get home and start.

A proud captain of the Wicklow Vocational Schools team receiving the Leinster VS Cup after we defeated Offaly in 1980; and the Blessington VS players on that team with our teacher, Paddy Hendrick (back row, right) were Pat Lennon, Peter Daly (back) and (front) Kieran Shannon, me and Jimmy Callaghan.

CHAPTER 3

I WAS NAMED at midfield for the 1989 'Home' league final against Dublin in Croke Park. In the dressing-room, I was thrown a No. 8 jersey – it was a new set with a special inscription for the final, but they were long sleeves and I hated that.

I had torn my ankle ligaments when I was young and I used to always strap them after that, so I had a scissors in the bag and I cut the sleeves. Because it was a final, we wouldn't have to give back the jerseys so it was fine.

Or at least it was until they looked at the programme and told me I was No. 9 and Teddy McCarthy was No. 8.

I threw the specially tailored jersey over to Teddy and he said, 'How the hell am I going to wear that thing?' They had to give him an old jersey but it didn't affect him, he had a great game. He kicked three points from midfield and we won by 0-15 to 0-12.

We played serious football that day.

Dave Barry hadn't been allowed play for a couple of years because he was playing soccer but Billy Morgan had got him back; Paul McGrath had a great game too.

Having lost two All-Irelands to Meath, it was a big thing to win a final in Croke Park. Okay, we had to go to New York to officially win the league, but it was a good bit of confidence injected into the team. When you do get over the line and get a cup, it gives you a boost.

A week and a half later and we were headed for New York, but not without some drama for me. Obviously, I had been going back and forth for a couple of years. I nearly knew every pilot and air hostess by that stage.

Not everybody was so lucky though and people had asked, innocently enough, 'How is it my son or daughter isn't allowed in… and this guy Larry Tompkins is over and back?'

The upshot was that a phone call was made to the county board by immigration and an official letter came from the embassy, saying that I couldn't enter the US again. Ordinarily, that wouldn't have been a huge problem, given that I had settled in Cork, but it was an issue when we had to go out for two games in Gaelic Park.

I told Frank Murphy that I had bought a business in Cork, that my New York days were done, and an agreement was made that when we'd arrive in Shannon the immigration officers would talk to me.

We arrived at the airport on the bus and there was a big delegation waiting, all in their uniforms. I thought I'd be checking in and taken for a chat, as had happened sometimes, but this was like I was a murder suspect. I couldn't even bring my bags with me!

I was escorted into a long room, with 10 or so people in there. The top guy was a Denis O'Riordan; American, but his people came from Clare. He knew the culture of the games at least and he started talking.

'Could you give me an outline of your time in America over the years?'

'I went over, I stayed for a few months and I came back.'

'Were you working over there?'

'Little bits of summer work.'

'Were you playing games in Gaelic Park?'

'Not much.'

Then he produced a photograph from a Donegal match against Cavan in 1986. 'Does that guy look familiar?'

I was kind of bluffing.

'Look, it was me… I played a few games. I was out there and I might have overstayed my visit once or twice but as you can see, I came back a good few times.'

'What do we tell the people that phone in saying Larry Tompkins is over and back?' he argued. 'That puts us under pressure.'

I had had business cards printed and I showed them, insisting I was coming back after the final. It basically ended with them saying that they'd be waiting to meet me when we landed back and if I wasn't on the flight, there'd be trouble.

I shook their hands and left. I got a fierce slagging from the lads, but I was in the clear.

▲▼▲▼▲

WHERE IN THE name of God was I going to find a gym in Kildare in 1981?

They weren't all that common.

I contacted Dermot Earley and asked if I could use the facilities at The Curragh Camp. While he said that civilians weren't allowed to use them, he'd explore a few avenues. I'd say it wasn't even a week later that he rang and said that two of their guys were opening a gym in Naas, on the Newbridge Road, near the Town House Hotel.

In the meantime, I was transitioning from school to full-time employment. I had it in my head all the time that I'd liked to have become a Garda, but I had given up Irish so that was a non-runner. My mother was always keen for us to have a trade and there was a guy involved with our club, Kevin McGoff who was a builder and he was looking for apprentice carpenters.

I gave him a call and started the next day, so that put paid to any notion of the guards!

Apprentices are slaves; you have to run for everybody, but I didn't mind, the work never bothered me. I was used to getting up and getting on with it. I had bought a Mini from a fella up the road, so I had some independence.

We were working on an estate in Kilcullen at the time and after work I'd go to the gym. I was very lucky to find these army guys thanks to Dermot Earley. They were very well trained instructors and they thought me how to use all of the equipment properly and how to push myself to the limit. I was working out for two hours, three times each week, after been on the sites all day. I would get home for 10pm and my mother, God rest her soul, would have the dinner on the table.

What was in my head was that I wasn't going to get pushed around by Kerry the next time – that day in Tralee, I had been marked by Jimmy Deenihan, Páidí Ó Sé and Tim Kennelly, and they were way ahead of me in terms of strength. On the nights I wasn't in the gym, I was training away with the club and the county.

After six or eight months though, I was in really good shape, eating right and, if I didn't have a game on a Sunday, I'd go down to Punchestown racecourse. There's a big hill there and I'd run up and down it for an hour or an hour and a half. Sometimes during the week, I'd go to Naas racecourse, beside where the pitch used to be, and run up and down there, using the streetlights to show the way.

My mother couldn't get over all this work I was doing.

'There's saner fellas locked up!' she'd say to me

I WAS ENJOYING putting in all of this effort, but playing for Kildare wasn't all that enjoyable for a lot of fellas. There were some fine players there like John Crofton, Paddy O'Donoghue and Ollie Crinnion, but the set-up left a lot to be desired.

The county board, in my opinion, was not losing any sleep over the fact that the senior team was losing, year after year. The board, in my experience, accepted that Kildare should be second best - and I placed the blame for that with the chairman, Pat Dunny and the secretary, Seamus Aldridge.

After training, Johnny 'Raw' Dowling would carry in crates of milk – it was supposed to be a pint for each player but, if you weren't in early enough, you'd get nothing as some lads would drink two!

That and a Marietta biscuit; there was no question of chocolate biscuits for us. My brother, Joe was a great player but he and a few others, like Gerry Power, decided not to bother playing because it had become a bit of a joke.

I'd be at training at 6.15 pm for a 7.30 pm start and there might only be 12 or 13 there. Before I bought my car, I'd have five and a half miles to get home and not one of them asked me how I was getting home?

I'd end up walking or thumbing, and get home at 11.30pm, with work again the next morning. In 1981, I played minor, under-21 and senior for Kildare, but none of the three sides made a Leinster final.

There was some solace with Eadestown, at least. The club had won the Kildare senior championship in 1970 – my eldest brother, Tommy was on the panel – but there had been a sharp decline after that and they had dropped to junior B by 1979. We got to the county semi-final that year, losing to Kill, but we won the Shay Dowling Tournament, named after one of our players who had tragically died in Australia in 1971.

Winning that gave us a bit of confidence and for 1980 my boss, Kevin McGoff took over. He wasn't a huge GAA man; he was more into running, but he had us super-fit and we got to the final against Nurney. We nearly lost but I kicked a free to equalise, and we won the replay by 2-14 to 3-9. My brother, Martin was captain and John and Joe played as well. Men were tougher back then. There were no dressing-rooms at most of the fields so we might tog out under a tree, and if we were lucky we might find a stream nearby to wash the muck off after a game.

Back up junior A for 1981, we made it to the final at the first attempt, against Naas – crazy to think that a town that size would only be junior – and they beat us, but we won Division 3 of the county league. It set us up nicely for 1982 and we reached a county final for the third year in-a-row, this time against our neighbours, Ballymore Eustace.

MY FATHER USED to go to Murphy's pub in Ballymore.

He'd dress up on a Sunday, go to Mass and then himself and our neighbour, Mick Fitzpatrick Sr, who was originally from Cavan, would head off and they might go to five or six matches, ending up in Murphy's, where the matches would be played over and over.

That was their kind of fanaticism – my father's brother, Dan was the same, he'd never miss a match. Before that final with Ballymore, my father told us in no uncertain terms that he couldn't show his face in Murphy's if we lost.

And we didn't – we drew with them, twice!

Martin was marking the Ballymore dangerman and he had been beaten the first two days. Before we left for the third match, my father said, 'Don't bother coming home here if you don't get the better of him!' Martin had to do a job and he laid him out early on.

We eventually won the second replay by 3-11 to 1-7. The pressure of playing our neighbours was huge, as I'd learn again with Castlehaven. They were big games with massive crowds and to come out on the right side of that was a real boost.

EARLIER IN 1982, I had experienced my first championship wins with Kildare, beating Kilkenny and then Wexford to put us into the semi-final against Dublin in Navan. The place was packed to the rafters and, just before the game, word filtered through that Brian Mullins – out for a year or so after an awful car accident – was starting for Dublin, even though he wasn't on the programme.

That lifted the Dubs, but Mullins hardly got a kick that day. He was marking Dave Kavanagh, an Eadestown clubmate of mine who had transformed himself. A couple of years before that, Dave couldn't get on our junior B team but he had been transferred to Tullamore in his bank job and started training with Tullamore Harriers and it brought him on a tonne. He was proof that attitude and application are the key attributes.

He was outstanding that day and early in the second-half we were four points ahead when I was caught with a heavy shoulder by Tommy Drumm. I had to go off on a stretcher; my shoulder was dislocated. Ten minutes later, John Crofton was sent off for a boot on Barney Rock and Dublin came back to win by a couple of points.

My mother was at that game and it was the last game she'd see me play. She couldn't handle the pressure of seeing me carted off on a stretcher. From that day on, she would walk the roads any time I was playing a match.

We lost in a Leinster semi-final in 1983 too, well beaten by Offaly, but it was a good year in the under-21 championship and we made it to the Leinster final against Louth in Navan. Pat O'Neill got an early goal to put us on top and Bill Sex was good too. I got five points and we won by five, 1-13 to 1-8.

We were looking forward to an All-Ireland semi-final against Derry.

However, I wouldn't be able to line out in that game as I was recovering from a coma.

Proudly displaying some Eadestown championship silverware with Martin, John and Joe; and reeling back the years in 2020 in Eadestown GAA grounds with my former Eadestown and Kildare teammate, Dave Kavanagh.

CHAPTER 4

THE REST OF the 1989 trip to New York went just fine. I played at midfield in the first game alongside Teddy and we won by 1-12 to 1-5. I was marking one of my great friends, Pádraig Dunne from Offaly, whom I had played with for Donegal, having also worked with him before emigrating. It was hammer and tongs throughout between us.

We were staying in Manhattan and the second game was a week later. We might have trained twice that week but there was a fair bit of downtime and we enjoyed ourselves. It was good to catch up with my buddies from my time there, even though I hadn't been gone too long! Teddy got itchy feet during the week and looked to travel up to Boston to meet a few friends. He said he'd be back by Saturday, and Billy Morgan left him off.

Saturday came and went with no sign of him and he wasn't back on Sunday, either. Steven O'Brien played midfield with me, it was another battle and we only won by a goal, 2-9 to 1-9.

Teddy showed up after 20 minutes – they wouldn't let him in at the gate so he had to pay in. What had happened was that he had actually come back on Saturday but met up with another friend of mine, JC Daly and they had enjoyed themselves. On the Sunday, JC tried to drop Teddy to the hotel but they missed the bus.

Billy wasn't too impressed with Teddy, needless to say; but there was another issue that had him even madder.

Colman Corrigan had suffered a nasty injury during the game, snapping his Achilles tendon. Everybody thought that it had been a dirty stroke off the ball by the guy he was marking, Willie Doyle from Carlow, but I knew Willie and it wasn't like him.

Afterwards, we went to a pub called Characters down the road from Gaelic Park; the New York lads were there too and there was a lot of aggro. Colman had been taken to hospital and Dr Con Murphy said it wasn't looking good, that he'd be ruled out for a year.

Billy saw Willie, and went bald-headed for him. There was a bit of a rumpus. When the thing settled, I was chatting to Pádraig Dunne and Willie, who was adamant that he hadn't laid a hand on Colman. Not long after that, my brothers were telling me about a match they were playing and the same thing happened. Martin had pulled up with nobody near him, his Achilles tendon after going. I was saying to myself… *Willie was telling the truth there.*

Later on, I was getting stuck into Teddy about not turning up.

'For God's sake Larry, you'd beat them fellas on your own!' he replied.

So we left it at that.

We had a good time out there and it built another bit of momentum ahead of the championship, waiting on the winners of Tipperary and Waterford. Before that, there were two sizeable pieces of business to attend to, within days of each other in early June.

I opened the pub on Wednesday, June 7.

It was the same day as the Epsom Derby, but I was far too busy to pay attention to Nashwan's win. The following Sunday, Tipperary were playing Limerick in the Munster hurling championship in Páirc Uí Chaoimh and the place was crammed. I still hardly had a clue about how to run a pub, I was only learning how to pull a pint.

I was lucky that Dan, a man in his 70s who had worked there under the previous owners, was behind the counter and trying to train me. It was bedlam but we survived; I'd say I was on my feet from 10 am until 1 am.

That day, I learned all about the business.

The previous night was arguably more important as I finally ticked an important box, a first championship win with Castlehaven.

Back in January, I had been made captain, but it was kind of strange as three of the four lads in New York who did so much to convince me to transfer – Martin Connolly and Anthony and Vincie Collins – wouldn't be coming back for the championship. Martin lived in San Francisco, which was double the journey New York was, and the Collins lads had a business that they couldn't leave. I felt bad for them; here was I as captain and they couldn't come home again.

We had been drawn against either St Nicholas' or Carrigdhoun and Nick's won that game in April, so we played them in Ballinascarthy on June 10. Nick's were never easy to beat and 10 minutes into the second-half, they were three points up.

John Maguire took a short kickout, the ball was intercepted and kicked into the net. Niall Cahalane was injured, he was on the sideline on crutches, and it looked like the curse was going to continue.

We got six points in-a-row to go ahead by three, but they got two back and we were hanging on by the end, 0-13 to 1-9. The relief was huge. Coming off the field, my jersey was ripped to pieces. It was a very physical game, and I was till revved up. I was pushing through the crowd and I stormed into the dressing-room and turned over the table in the middle of the room. Then I put it back upright, and jumped up on it.

'No one go into that shower!' I shouted. 'I want to talk here!' Needless to say, there were a few curse words thrown in.

'This is my first championship win... but by God, we're going to win the county this year!' They thought I was off the wall, but I was convinced that it was going to be a serious year for us. Later, Finbar McCarthy told me his wife, Mary saw me coming off and said to him, 'That Tompkins fella is a mad man... I wouldn't like to cross him'.

▲▼▲▼▲

WHEN WORK WITH Kevin McGoff had gone quiet, I got a new job with Martin & O'Shea, so I did the last two and a half years of my apprenticeship with them. My sister, Jean was working in the office there, so she had got me in.

The 'Martin' side of it was Brendan Martin, who was a real GAA man.

He was a big supporter of ladies' football and the cup presented for the senior ladies' All-Ireland was named after him. He employed Pádraig Dunne from

Offaly as well and that's how I got to know Padraig and become friends. We were building a lot of schools at the time, in places like Jobstown and Clondalkin, as well as Cheeverstown House in Templeogue, a facility for providing services to people with intellectual disabilities.

When I was doing my time, you had the option of doing a three-month stint in the College of Technology in Bolton St or doing one day a week and I opted for the latter. I used to go in on a Wednesday and undertake the various studies in mechanical drawing, maps, designs of houses, foundations and so on.

On rainy days I'd get the bus and sometimes I'd run into Eugene McGee, who had been my manager with Leinster for three years by this stage, but he'd walk past without hardly saying hello.

I'd be wondering if I had done something wrong but the Offaly lads put me at my ease; they said he was the same with them! When I was in Dublin, I'd often go into Easons on O'Connell St and browse through running books to teach myself how to improve my fitness. It was there I read about people who excelled, from Mick O'Connell to Muhammad Ali. I also kept a few quotes from Ali, to live by.

So things were going well again on the work front and they were as good as ever for Eadestown in 1983 as we made it to a county final for the fourth year in-a-row. The jump to intermediate after winning the junior A didn't really faze us and we beat Naas in the semi-finals to get revenge for the loss in 1981. We were up against Castledermot in the decider and it was obviously a huge game as we felt we could compete at senior.

We proved that with a great win, 3-11 to 1-9, and I scored 1-6 – but I can't remember much, or any, of the match. Just before half-time, a Castledermot player came running from the other side of the field and lamped me with an elbow into the head. I was blindsided and staggered a bit, but I played on after having a drink of water.

I've seen the match back on video and, after we won, you could see in the presentation that I wasn't really with it. I must have had some of my senses as I made it to the dressing-room. One of my brothers came over to check if I was okay.

I told him that I was kind of seeing black spots, and my vision was blurred.

I decided I'd go in and have a shower... that's the last thing I remember.

I COLLAPSED AND an ambulance had to be called.

It had to go through the crowds leaving the stadium with the sirens blaring. Thanks to Ger Kavanagh, I was rushed to Naas General Hospital, where I was in a coma for nearly 36 hours. It was awful for my family.

My mother had to come in to sign documents and I was having scans and MRIs. It turned out that I had a hairline fracture to the temple bone. I woke up two days later. I didn't know where I was, my head was bursting. I couldn't speak or get my focus for a few hours but I could see an outline of my mother and Martin. They were asked to leave while the doctors checked me out and it was a good few hours later before they were let back into the room. Then, Martin told me how and why I was in the hospital.

The joke about the hospital in Naas at the time was that you'd go in well and come out sick, but I can't say enough about the treatment I received in there.

I went to Dublin to see a specialist and I was told that it was a case of seeing how things went in terms of me playing ever again, never mind in the All-Ireland under-21 semi-final against Derry.

We all knew who the culprit was but I never met him or got an apology from him. That was the way it was back then, you went out on the field and you accepted that it was going to be a battle. In any case, my mother blamed my brother, Joe, who was supposed to be the enforcer looking after the rest of us.

'How did you let this happen?' she was asking him.

I travelled up on the bus with the Kildare under-21 team for the game against Derry, which was played in Clones. It was tough to watch and not be able to influence things. It was nip and tuck and went down to the wire, but Kildare lost by 0-11 to 1-6. Derry went on to lose to Mayo in the final after a replay and it felt like one that had got away.

I felt very sorry for Tony Keogh, who was in charge of that team. He was a football fanatic; he would go to watch the top teams train in order to get ideas. I can remember being at Leinster training in the pouring rain and he'd be there on the bank. He nurtured a lot of Kildare lads to a level of football they didn't think they could play and it was a pity that there wasn't an All-Ireland as a reward. He was the one fella driving the whole thing.

For me, it was a case of rest and recuperation, though there was some joy as I was named the Kildare Footballer of The Year. I was out of work for six or seven weeks but Brendan Martin was a great guy, he understood the severity of it and he told me to take things easy, though I was always keener to work than to put my feet up.

Gerry McEntee, the Meath player, was working in the Mater Hospital at the time and he ensured I got the best of treatment there. He was keen that I take things slowly, but obviously that was frustrating.

For a couple of months, I followed the guidelines but then I started going back to the gym, doing a small bit to get gradually back into it.

I said to Gerry that I felt good but he reminded me that, when you push things, your head will always find the weakest spot. I realised I had been getting headaches when I worked too much so I had to ease back again.

After Christmas, I was feeling better and more confident.

At the beginning of February, Kildare played Dublin in the league in Croke Park and I was named as a sub and came on after quarter of an hour. I was a bit wary and there was talk of me wearing a helmet, something like the scrum caps that rugby players wear now, but it was felt that that would make me a target. The best thing was just to play away like normal and thankfully everything went alright.

That game helped to convince me that things would be alright again. I bought a bicycle to help with my training and on the days I had college in Dublin, I cycled in – it used to take about two hours. The fresh air definitely helped from a psychological point of view and I went back out pounding the hill at Punchestown too.

Looking back during that time, I felt that I might never play again. I was having headaches, and there were black spots in front of my eyes. I was often dizzy and disorientated. But, I did not tell anyone and kept on pushing forward, hoping the symptoms would simply go away.

I HAD MY first foray into coaching with Eadestown that year.

Even though I was still only 20, I wasn't afraid to demand a lot from lads and maybe they found me a bit too direct at times! At the same time, I had seen how someone like Dave Kavanagh had developed so well and I was keen for guys to get the most out of themselves.

It was a short year for Eadestown back at senior level as we lost to Kilcock in the first round of the championship in early June. I obviously didn't know it at the time but it was my last championship game for the club.

Unfortunately, they would have no Tompkins on the team within a few years as a dispute arose when Joe was wrongfully sent off in a game and the club didn't back him up. The rest of the lads ended up transferring to Two Mile House.

A week prior to that Eadestown-Kilcock match, Kildare played their only senior game of the summer of 1984, beaten by Laois, and the under-21s lost in the middle of June, 0-10 to 0-9 against Dublin, who would go on to win Leinster. I was captain of St Oliver Plunkett's, the Eadestown and Ballymore Eustace underage combination, as we made it to the Kildare under-21 county final but we lost by 2-10 to 0-11 against Naas.

KILDARE HAD JUST about stayed up in Division 1 of the league at the end of 1983-84, needing to beat Offaly in a relegation play-off, but we started well in the following campaign in the autumn of '84. One game that stands out is a win over Kerry, played in Athy to mark the opening of their pitch. I scored 1-6 and, given how tough I'd found it against Kerry in Tralee back in 1980, it really felt like I had got myself to a higher level.

For 1985, Bobby Miller was in charge of the Leinster team for the Railway Cup, replacing Eugene McGee, who had been in charge since around 1978. We were training away in Clane, preparing for the semi-final against Ulster, and there was a challenge game arranged against Dublin in Parnell Park.

Brian Mullins had an absolute blinder for Dublin that day, so much so that Bobby asked him on to the panel. It was the only thing Mullins had never won in his career and he said that he'd play if he was made captain, that he'd guarantee Leinster would win it – which hadn't happened since 1974.

The crowds were waning but it was still a prestigious competition among the players. Mullins brought a real intensity to training – one bad pass and he'd bawl you out of it. Guys were in awe of his presence. We beat Ulster in the semi-final and we were down to play Munster in the final on St Patrick's Day.

We met in The Ashling Hotel, just across the road from Heuston Station, and Mullins was geared up. He spoke to each of us individually.

'Your job is to kick the ball over the bar,' he informed me. 'I'll do the ploughing.'

When we got to Croke Park, the place was locked but Mullins wasn't in the mood for waiting and he hopped over a fence to get in. In his team-talk before the game, Bobby Miller spoke a lot about Jack O'Shea. This did not go down well with Mullins, who turned over the physio's table with annoyance.

'Don't ye worry about Jack O'Shea, I'll look after him!' he roared.

In fairness to him, he backed it up. He put in a Man of the Match performance that day. It wasn't a great game and Munster were poor but we did the job; we won by 0-9 to 0-5. This was the last time that the Railway Cup was played in Croke Park, with the All-Ireland club finals taking over from the following year. Still, we had done it.

Afterwards, we were at the victory function and I was chatting to Jack Boothman, a great friend and neighbour of my family and a man who would go on to become GAA president a decade later. Mullins came over with the cup and plonked it on the table.

'I don't want to rub it in your faces... but ye don't win too many of these, so take it away,' he said to us.

He had done what he had to do. I suppose he saw that Meath were coming and knew that this was his swansong. I brought the cup to Blessington and a few other places.

I had it for a few months before anyone came looking for it.

Unfortunately, while things had gone well on the pitch that spring, work was slackening. Things had bottomed out and, whereas Martin & O'Shea had around 1,300 workers at one stage, it was down to the bare bones. In fairness to Brendan Martin, he kept me on for an extra month or so to see out my apprenticeship. Around the time of the Railway Cup, I finished up and was let go.

It was the same for my brothers as the recession bit. Joe was the only one of us working; he was in Roadstone where my father was. My father had got him in initially as an apprentice fitter mechanic, but otherwise it was complete and utter wipeout everywhere.

Imagine a winter's day and it raining, and all of us tradesmen at home, looking out the window with nothing to do.

One saving grace was that there wasn't a huge problem with people over-borrowing like the recession in the 2000s; you just worked and made your few bob and saved your money. Still, Dublin just shut down. It started around 1983 but by '85 it was widespread and there was massive emigration.

It never really entered my head to leave, even though it'd be on the news every night. I had the feeling all the time that something would pop up.

One day, I got the bus to Dublin, just to go in for a walk around the place.

I was walking over O'Connell Bridge and I met Mick Wright, who played for Offaly. He was a journalist and worked nearby. He asked how I was getting on and, when I said I was out of work, he mentioned he had played in America the previous summer.

He had played for Donegal and really enjoyed it, and said that they were always looking for players.

He asked if I'd be interested and I didn't rule it out, but we just kind of left it at that. Then, a week or so later, I got a phone call from Donal Gallagher, who was involved with Donegal. He had got my number from Mick.

'We're playing Sligo at the weekend... will you come over?' he asked me.

'I will,' I told him, immediately. 'Sure I'll see how it goes.'

Scoring a point from a free for Kildare in Croke Park in 1981; and playing against Kildare some years later when I returned from New York (here I am challenging Martin Lynch as Niall Cahalane comes in to support).

CHAPTER 5

WE WON OUR 1989 Munster football semi-final against Tipp in Páirc Uí Chaoimh and the final was in Killarney. It's amazing, but Cork had never before won three in-a-row in Munster. They did two on the bounce twice when Billy Morgan played but, in 1968 and '75, Kerry came back to deny them the three.

Kerry started well and they went 0-4 to 0-1 up but we got going, slowly enough. It was level at 0-4 each when they had a great chance. Timmy Fleming and the Bomber Liston linked up well and Fleming tried to put Maurice Fitzgerald in for what would have been a certain goal. I was midfield that day but I was back there defending, and I just got a hand in and tipped it over his head.

We only won by three points in the end, 1-12 to 1-9 – it wasn't a cakewalk but I felt that we had played really well and to win three in-a-row was sweet.

Of course, that wouldn't matter much if we didn't go all the way.

We had built ourselves up for Meath again in our heads, except Dublin won Leinster so we'd be playing them in the semi-final. Mickey Kearins, the Sligo great, would be refereeing it and a few of us had got to know him from the All Star trip in America earlier that year, out around New York, Cape Cod and Boston.

There was a good social side to that and we got on well with him.

Jokingly, I said to Frank that he should get Mickey to ref all of our games! He would end up being a busy man for the semi-final against Dublin.

▲▼▲▼▲

ON CHRISTMAS NIGHT 1984, Dave Kavanagh rang with some horrific news – Matt Connor of Offaly had been in a car accident.

Matt was somebody I had become very good friends with through playing for Leinster in the Railway Cup and there was a good rivalry between us as the papers would list the national league top scorers and we were always battling each other near the top. What a footballer he was – you'd go to a Walsh Island game just to see Matt, he was worth the admission alone.

He could do extraordinary things with a football. He was only 24 at the time and only reaching his peak and this news hit everyone.

On St Stephen's Day, Dave came up from Tullamore and we went to see Matt in Dr Steevens' Hospital in Kilmainham. At the time, he was in good spirits; he thought that he would be fine. Soon after that, though, he was moved to Dun Laoghaire as things weren't looking good and it emerged that he would be paralysed from the waist down.

Two charity matches, hurling and football, were arranged for Tullamore on Easter Monday, April 8 – the All Stars against the Rest of Ireland in each case. I was chosen on the All Star football team as a replacement for Mikey Sheehy, who was unavailable.

It was in early April of 1985 when Donal Gallagher rang me.

Donal was an accountant from Killybegs and he was the man in charge of Donegal GFC in New York. The way the championship in New York ran was a league system before the knockout stage, and their first match was Sligo. I agreed to go to New York to play that game and see what it was like.

But, before that, I had the fundraiser for Matt. It was an important game and an emotional one. It was a scorcher of a day and O'Connor Park was flooded with people. It was an occasion that I'll never forget. The reception that Matt got showed just how special he was to so many people all over Ireland.

A few years later, I met Matt again.

He was invited out to New York by the Offaly Association to be Grand Marshall for the St Patrick's Day parade. The same week Pádraig Dunne, the former Offaly All-Ireland winner, organised tickets for Madison Square Garden, for a boxing event.

The three of us headed off to the Garden. We had great seats and watched a few of the early fights, but when it came to a match in the middleweight division there was some friction in one section of the crowd and some fighting broke out there. We were caught in the middle of the action.

Myself and Padraig were in our seats, and Matt was situated in the aisle in his wheelchair. We panicked, worried for Matt's safety, and our own in all honesty. Chairs were being thrown through the air at this stage. Within minutes, police and security were everywhere. Sirens were wailing and whistles were blowing, and people were being dragged out and arrested.

We rushed out of our seats; Padraig on one side, me on the other, and we grabbed Matt's wheelchair and lifted him up into the stand, towards an elevator. The elevator doors opened, and we squeezed inside, just in the nick of time.

TWO WEEKS LATER, I played centre-forward against Sligo and we won.

Donegal were keen to hold on to me and they said that they'd sort me out with work over there. It was a tough decision as I was a real home-bird.

Nowadays, when someone goes to America, it's like going up the country but back then it seemed a whole world away. At the same time, another part of me was thinking that I'd go over for a few years and save a bit of money.

I was 21, going on 22. Here was a chance, an opportunity. My brother, Tommy told me to go for it and I said to my parents that I'd go over for the summer and see how it went.

When I was back home, Donal rang me again to see what I thought? I said to him that I would love to go back but I was committed to playing with Kildare in the first round of the championship. However, just after that, as a replacement All Star, I would be going to America on that trip a few weeks later for a couple of games against Kerry, who were the All-Ireland champions.

The plan was that I would stay out there after that rather than come back. The Kildare manager, Eamonn O'Donoghue had been very disappointed when I told him that I was going to America. I told him that he was a gentleman and that I felt that I was letting him down, but explained that I had to make the move. I said, however, that I would commit to coming home for the Leinster quarter-final against Meath in Pairc Tailteann at the start of June.

I just had one condition; he had to make sure that the county board had a return ticket to New York for me on the Monday after the Meath game.

Four weeks later, Kildare played Wicklow in Newbridge in the first round of the Leinster championship and we won by five points. I had been made captain for 1985 and I obviously didn't know it at the time but it was the last winning match I would play for my native county.

I headed off on the All Star trip, San Francisco first and then on to New York. John Crofton was the other Kildare player travelling.

THE MIX OF hurlers and footballers meant that I got to know the likes of George O'Connor from Wexford and Christy Heffernan of Kilkenny, guys you wouldn't otherwise get a chance to meet. Jimmy Gray, a former Dublin county board chairman, was part of the travelling party too and I was telling him of my plan to stay over.

'Jesus, you'll get killed!' he said,

'New York football is tough… there might be a referee, but he won't blow the whistle.'

My mind was made up, though.

I moved into a place in the Bronx. Donal had an apartment on Godwin Terrace – a few years later, the actress Saoirse Ronan would spend some of her early life in the same apartment. Pádraig Dunne had also stayed out after that first trip and he was there with his wife, Mary who had come out as well.

I was on the bottom floor, on the left-hand side, 1F I think it was. There was no elevator there, so I was glad not to have to climb the stairs – it was a long way up after a hard day's work or a training session!

My first job was gutting out the basement of a travel agency, along with another carpenter, Mick Hannon who had played for Cork. The travel agents were expanding and wanted to use the downstairs so we were clearing the whole place out to put in shelves and worktops.

While the football might have been tough in America, the carpentry was fairly straightforward. All you needed was a level because everything comes like a jigsaw, something like you'd get in Ikea, you just slot it all together. Back home, you'd have big sheets of timber and have to cut them up and join the parts together.

The more we cleared out this basement, the more we were picking up this smell.

Eventually, we found the source in the corner… a dead snake, five or six feet long. Seemingly, he had come in through the downpipe from the sewers and we had to call a pet store to get him removed.

The stench remained, however, and people in apartments three or four floors up from the travel agents had to spend fortunes to get rid of the smell. It was a nice eye-opener!

The money was an eye-opener, too.

I was on $18 or $19 an hour and if you went over 35 hours for the week, you were on double-time. The highest-paid were electricians, on around $21 an hour, and a dollar was close to a punt at the time – I can remember, as I was sending back a good bit to my mother. Back home, fellas were on IR£5 or £6 an hour, it was a different world.

Another thing about New York was that the connections I made were unreal. Even if you weren't into GAA, you'd go along to Gaelic Park as it was like a community centre. People looked out for each other with jobs and the like.

THE TIME CAME for me to fly home to Ireland, and play for Kildare against Meath.

I still had the return part of the ticket from the All Stars trip and had checked with a travel agent that I could transfer that for a minimal charge. I did that to come home, thinking I'd get a return ticket the other side to come back.

After I changed my ticket, I met Donal for lunch in the Piper's Kilt. I had often mentioned to him my worries about the Kildare county board and the way they handled things. That day was no different, and I was concerned that there would be no ticket back to New York for me after the game, and that I would be left high and dry.

Two days before I was due to fly home, Eamonn rang me and told me that everything was organised. The board had assured him that they would have a return ticket. I stressed to Eamonn that I had to be on that flight on the Monday, as I had to be back at work in New York on the Tuesday morning.

I left New York on the Friday, and my brother, Tommy picked me up at Dublin airport. I was not feeling the best. I was suffering from a stomach bug, but I had to play the game.

I did okay in the game, but Meath were turning into a force in Leinster and they beat us, 0-13 to 0-7. I came out of the shower in the dressing-room and I could see Eamonn heading towards me with a face of dismay. For a minute, I thought it was because we had lost.

Then he hit me with a bombshell.

'They've told me they have no ticket for you to go back to New York!'

Eamonn was distraught on my behalf.

He told me that the board said they would see me in The Beechmount Hotel, in the middle of Navan town, where we were having our after-game meal. I got dressed, and stormed out of the dressing-room, not saying a word to anyone. Tommy drove me to the hotel.

I walked in and went straight to the room where the food was being served. The minor football team, and the two members of the board I needed to see were in there, Pat Dunny the chairman, and Seamus Aldridge the secretary. They were eating.

'HAVE YOU GOT my ticket?' I immediately asked them. Aldridge did all the talking. There were heated words. Bottom line, there was no ticket. I was so angry. Finally, they agreed to write me a cheque for a ticket. I told them they would never see me in a Kildare shirt again. I stormed out of the hotel and went straight home.

The next morning, Tommy brought me to the airport. As I was checking in, the lady behind the desk asked me if I had booked twice?

I had no idea what she was talking about.

It quickly transpired that Donal Gallagher in New York was after booking me a ticket. That gesture meant the world to me, and it also told me everything about the quality of people I was going to have in my life in the immediate future.

I gave Tommy the cheque and he knew what to do, he returned the cheque to the county board and made it clear I would never return.

But I got on the plane heartbroken.

I was thinking of the great players I knew in Kildare, people like Paddy O'Donoghue and John Crofton and, of course, Dave Kavanagh from my own club. They were just a few, but there were so many players I knew I would miss. Also Billy Dunne, whom I'd miss for our chats after games! What would they think of me…

After the seven-hour flight, we touched down in JFK Airport, I knew I had a new challenge in my life to look forward to and meet head on.

Parading around the field in Gaelic Park, New York before the 1985 senior championship final against Sligo, which we won (here the celebrations begin out on the field). And (below) enjoying the victory with Offaly All-Ireland winner, Padraig Dunne who also travelled out with me to the Big Apple in '85.

PART 2

BUILT IN NEW YORK

CHAPTER 6

CORK WERE MOTORING well in 1989 and so too were Castlehaven, with the false starts of 1987 and '88 forgotten.

In July, we had played Carbery, the west Cork divisional side, in the quarter-final of the championship down in Bantry and we beat them off the field. To me, it was the first sign that, even though we were missing the New York lads, we were serious.

We were winning matches and gaining momentum.

Duhallow, another divisional team, from the north-west of the county, were to be our opponents in the semi-final, but before that game would take place, it was back to the quest for Sam Maguire with Cork.

WE PLAYED DUBLIN in Croke Park on August 20.

It was a savage day, with a gale blowing. Dublin had it behind them in the first-half and they were all over us early on. After a quarter of an hour, we were seven points down.

Vinny Murphy had got a goal for Dublin and we were really on the rack.

Our friendliness with Mickey Kearins didn't necessarily mean favourable treatment, either. According to Jim O'Sullivan's report in *The Cork Examiner*, there was a blatant charge on me and a sliding tackle on Jimmy Kerrigan that went unpunished. It was fairly robust stuff.

Nearly 17 minutes had gone when I got our first score and, despite such a slow start, we were ahead by half-time, thanks to two penalties.

John O'Driscoll was fouled for the first one; he waltzed through and would have scored a goal only the whistle had gone. John Cleary took the penalty and he was cool as a breeze, he gave John O'Leary no chance.

Then he did it again when we got another penalty, even if that one was a bit more debatable; I think it was O'Leary who was punished.

Teddy McCarthy put us ahead, 2-2 to 1-4, and just before half-time Dublin's Keith Barr was sent off after a tussle with Dinny Allen. Dinny was our captain and, at the start of the second-half, he and the Dublin skipper Gerry Hargan were called together by Mickey Kearins and told that if the game continued the way it was going, he'd have to take serious action.

That helped to calm things down.

I acted as our spare man.

I stayed around the half-back line and we were on top at midfield. Dublin pressed late on and we only scored one point in the last 13 minutes.

The lead was down to three points near the end when Joe McNally pulled on a ball and it just trickled past the post and wide. I kicked a late free and we won by 2-10 to 1-9.

It wasn't a convincing win, given the strong wind and them being down to 14 but we had got into an All-Ireland final and that was the main thing.

▲▼▲▼▲

OVER IN NEW YORK, Donal Gallagher had apparently canvassed the opinion of the Donegal team as to whether they'd be willing to have me on board. Martin O'Mahony's first question was whether I was a back or a forward and, as an attacker himself, he nearly voted against me joining!

Gaelic Park was on 238th St and for training we were two blocks further down on 240th, a place called Van Cortlandt Park, where you'd see a pile of teams training – American football, baseball, Gaelic, soccer; you'd get a patch and work away.

There was also a massive cross-country running trail through the woods; I got to know that during the time I was there. Later on, we found a place in Randalls Island, down near Giants Stadium. We felt it was better to be away from Van Cortlandt Park as you could be training alongside the team you were playing the next week.

Donal was a perfectionist in terms of organisation.

Donegal hadn't won the championship since 1978 so there was a big push on when I got over there. As well as Donal, you had a lot of other good guys. There was Mike Cassidy, a retired police officer who owned a few bars; Danny Doohan, who owned a business or two as well; and Mike Meehan, another great fella from Donegal. Phil Brennan too.

They knew what it was like to leave home and New York wasn't called the city that never sleeps for no reason – you could go wrong just as easily as you could go right. Having a good structure was important, to make sure guys were organised.

I'm not saying every fella went right, but our team was full of guys who were committed to succeed, on and off the field. These people were giving you the start but after that it was up to yourself.

New York changed me, hopefully for the better.

This was my new challenge and I was determined to be the best. I was driven to succeed. I was hearing stories that Frank McGuigan, the former Tyrone legend, was the 'King of Gaelic Park' but I wanted to change that.

The Bronx became my new training ground. The cross-country track in Van Cortlandt Park became my daily run. I would often have strong challengers against me, the likes of Kevin Madden and Padraig Dunne, with JC Daly trailing just behind them. The team, would train in Randalls Island twice a week, and myself and Padraig had two big station wagons and we would race down the highway with often 10 men in each car, to see who would get there first. Great stories came from training on the island.

There was a guy called 'The Big Buc'... his name was Frank Molloy. His job was to test all the newcomers and take a few lumps out of them. He tried with me one night, but he ended up in a ditch. Training was hard and tough. We would work out for two hours, though one particular night when Donal was away and I took over the training, we stayed at it for the guts of three hours. We finished training, and we could barely get into our cars.

That evening I dropped Eunan McIntyre to his apartment. A few days later he admitted to me that it took him half an hour to get up the stairs as his legs were seized up. I had a similar story, as when we got to our own apartment on Godwin Terrace the stairs was also a problem!

Kevin Madden and Martin Connolly and myself, we had to get to the fourth floor. Martin could not budge. I grabbed him, threw him over my shoulders and carried him up the four flights. And I put him to bed!

Contrary to the scene I was used to in Kildare, here I was seeing a club in New

York that was very well run. Nobody missed training, everyone was committed.

It was a very strong team. Pádraig Dunne was in midfield and you had other top players like Eugene McNulty from Down, another Kildareman Kevin Nolan in goal, Pat O'Toole from Wicklow. Eunan McIntyre had won an All-Ireland under-21 medal with Donegal, and Tom Ross from Dunmanway had won one with Cork. Sadly, he would die at the age of 49. Connie Molloy was captain; Lanty, his brother, was a super player, as was Kevin Madden, who was to prove to be one of the great players in Gaelic Park. Another Corkman, Martin Connolly would go on to play a big part in my decision to join Castlehaven. PJ Buckley was out from Dublin and we had a few weekend players, but not too many.

Anthony Molloy came out and Brendan Searls, who would be a colleague of mine on the 1990 Cork panel, used to commute from Boston for the games. Kerry's Pat Spillane travelled over, but, when we got to the final in 1985 against Sligo, that was a source of conflict.

Mick Wright, the man who had been the inspiration for me to take the plunge and leave Ireland, had come out again that summer and he had history with Pat but none of the rest of us realised it.

THE NIGHT BEFORE the final, I got a knock on the door from Mick.

'Any ball you get tomorrow, don't pass it to that fella at all! He's a mé féiner... he'll only be out for himself,' he said, quickly followed by... 'If I'm coming up the field, I don't give a damn if he's through for a goal... I'm not giving it to him.'

I tried to talk him around but he was defiant.

The next day was a huge occasion, there was a parade beforehand and commentary on the speakers. Spillane was shouting for a few balls from Wright early on, but no passes were coming.

Just before half-time, Spillane bawled Mick out of it for not giving him the ball.

It nearly became a boxing match in the middle of the pitch.

Inside in the dressing-room, Pádraig Dunne and I had to step in, reminding lads of the bigger picture and that a different attitude would be needed in the second-half.

The game finished in a draw, 1-10 to 0-13; I kicked 1-9 for us and Connie Molloy got a point. Pat Spillane stayed over in between that game and the replay and things were sorted out.

We beat them by two, 1-12 to 0-13.

Spillane got a couple of points so he was happy and Wright passed him the ball a few times, for which he got a fierce slagging afterwards!

It was a massive game for us to win.

People had said beforehand that Sligo were unbeatable so to come through gave the club a strong foundation and it was a really good starting block for the likes of myself and Pádraig Dunne. There was a real togetherness and a lot of that had to do with how Donal Gallagher ran things.

I always say that I could never shake Meath off and it was the same when it came to the work side of things in New York. Obviously, I was illegal, so the name I worked under was that of a Meathman, whose name I shall not mention. He had played for them back in the 60s, and had worked in America and had the 'green card'.

He had returned home but the card could still be used – nobody would ask who he was, all they wanted was the social security number.

I was working for a construction company.

We had been renovating a hospital and that came to an end and I was shifted to Harlem, for a big job on the famous Apollo Theatre. I used to get the subway at 5 am and arrive in Harlem a half hour later, just a bag of tools on my back initially.

I was told to stay on the main streets which was daunting for the first few mornings. I was the only white person around.

I'll be honest, I was nervous.

I WAS PRETTY much the only white fella on the job.

On my second day, the boss asked me if I'd go to a hardware store nearby. I went up and stood waiting to be served but I was kept waiting and eventually I went back with nothing. I explained the case to the boss and he had to go up to explain the situation to the guys in the hardware store.

As the job went on, a lot of locals were hired. I got to know them and they became my protection, really. In the end, it was a job I ended up massively enjoying. If you can overcome something like that, you can overcome a lot of things.

Whether it's work, sport or life, you meet challenges but if you meet them head-on but with respect, you tend to be rewarded.

A lot of Irish took St Patrick's Day off work, but I had to go in – though we didn't get much done! The Harlem lads had two bottles of Jack Daniel's and I'm not a man for drinking shorts by any means but we had a few that day and a gang of us ended up going into Rosie O'Grady's in Manhattan.

AS MUCH AS the football, that camaraderie is what stays with you. I can remember the day of the 1985 All-Ireland final, between Kerry and Dublin, practically every Irish person in the city went down to Lehman College to watch the game.

It was $20 to get in but the place was packed.

On Monday nights, you'd go to the Celtic House pub – they used to get tapes of *The Sunday Game* flown over and there was always a huge crowd to watch the games. That sense of a shared experience is very strong.

I became very friendly with the Kerry legend, Mick O'Connell.

He was working on a building site by day and in Moynihan's bar by night. On a Saturday morning, we used to meet for breakfast in the Riverdale Diner and the friendship endured after we both returned to Ireland.

I FOUND THE New York lifestyle suited me, the fast pace and the early mornings. Popping in for a coffee and a donut on the run to the subway. We could never find a decent cup of tea!

I did miss the Irish food, but when someone was 'coming over' from Ireland there would always be an order put in for tea bags. A big fry up would always happen in some apartment and everyone would turn up for a taste of home.

I was always looking ahead. I was driven to train and when you reach a certain level, you have to look for consistency. You want to stay there, and then move forward again.

I always made sure I had downtime too. There has to be a balance. After all, I was living in the Big Apple, the greatest city in the world. I loved going to Madison Square Garden. I saw everyone, from Elton John and Bob Dylan to Madonna, perform there. I got to watch the greats in basketball too, from Larry Bird to Michael Jordan.

But the most exciting sporting event I attended in the Garden was Eamonn Coghlan winning the Wannamaker Mile in the Millrose Games. He was the 'Chairman of the Boards' and he ruled the world from New York City.

AT THE START of the 1986 season Donegal were invited to play an exhibition match against Sligo to promote the quality of Gaelic games. Myself and the lads headed off to Coney Island, and arrived to find a huge tented village erected around the pitch. It was festival time on Coney Island.

We togged off, and the ball was thrown up. But Sligo were well up for the game, since we had beaten them in the New York final the year before. It started getting niggly, then downright violent. And a free-for-all developed before too long, and a section of the crowd joined in. I turned around at one stage and all I saw was 'Moggy' with two legs in the air and he sent Jigger O'Connor (the legendary Roscommon forward from the 1980 All-Ireland final) into the marquee.

The whole marquee collapsed.

The fight continued. Tables were broken, and food and drink was flying everywhere. Then we heard the whistles; the police had arrived in force. They tore everyone apart, and calmed us all down. And, to assure the officers that we had had enough fighting, we all shook hands.

If we did, wasn't there a huge roar from the 'locals', who thought that the whole carry-on was part of the entertainment on offer.

AFTER WINNING THE championship in 1985, we were the favourites in '86 and we got through our group fairly handy and into the quarter-finals. April and May were lovely months but June, July and August could be a killer.

Walking up Broadway, there was a big clock that would tell you the temperature; some days it might be up around 110° Fahrenheit. The sweat would be pouring out of you.

Out on the Gaelic Park pitch, it felt hotter still. We were playing Monaghan in the semi-final. They had a lot of Scotstown lads and were a strong team. They were out for our guts. In the second-half there was a collision of players and all hell broke loose. Supporters came in over the wire. The first two in were Connie and Liam Molloy from Donegal, two guys well able to handle themselves. I turned around and there were bodies everywhere and Spike Nolan was sprinting from the goal to join in. This lasted for 20 minutes. It was a free-for-all. Supporters, players, linesmen and all. When everyone got tired, the ball was thrown up and the game resumed. A song was even written about the event by Maeve O Grady.

After the match the veteran (Donal) was smiling all night and said it was a great match to win but a bloody great fight to win too.

I was captain and we reached the final again, beating Leitrim along the way. Billy Morgan, who worked in Rosie's was playing for them. In the final, we were up against Cavan, who had 13 inter-county players, including Ger Power and Eoin 'Bomber' Liston.

Obviously, myself and Pádraig Dunne had played senior for our counties but we prided ourselves on being a home-based team, guys who might have played under-21 for their counties but were living in New York now.

In 1986, we brought over very few, if any, weekend players.

Unusually, the forecast was for rain on the day of the final. Donal Gallagher suggested to me that we should go up to Van Cortlandt Park at around 10 am and have a kick-around in the rain, come back and have a light breakfast.

It set us up brilliantly because we were used to the conditions; we went out and absolutely beat them off the field. It was one of the best exhibitions of football from one to 15 I've been involved in.

The final score was something like 4-14 to 1-4.

To get a sense of how strong a unit that team was, you look at the guys who came on as subs that day – Anthony Molloy and Martin McHugh, who went on to win All-Irelands with Donegal in 1992, and Pat O'Toole, a superb player for Wicklow.

After that, we were the target in everybody's sights.

The big aim was three in-a-row, which hadn't been done since Kerry managed it in the 50s, and obviously everybody else was keen to stop us.

Teams started bringing in more and more big names; you nearly had to go to JFK airport to see who was coming in each weekend.

OBVIOUSLY, CHRISTMAS TIME in 1986 was a turning point in my life. Vincie Collins had come over from Castlehaven in 1984 with Anthony following in 1985. They were good players and like Martin O'Mahony and Martin Connolly, they were incredible guys to train hard. Not everybody enjoyed the sessions I used to put on – Timmy Dowd, who had won an All-Ireland with Kerry, used to say that Mick O'Dwyer's training felt like a stroll compared to mine!

The way the Collins' and the two Martins talked about Castlehaven, you knew there had to be something special about the place.

It wasn't anything serious at first – the usual, you'd be out after matches and having a drink, people would ask why I wasn't at home when I was playing such serious football. They'd say that the Haven would be a perfect place for me, jokingly at the beginning but there was something there. When Francis Collins was over in the autumn of 1986, I had said I was thinking about it.

They mentioned Niall Cahalane and John Cleary, guys who I would have been aware of as they had played under-21 for Cork, and Michael Maguire had come out and played a bit in goal for Donegal – I couldn't believe how long he could kick the ball.

I was thinking if they had the four New York lads and had these other players back home – Denis Cleary was another who had been a Cork under-21, and there were more Collins brothers – there was the makings of a serious team.

I was training away as fanatically as ever.

In late 1986, JC Daly came out to America and he would become one of my great friends. He was from Drinagh and he was only 18, as green as grass at the time. We were working together and at the end of one long day he was concerned that a door saddle was a quarter of an inch too short.

I tried to reassure him.

'JC, in a country this size… nobody will notice a quarter of an inch!'

He played for Cork rather than Donegal but he was fascinated with the training I did and he wanted to build himself up. He wasn't used to the level; we'd go to Van Cortlandt Park and shoulder the goalposts to toughen ourselves up. He started trying to stay with me and a few nights he nearly had to be hospitalised, but he wouldn't let go. He was mad determined. He would come with me to Jack LaLanne's Gym and after run up Eucon Park hill. I nearly had him killed.

Just before Christmas 1986, the Donegal team met to discuss the possibility of a trip to Ireland, playing a few games over there. We decided May would be an appropriate time to go, before the New York championship started properly. The names were needed for the start of January but the problem was that so many of the team were illegal in the country.

The answer was… 'We'll get *back in* some way!'

At that time, the Castlehaven lads were really going with the hard sell and after that snowy night in January, it made sense that I would stay on in Ireland after that Donegal team trip. The four Haven lads would be doing the same, staying around for the summer in the hope of winning that elusive county championship.

We flew into Shannon on a Thursday and it was a huge thing for a lot of lads as they hadn't been home in a good while. Just even to land in Shannon was special, I'll always remember it – you'd be so used to the fast pace of New York and this was all so slow.

There was a cousin of Donal's called Jack, who came along with us. He had brought wigs for us and we'd put them on going through every place we passed from Shannon down to Fernhill House Hotel in Clonakilty, where we were playing our first match on the Saturday against Cork.

It was a massive game to kick off the tour. Donegal NY always had great affinity with west Cork so this game drew a big crowd. It was tight to begin with, but we won comfortably in the end.

Even though it wasn't far from Clon, I didn't get a chance to actually visit Castlehaven as we were moving on to Castlebar to play Mayo in midweek, and we won that too. We continued to zig-zag the country as, after that, it was Laois, who were very strong at the time – they had won the league in 1986. It was a tough game but we won by two points.

On the Monday or Tuesday, we travelled to Donegal, with our final game the following Saturday evening in Ballybofey. They were probably the weakest of the four teams but it was a heavy week of celebrating. We went to so many places and were treated like royalty, so lads were a bit tired. We scraped a draw but it meant that we finished the trip without losing any game.

Most of the lads headed back to America after that. I dropped in home to my parents for a week or so, my first time back since leaving.

After that, I was headed for Castlehaven.

With my great friend, Donal Gallagher in early 2020. It was Donal who first invited me out to New York in 1985 and helped me make the city my home, and the Donegal New York team my family. And (below) with two of my brilliant teammates from that Donegal team, Martin Connolly and Kevin Madden.

CHAPTER

WE HAD A great core of people that supported us with the pub, people who'd still come to the place I have now. I hope that that loyalty was because I am genuine. I think I'm as straight as a die.

In business, you need to take an interest in people. If someone has a problem or their wife isn't well, you listen and the next time they come in you ask how things are? Simple, basic things.

At the same time, running a bar in 1989 was tough because it was hands-on and I had Cork and Castlehaven as well. It was something we had put a lot of money into and we had to clock in the hours. The late nights meant I found it draining and it's not the ideal business to be in if you're playing at the top level.

I would look back now and think it probably took a chunk out of me. I had to put a lot of time into it and get to know people to make sure it was run right.

There was a guesthouse as well, so it was two businesses. We had nine rooms and we were very well supported by people coming into Cork during the week for work. Lord have mercy on my mother; she'd hop on the train and come down and give a hand, and my father would come down an odd time too. We used to do full board, breakfast and dinner.

My mother was a fantastic cook and people loved it. She used to make bread and scones, it was like a feast.

The first thing people would ask was, 'Is your mother here?!'

People liked the pub and they liked coming in to have a chat but I was going to bed at 3am or 4am. As the owner, the buck always stopped with me. An employee mightn't show up and I often had to get up to do breakfast but that was no bother with the way I was reared.

▲▼▲▼▲

ONCE I SIGNED the transfer form with Martin Connolly on that snowy night in New York, in January of 1987, Francis and Christy Collins quickly approached Frank Murphy, the Cork county board secretary, who is an expert on the rules of the GAA.

Frank was quick to point out that I was playing illegally for Donegal NY as I had never got a transfer form from Eadestown. So, first up was to send a letter to Croke Park and admit that I was not aware that I had to transfer. I duly got a 12-months suspension, which definitely wasn't part of my plans. It was February, 1987 and my plan was to come home in May to play for Castlehaven for the summer. And go back to New York once I was done.

The lads in Castlehaven lost the rag with Francis, but he told us we had to trust Frank.

The next step was to write a letter to the 'Mercy Committee' who met at the GAA's annual congress every Easter. I wrote to them, and made my case.

The suspension was lifted.

I was back on track to leave New York in May and play with Castlehaven. Frank suggested that an inter-country transfer would be faster. I knew I would never play with Kildare again, so I had no problem with that. But at the same time, my ambition was to play for the Haven; playing for Cork didn't come into my head.

Little did we all know how frustrating things were about to get.

Central Council had no problem with the transfer, but the Kildare county board made it awkward. Every time the form went up to them, it seemed to come back with a fresh request. I needed everything... letters from the local sergeant, who luckily was Ned Cleary, John's father, the local parish priest, who was a man from Donegal... and this went on and on.

At this stage I had moved back to Cork, to a house in Union Hall.

Eventually, Frank rang me on that evening in June, the night before my 24th birthday, asking if I'd travel to Dublin to play in the challenge game for Cork at Parnell Park.

'It would look good,' he had said.

Getting the news just before the match that the transfer had finally gone through was a huge relief and I went out and played fairly well. I was on Eamonn Heery.

On the train back down to Cork, Billy Morgan asked me to join the panel and to come up to training the following Tuesday evening. I was open to the idea.

WE GOT BACK to Kent Station in Cork.

Little did I know I'd be living across the road from it before too long. And I set off for west Cork.

On the Tuesday night, I went up to Páirc Uí Chaoimh with Niall Cahalane, who was working as a courier at the time. You could hardly get into the van with all of the stuff, we had a few deliveries on the way!

I told him that I was dreading the session and he said it would be a hard one as Billy liked to do that early in the week. That made me more nervous. To think I was going to Páirc Uí Chaoimh where guys like Jimmy Barry Murphy, Ray Cummins, Billy Morgan and Declan Barron trained. I watched these guys play in Croke Park, legends every one of them. I looked at Cork as being one of the top counties.

We wound up in the old gym in Páirc Uí Chaoimh before we went out onto the field. Billy pulled me aside and told me I could fall out whenever I wanted, as the guys were at a very high level of fitness. We did four laps, and I lapped every one of the lads comfortably. We then did a number of other drills and exercises, and then Billy ordered another four laps.

I think Billy thought I would not be up to doing the second set of rounds, but I lapped everyone even worse the second time. At that stage Billy had another private word with me and he told me I was in great shape.

'I'm only okay,' I replied. 'I have a bit more to go!'

But I needed to tell him something else!

'You have a long way to go with these lads!' I bluntly informed him.

This was my first session with cork, just to see how it would go. Later the management team asked me to come onto the panel. I told Billy I was ready for the challenge ahead, and that I would give it one hundred percent, but I told him we needed to step up the training. I told him we would not beat Kerry with the shape the panel was in, and as for Meath?

I told him Meath would eat the whole team for breakfast!

At that moment, I think Billy realised I was not a man for wasting anyone's time, or for messing around. I also think the players knew I was in this fight with them. All that was in my head was to win.

I wasn't expecting to be picked for the Limerick game but Cork had a few injuries and I was named at centre-forward.

A lot of people from Castlehaven were going up to it as they still hadn't seen me play for their club and people were telling me we'd beat Limerick by 30 points. That talk probably made me lose my focus a little bit and I didn't have a great game even though I kicked a few frees, though Shea Fahy – also making his debut – did play well. Limerick were dogged and we needed a deflected Paddy Hayes goal to come through it.

Naturally, I was fairly disappointed walking off and things got worse when this guy shouts out at the top of his voice.

'Go back to Kildare... YOU'RE USELESS!'

I didn't go for any drink afterwards.

I got back late to Union Hall and I was so restless and frustrated that I got up at 6am the next morning and went down to the Black Field.

I kicked and ran, eager to put the memory of the game behind me and prepare for Kerry. The fella that was roaring at me, I could picture him in my head and I was thinking... *I want to see that fecker in four weeks' time.*

When four of the Collins' brothers – Bernard, Dinty, Vincie and Anthony – were driving home, there was hardly a word spoken until they were about half-way home. Then Bernard piped up from the back.

'Begod boy... I suppose we were expecting a bit much.'

The wider consensus seemed to be that, while I might be some good for the Haven, I'd be no good for Cork.

The following Friday night, we were playing St Finbarr's in the Kelleher Shield, the Cork senior league. The Barrs, from the southside of Cork City, had been Castlehaven's Achilles heel for a while, they just couldn't beat them. This went all the way back to 1979, the Haven's first year up at senior level, when they made it to the county final but lost to the Barrs by 10 points.

FOR ME, THIS was what I had come home for.

It might have only been a league game but it was a big match for the Haven and there was a massive build-up. Even beyond Castlehaven, we used to get support from places like Goleen and Ballydehob.

It was a glorious evening and, as I walked down from the house to the Black Field, I could sense that there was a good bit of traffic. There was such a crowd that the game had to be delayed for 20 minutes or so, which was completely unheard of.

The Barrs were the reigning All-Ireland club champions – though they had actually lost the 1986 county final to Imokilly, a divisional side who couldn't progress to the Munster club championship – and they had a strong team. I was marking Gene Desmond and they had Christy Ryan, Dave Barry, John Kerins, Mick Slocum, Paddy Hayes, Tony Leahy... all serious players.

It was a total contrast to the Limerick game and I was on form.

We won by 1-15 to 2-8 and I kicked nine points. When I was coming off the field, this old man was coming out to meet me, brushing people aside.

'That's the best performance I've ever seen from any player in my lifetime,' he said. Mike O'Brien, one of our defensive stalwarts, told me that it was Dan Collins, the father of all of the brothers on our team.

He had been a founding member of the club with Ned Cleary.

THE MUNSTER FINAL against Kerry was on July 26 in a searing Páirc Uí Chaoimh. I rested for a few days beforehand and, coming up to the game, I had a sense that something good was going to happen.

The west Cork fellas used to come up to Jurys Hotel the night before games like this so as not to be making a big journey on the morning of the match. Everybody was fairly relaxed, it was four years since Cork had beaten Kerry but they had won three under-21 All-Irelands in the meantime.

Billy had had a good impact and Kerry had to pass their peak eventually.

The following day, things could hardly have gone better, at least up to the last minute. I scored a point after 30 seconds and that settled me. I was on Tom

Spillane but it didn't matter who I was marking, I felt like I could play as I pleased.

I kicked seven points that day and we were two up going into injury time.

Then, Mikey Sheehy got a goal at the City End.

He was nearly on the end-line but he jinked around a couple of challenges and squeezed the ball past John Kerins at the near post; I think there was a deflection.

There was bedlam when that went in. The Bomber Liston was hanging out of the crossbar celebrating. Billy had been standing right where it happened and he was plonked on his knees, but John Kerins kept his head.

He kicked the ball out quickly – with his left foot, which was amazing when you think about it. John Cleary picked up the break and got it in to John O'Driscoll, who was fouled. It was a straightforward kick for me, 25 or 30 yards out, ideal for a right-footed kicker.

We had avoided defeat but it felt like a game that we should have won.

We were fairly down afterwards but Billy was bullish. He came in with a positive attitude and told us we'd finish the job in the replay. We heard that night that the game would be a week later down in Fitzgerald Stadium, the August bank holiday Sunday. And the two nights of training during the week were very positive.

I had never played in Killarney; any game with Kildare away to Kerry had been in Tralee.

I was chatting to Christy Collins about it and wondering if there was any way I could get in for a bit of practice. He knew the O'Sullivans, who owned the famous Tatler Jack's pub in the town, and Patrick O'Sullivan was able to sort it for me.

I went down with a bag of balls and got to kick frees there for an hour, which was great in terms of getting my bearings for what the place was like. Kerry were training later that evening and Mick O'Dwyer was livid, I believe.

'How did he get into the pitch?'

It showed that we had got in their heads a bit, and that could only be a good thing for the replay.

We dominated them the second day.

Conor Counihan and Denis Walsh were massive in defence and Kerry were down to 14 men when Ger Power was sent off for a late tackle on Tony Davis. Tony became the spare man then and got two points.

We won by 0-13 to 1-5 in the end and their goal came fairly late on. It was comprehensive, the kind of beating that Cork lads had been on the end of against

Kerry too often.

I think it helped the team, going to Killarney and winning there; it brought us together more. It had a huge bearing on a lot of the players; they felt that this team was going places. You had a massive backroom team – Frank Murphy was a selector, Bob Honohan would have been involved with a lot of the lads coming through from the under-21s, Seán Murphy and Mick Keating were great men to have involved too.

I was named Man of the Match after the replay, even though I would have felt I played better the first day. Denis Walsh was in a lot of ways an unsung hero. He had gone out and held the Bomber in Páirc Uí Chaoimh and he got Man of the Match in that game. I told him I'd have to beat him the next day and I did, even though he played just as well!

After the game, we really got the sense of how big this was.

We were going down to the hotel on the Killorglin road, beside the golf club. Someone was asking where the bus was and Billy said, 'Forget the bus… we'll walk through the town!'

It was Cork's first win there since 1974.

In Van Cortlandt Park in the Bronx where so much of the hard work was done as the Donegal team set out on course for four New York senior championships in-a-row (1985-88). Here I am with the great JC Daly, one of my teammates and (below) the famous hill in Ewen Park where we often met hell on earth in training.

CHAPTER 8

A WEEK AFTER the Dublin game in August, 1989 there was another semi-final as Castlehaven took on Duhallow in the county championship in Macroom.

There's a large grass bank in Macroom but you couldn't see a bit of green, people were jammed in everywhere.

Duhallow are regarded as probably the strongest divisional team in Cork, taking players from the junior and intermediate clubs in the north-west of the county.

They were coming on strong, they had lost to Nemo Rangers in the 1988 final and they would win the championship in 1990 and '91. They weren't far off doing it in 1989, either.

Niall Cahalane had been out injured but he was back and he had a huge influence. I started full-forward but I was moved out to midfield for the second-half after we went in at half-time trailing by 1-4 to 0-4. I was alongside John R O'Donovan and we were up against my Cork colleague, Danny Culloty and a guy called Jerry Casey from Rockchapel.

It was a real battle, that game. Danny probably got the better of me but we stuck at it and we got two late points, one from Edmund Cleary and a free by me, to level it.

The replay would be in Páirc Uí Chaoimh as part of a double-header with the other semi-final between Nemo Rangers and St Finbarr's but it wouldn't take place until the middle of October.

We had other business to attend to before then.

▲▼▲▼▲

IN THE 1987 All-Ireland semi-final we were up against Galway, on one of the warmest days that I ever played in Croke Park. Truthfully, they should have caught us.

We weren't as good as we had been against Kerry in the Munster final and Galway were a point ahead near the end. They nearly made it two but Pádraig 'Dandy' Kelly, who died a young man, was unlucky with an attempt.

They got a sideline kick underneath the Hogan Stand but John O'Driscoll fielded an unbelievable ball and was fouled. It was towards the Hogan Stand, into Hill 16, way back from the '45'. I'd played really well and I just said to myself... *I know I'm going to put this over the bar.*

It was one of those ones which I struck perfectly.

The ball went a mile over the bar for a final score of 1-11 each. Johnno always said afterwards that he helped to create my 'legend' as he was fouled against Kerry and against Galway! It was after that second one that I acquired the nickname, 'The Equalizer', after the television show starring Edward Woodward, which was on at the time.

Thankfully, we were on song in the replay and we won by 0-18 to 1-4.

I kicked 11 points, five from play, and I was really happy with the performance. Colman Corrigan stood out in defence and Colm O'Neill did well in attack too. Donal Keenan in the *Irish Independent* wrote, *"King Larry rules Cork and he doesn't even have a Leeside lilt to his voice".*

There was certainly a sense that I was becoming known nationally again. I had played five years of Railway Cup for Leinster but you get forgotten fairly quickly and I had been off the scene while I was in America.

IN THE SAME YEAR, my Castlehaven championship debut – the quarter-final against Muskerry, the mid-Cork representative side – was scheduled for a week later. The game had been postponed more than once that summer due to Cork's replays and Castlehaven hadn't played since a big win over Seandún, the city divisional team, back in May.

Clonakilty was packed – Francis Collins, travelling down from Cork, was nearly late arriving due to all the traffic – and talk about a comedown. I just couldn't kick the ball over the bar that night.

I hit the post… hit the crossbar… I was missing frees I'd kick with my eyes closed.

I had to give John Cleary the frees before the end and we got beaten by a point, 1-9 to 1-8. It was just so hard to rationalise after what had happened the week before, when I was kicking points from all angles. This was the reason I had come home, to try to win a county championship with Castlehaven, and it was over after one match.

I went into the dressing-room and I just sat there, dazed.

I must have been in there for around two hours on my own.

The man coming to lock up saw me and said he'd come back in a while. I just couldn't get my head around it. I went back to Union Hall and, just like after the Limerick game, the following morning I went out early and I just ran…

The other lads who had come home, the native Haven fellas, were heading back and I felt guilty. Here I was, an All-Ireland final coming up, but Castlehaven were out of the championship and the lads had to go back.

I felt I had let them down, it was a huge disappointment; I couldn't explain how gutted I was.

I wasn't the only one, either. It's not too much of an exaggeration to say it was like a death in the parish.

Christy Collins was at the creamery on the Monday and was chatting to John 'Butcher' Browne.

'We'd better go home… have a bite of dinner,' Christy said, as the conversation ended. To which the 'Butcher' replied, 'We'll go home alright, but I don't know if I'll be able to eat!'

I knew how he felt.

We believed we were good enough to win the championship but we didn't get to prove it. Instead, all the focus was on proving Cork were good enough to win the All-Ireland, with my old adversaries Meath standing in the way after they beat Derry in the other semi-final. Between the semi-final and the final, our training went well but there was a doubt about whether we had the edge to beat them.

They were hardened, a few years further along in their development than us and, while they had taken a beating from Kerry in the 1986 semi-final, they had learned from it and improved. A week before the final, I stood up in a team meeting and I told the lads that this would be a different kettle of fish altogether. Meath were a different animal to Kerry.

I don't think they believed me.

WE STAYED IN the Spa Hotel in Lucan, a place where I had worked doing my time with Brendan Martin, undertaking renovations. On the Saturday night, I went for a walk with Teddy McCarthy.

We went into a pub and I was saying we'd have a lemonade but sure didn't Teddy order a pint! After our stop, we walked on, into another pub and the same thing.

Teddy was working in Beamish at the time but he had to make do with Guinness in Dublin!

I was getting a bit anxious now.

'Come on,' I said, 'I don't want to be carrying you tomorrow.'

'Don't worry,' he replied.

'You won't be carrying me at all.

'Two or three pints makes me sleep better.'

True to his word, he had a blinder the following day.

Early on, it looked like we'd all have blinders. We started like a house on fire and we were 0-7 to 0-2 up after 22 minutes, and it could have been even better – at 0-5 to 0-2, Jimmy Kerrigan had a goal chance but Mick Lyons made a heroic block-down.

Colm O'Rourke's goal brought them right back into it and they were up by 1-6 to 0-8 at half-time. Brian Stafford kicked a '45' just after the restart and I had a free for us but we went nearly a half-hour without a score after that.

Meath were energetic guys and they had been chipping away for a few years. I knew they were good players, fit and strong; they'd take it any way you wanted.

We weren't used to the physicality, we were just learning. And they really asserted themselves. It was 1-14 to 0-11 in the end and you couldn't really argue that we hadn't been beaten by the better team. When that happens, you just take it on the chin, try to learn from it and move on.

We came back to Cork and went to the old *Examiner* office on Academy St for the speeches. There were close to 30,000 people in Cork that night to see a team that had been beaten; you could sense that the supporters were getting behind the footballers in a way that normally only happened for the Cork hurling team.

The speeches were made from the verandah looking on to St Patrick's St. We made our way out on to it through the old sash windows, but there was only room for a few people.

Most of the players were inside, and we couldn't see anyone!

Conor Counihan was the captain and when he finished his speech, the crowd were shouting my name, so he called me out. I spoke from the heart.

I said that for myself and Shea it was an honour to be involved with Cork in 1987. I said that I respected each and every one of them for coming out and that we'd have the real deal the next year. My future, in the immediate term at least, was with Cork.

I had seen from the supporters and the people how proud and passionate a GAA county it was. I had had a serious year with Cork in 1987 and, apart from not winning the All-Ireland, I couldn't have asked for more. I felt there was work that was unfinished and it would have been a disaster if I didn't go back.

LISTOWEL RACES USED to be on the week after the All-Ireland and I headed there with Mick McCarthy; we spent a lot of time in Tim Kennelly's pub. I planned to go back to America the following week.

There was also the chance to try to win some silverware with Donegal as the New York championship resumed.

Before I came back, the team had played Connemara Gaels in the group stage and they gave us a good game as they were starting to make a resurgence. They proved that by making it all the way to the final, trying to stop us doing the three in-a-row.

By now, I was considered a 'weekend player', with Niall Cahalane and Jack O'Shea the other two – not a bad trio!

As it happened, the game at the end of October finished in a draw. I was getting used to them that year – and the replay was scheduled for the start of November. However, there was a dispute between the New York board and John 'Kerry' O'Donnell, who owned Gaelic Park.

The game was postponed and then voided.

It means that there are no 1987 New York champions in the record books so, strictly speaking, we didn't do the three in-a-row. But, if you apply boxing logic, we were champions and weren't beaten! In the end, we were awarded the title.

I came back for the All Stars before Christmas and was delighted to pick up my award. It was only a flying visit home and I was in New York again when news came through of the draw for the first round of the 1988 Cork senior football championship – Castlehaven had drawn Nemo Rangers, the county champions.

A game that I and the Haven contingent in New York would be looking forward to during that winter.

Before thinking of anything else, the Cork team I joined in 1987 had to deal with Kerry, the greatest team of all time which had eight All-Ireland titles in the bag (above, Mick O'Dwyer and Jack O'Shea enjoy one of those victories). That first summer of '87 we defeated Kerry after a replay (right, O'Shea and Pat Spillane receiving the close attention of Tony Nation and Conor Counihan). I was still fighting it out with Kerry long after Micko left to manage Kildare (below, shooting for a point in 1998).

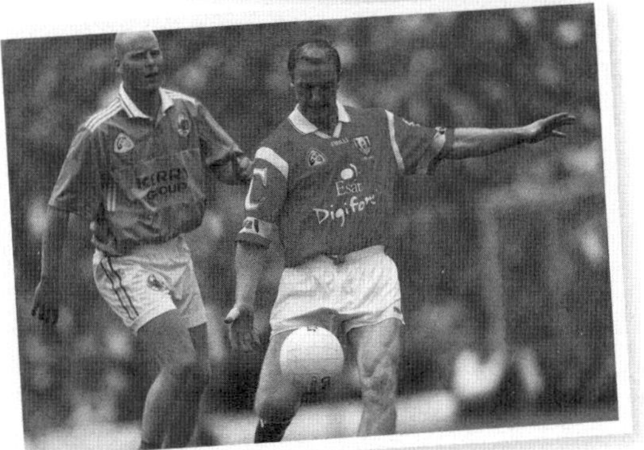

CHAPTER 9

DENIS CONROY FROM Carrigtwohill became chairman of Cork county board in 1988 and he was someone with whom I became great friends. In 1989, through Denis, I met a Glen Rovers man by the name of Paddy Walsh – who revealed himself to be the fella that shouted at me after the Limerick game to go back to Kildare.

Paddy never missed a Cork hurling or football game and he, like so many others, lived and breathed the GAA. Thankfully, with an All-Ireland final on the horizon for the third straight year, he held me in higher regard than he had in June of 1987!

By this stage, we knew the September routine quite well, though the big difference this time around was that Meath weren't there. Instead, we were playing Mayo, who had beaten Tyrone in the other semi-final.

Naturally, we would have been strong favourites after beating Dublin, but the other side of that was, after losing the previous two finals, there was a lot of pressure and a lot at stake. Winning the league had been a big boost for us, you can't over-estimate the power of winning a national title, and going into the All-Ireland final. We expected to win.

Mayo had a very good team, a lot of strong players like Peter Forde, TJ Kilgallon, Liam McHale, Willie Joe Padden and Michael Fitzmaurice. John O'Mahony was over them, he was only 36 at the time, but, while they had the talent, at that time they might have just lacked the belief.

It was their first time in a final since 1951, whereas getting to the final meant nothing to us unless we finally won one.

That said, it was nip and tuck for a long way.

I kicked a free early on, a good 50 yards out on the Hogan Stand side into the Canal End. It was one of the best I'd kicked, the 'opposite side' for a right-footer but it sailed over. It was the first score of the game but, amazingly, I never got a kickable free afterwards. Mayo were very disciplined, they didn't give away frees and they hung in there.

We were leading at half-time, 0-10 to 0-8, but we just couldn't pull away from them.

And then, there was a period where it could have gone from us.

Anthony Finnerty had come on as a sub for Mayo just before half-time when Jimmy Bourke got a nasty injury and, three minutes into the second-half, he scored a goal to put them ahead for the first time.

We knew not to panic, though. Dave Barry and John Cleary got important points to put us back in front and Teddy McCarthy was outstanding too.

Mayo actually went back in front, getting three points in-a-row, but Finnerty had another goal chance only to put it wide. In the final 15 minutes, we showed our experience.

We got the final four points; Mick McCarthy got two and Paul McGrath and Teddy one each, and we won by 0-17 to 1-11.

It was just a massive relief.

That final had been a case of 'now or never', a time when you know... *This is our chance*. The hallmark of that team was that, when the chips were really down, we had a very strong finish. John Cleary had a great game with three points from play.

The slagging afterwards was that he was heading for Man of the Match and they had taken him off!

I can see now how our training over the previous few years had helped the team to become stronger. Each one of the lads pushed themselves to the limit every day. Always finding time to get that bit extra in, nothing else mattered. Looking back, if I am asked what was one of the greatest things I brought to Cork, it was to help the whole team to believe in themselves and be the best they could be.

▲▼▲▼▲

I RETURNED TO Cork in the spring of 1988 and played a few of the national league games, though Cork finished bottom of Division 1 and were relegated. I was back working with Christy Collins, getting the ferry out from Baltimore to Sherkin Island each morning.

Christy was still playing at the time and in the evenings we'd come back over on the boat and jump into his pick-up truck to go to the gym – I had convinced him of the need to get fit!

There was no gym in Skibbereen at the time, so we had to go to Clonakilty, where there was one above the famous De Barra's pub. We used to stop in Leap and get a Mars bar and an apple, and then do a good hour and a half in the gym. His wife, Mary later confided in me about a particular week when he did not turn up for work, for days. Christy had told me at the time that he was very sick.

But Mary revealed that he was in bed, because of all the training with me! He could not move. His arms were seized up, and he was coughing up blood. It reminded me of the time in New York when I nearly killed JC Daly; when I thought I'd be brought up for murder.

I'd only be sitting down to have a proper bit of grub at eleven o'clock at night, but I was used to that. The idea of going home to rest never even entered my head!

Later, after I moved to Cork city, Christy was off the hook, but I rounded up another of the Collins clan. Francis was multi-talented – he played hurling for Blackrock and had featured in two All-Irelands for Cork – and we used to have kicking sessions that might last an hour and a half or two hours.

Hill-running had always been a central part of my regime and Vernon Mount near Douglas fitted the bill. It was a place used for motorbike racing and there were some ferocious hills. Francis used to dread it but I would tell him that it was all about the last five minutes.

'The tongue will be hanging out of the fella marking you... but you'll have this work done and he won't.'

That extra little bit would always be key. Jim Nolan used to join us there too.

In 1988, the Nemo Rangers game in the first round of the championship at the end of April was jumping off the calendar. Back then, it was make-or-break, straight knockout, with no back doors. We were training well and I felt that I was in really good shape again, but Nemo are Nemo – the one guarantee is that there'll be nothing easy from them.

It was back to Clonakilty, the scene of such personal disappointment the previous autumn against Muskerry. While I would play a lot better this time, unfortunately the bottom line would be the same.

It was a horrible day and we conceded a freak own goal early on, after a mix-up between 'Moggy' and Niall, and the half-time score was 1-4 to 0-4. But we had the strong wind to come.

I had been going well in midfield but they pushed on after half-time and I was moved to full-forward. We turned things in our favour again and had it down to three points when I got a chance.

I raced through and let off a good shot. I thought the ball was heading for the top corner but it took a deflection, hit the crossbar and went over.

It finished 1-7 to 0-9. That was Christy's last game. He played well, the training had done him no harm!

From such a narrow margin, Nemo would go on to win the county, Munster and All-Ireland championships and we were out. It meant a very short stay at home for Anthony and Vincie Collins, Martin Connolly and Martin O'Mahony, but I was around for the summer with Cork. I was staying in the bungalow in Union Hall again and, because the Haven weren't training, I had a good bit of time to myself.

OFTEN, I'D GO down to the Black Field for an early-morning session – you'd feel good for the day after that. There was hardly ever a day where I wasn't doing some kicking. Mick Burns' young fellas would be there, kicking the ball back to me, or Brian Collins, Dinty's son too.

All the same, it was still an area I didn't know very well and it was trying at times, especially with the other lads gone back to New York. I was extremely lucky that Nora Maguire was like a second mother to me. Her house was a home from home; I'd call in to say hello and I'd hardly have sat down before she'd have a dinner out in front of me.

'Moggy' used to say that he never got dinner because he'd come home from work and I'd be after eating his!

Christy Ryan had retired, but we had two new additions, or re-additions.

Dave Barry had missed the 1987 championship as the county board weren't keen on him playing Gaelic and soccer, but Billy managed to get him back for

1988. And Dinny Allen was back on the scene too after a few years away.

It meant that we had huge competition for places – so strong that neither of them started our first championship game, against Limerick in Askeaton at the end of May.

Danny Culloty, Barry Coffey, John Cleary, Mick Slocum, Colm O'Neill, Steven O'Brien, Paul McGrath – these were all serious players and they couldn't get in the starting 15 for that game, but it wasn't an easy ride.

Limerick were very good at the time and we won by 0-9 to 1-3 – I'll always remember the headline in the *Examiner*... *"Escape from Askeaton"*.

My father was chatting to our masseur John 'Kid' Cronin afterwards.

'Jesus, they'd beat nothing,' my father said, but the 'Kid' was confident, like he always was, to be fair.

He told my father that Cork would win the All-Ireland.

IT'S ALWAYS THE case in Cork, though, that nobody remembers how well or how badly the Munster semi-final went unless you beat Kerry. After the draw and replay in 1987, it was back to Páirc Uí Chaoimh for the final. It was a real test of our credentials to show that the previous year hadn't been a flash in the pan and that the balance of power had swung our way.

We had a totally new full-forward line for the final – Dinny was back in for his first championship appearance since 1984, alongside Dave and Mick.

Kerry had lost Mikey Sheehy but they still had Pat, Mick and Tom Spillane, Jack O'Shea, Ger Power and the Bomber Liston, while a teenage Maurice Fitzgerald was in his first year.

For the Munster final, Billy Morgan and the Cork selectors put another teenager, Steven O'Brien marking Fitzgerald. I started at centre-forward but Kerry were on top for the first 22 minutes and led by 0-7 to 0-2.

I was moved to midfield then and by half-time we had cut the gap to two points.

There was an improvement all over the field, with Tony Davis, Denis Walsh and Conor Counihan very tight in defence. We went ahead when Mick McCarthy sent in a high ball and Colm O'Neill, who had come on as a sub, took it down one-handed before laying off to Dinny, who finished.

That put us ahead again; it was huge psychologically, and we stayed in front until the end. We won by a point, 1-14 to 0-16, but the last Kerry point from Maurice Fitz came deep into injury time. To come out on the right side of a game like that showed that there was no longer any fear of Kerry. The way we saw it was that it was another step on the way to trying to win the All-Ireland.

We were playing Monaghan in the All-Ireland semi-final in mid-August, a very windy day. John Kerins was injured so 'Moggy' was in goal, but we were confident. Monaghan won the toss but opted to play against the wind and we were 0-8 to 0-1 up at half-time.

Brendan Murray was marking me and I challenged him hard. Some people said I raised an elbow but it was a fair challenge, though he ended up breaking his jaw. We drove on from there but could have won by more. Though winning by a big enough margin was a worry going into another final.

Once again, we would be up against Meath, who had beaten Mayo. They had dogged it out but probably weren't as impressive as us. I don't think there was much between us in terms of the betting but we were certainly in a good place.

Cork were probably playing their best football in the time since I had arrived. Our training was competitive, with a real edge to it.

TEN DAYS BEFORE the final, we were training in Dunmanway.

I had been up in Kildare for a couple of days beforehand and I drove straight down. I said I'd get there early and kick a few frees. When I got out of the car, my legs felt kind of tired and during training I pulled up with a hamstring problem, something I had never had before.

I had to go to a physio nearly every day; there was a doubt as to whether I was going to play or not. I was named in the team – the only change from the semi-final was that John Kerins was back in – but it was going to be touch and go as to whether I'd make it.

The weekend of the final, we travelled up on the Saturday and when we got to Dublin, Dr Con Murphy brought me out to Belfield for a fitness test. I came through it fine, though I didn't do any sprints, just half-pace running and kicking a ball.

I seemed fine and I was delighted.

Little did I know what lay ahead the following day.

On our way to the 1987 All-Ireland final we had to fight long and hard with Galway, and this free (above) from outside the '45' metre line earned us a replay. From day one, I found Billy Morgan one of the most passionate men I had ever worked with in the game, but as Cork manager I told him straight that his training was not nearly tough enough to earn his team an All-Ireland title.

CHAPTER 10

COMING DOWN FROM Dublin after the 1989 All-Ireland final was such a great feeling. Everybody was just so relieved to have finally got over the line.

There was a massive sing-song and we stopped in Mallow, where there was a huge turnout. Arriving into Kent Station was another story altogether. It felt like the whole of Cork was at the station; we could barely get off the train and onto the open-top bus. There was no Health and Safety back then and it took the bus nearly an hour to get to McCurtain Street.

When we came around 'Paddy Barry's Corner' and down towards St Patrick's Bridge, we were blown away by the amount of people that had come out. It was a really special night and naturally we enjoyed that and a couple of nights afterwards, but at the back of my mind and those of the other Haven lads was the county semi-final replay against Duhallow.

As well as Niall Cahalane, John Cleary and myself, Michael 'Moggy' Maguire was back-up goalkeeper to John Kerins and Mick Burns was on the panel too. All of their hearts were in the club and that's a massive thing to have.

It's something for which I'd have huge respect.

Niall was living in Cork city too and we used to travel down to training together. Often, on the way down in the van, we'd be plotting to see how we could beat MC O'Mahony in running laps. In sport, you'll always find someone to raise it to another level, someone that'll bring you back down a peg or two and MC was like that for us.

We used to be doing 10, maybe 15, laps in the Black Field through the muck and he'd be out in front, hardly even panting, putting myself and Niall to shame!

Invariably, Niall and I would end up on opposite teams in training and we'd be marking each other. It meant we'd get the best out of each other but occasionally we'd come to blows and there'd be no talk in the car on the way back until we'd get to Bandon.

We might stop at a shop and get a bottle of Tanora, and then we'd start chatting again!

The replay against Duhallow was on October 15 and it was in Páirc Uí Chaoimh, a double-header with the other semi-final, between back-to-back champions Nemo Rangers and St Finbarr's. The city clubs had won two of the previous three All-Ireland club titles between them, but that was the curtain-raiser for our game, with massive crowds coming from Duhallow and Castlehaven.

As it happened, that first match finished in a draw as well, but at the time that was none of our concern. We were just focused on improving from our drawn game and we did that, eventually.

There were less than 30 seconds gone when Duhallow got a goal and it was the difference for most of the game. With a quarter of an hour left, they were still ahead at 1-4 to 0-4, but Martin O'Mahony – the only other one of the 'Americans' who was playing that year – levelled with a goal and we got four points on the trot after that. John Cleary and Francis Collins finished things off with late points and we won by 1-10 to 1-5.

We were in the final and my prophecy coming off the field after the St Nick's match back in May was only one game away from coming true. A week later, the Barrs ended Nemo's hopes of a three in-a-row, meaning that the decider would be a repeat of Castlehaven's only previous appearance in the final, in 1979.

▲▼▲▼▲

WE GOT A great start to the 1988 All-Ireland final against Meath.

I was doing okay physically but then a ball broke around the middle and I felt the hamstring go. I headed for the sideline to tell Billy I was gone, but before I got my words out, Billy was roaring at me to swap with Teddy.

I said to myself... *If this is the last game I play, I'll wipe the pain out of my head.*

As a forward, you're looking to get off the mark, anticipating a break when the ball comes towards you. At midfield, you're going for the ball in the air and you're at a different pace, so that suited me rather than having to sprint for the ball.

We owned the ball in the second-half, but we did not capitalise on all our opportunities. On the 70th minute mark Dave Barry was fouled and a free awarded. Dave gave me the ball.

'Whatever you do... put it over!' he said.

Tommy Sugrue from Kerry was refereeing, and I thought I heard him say, 'Time is up!'

I put down the ball and I turned to Hill 16 and I blessed myself. I knew as soon as I had kicked the ball that it was going over.

I didn't even have to look at it

Dave jumped up on my shoulders and I fell to the ground.

Then, McQuillan kicked the ball out and the ref let play go on.

Shea Fahy caught it cleanly and went to fist it to Tony Nation, but the ball went out over the sideline at the Cusack side.

Still, he still let play go on.

Martin O'Connell sent a massive kick in and everyone went for it, before David Beggy threw himself on the ball. And Sugrue gave a free.

It was easy for Stafford and that was it, a draw, 1-9 to 0-12. Sugrue came in for some stick, I remember Conor trying to keep the peace.

THERE WAS HARDLY a word spoken in the dressing-room afterwards.

The only noise I can remember was Dr Con Murphy bawling crying, something I had never seen before. I was banjaxed.

I could hardly walk and Dr Con was saying that there was no way I'd be able to play in the replay. The one saving grace was that we had a three-week window – normally there would be two weeks until the replay but the Nissan International Cycling Classic was finishing in Dublin on October 2, and so the game was put back to October 9.

In the lead-up to the final, a local band called Riordan's Fancy had brought out a song called *The Ballad of Larry Tompkins*. Con Riordan was a lovely fan and he had got in touch to ask if it was okay and I had no problem – even now, the song would still be occasionally requested on the local radio station, C103.

When we got back to the railway station on the Monday night after the drawn game, the band were there playing the song and there was a crowd to greet us, but we were fairly deflated. I was expecting to have to get the leg iced on the Tuesday by Dr Con to get the rehabilitation going, but I got a phone call late that night from Frank Murphy.

He asked if I could be at Cork Airport the following morning. Dan Hoare, the county board treasurer, would meet me with money and a plane ticket to Manchester – I was being sent to Manchester United for treatment.

The pilot on the flight over was a man by the name of Con Foley, a brother-in-law of Barry Coffey's. Con's uncle, Donal Foley was chief pilot in Aer Lingus at the time and the two of them used to fly us all over the country to national league games.

I was brought up to the cockpit, though it was still quite difficult to walk.

When I landed in Manchester, I was met by former Manchester United player, Paddy Crerand, who had been a member of the team that won the European Cup in 1968. That was around 10am or 11am and he took me straight to the training ground, known as The Cliff. I was to be staying near Old Trafford in the Copthorne Hotel, which was owned by Aer Lingus.

I couldn't get over the size of the training ground, there were loads of pitches and the main building was nearly all glass.

Bryan Robson, the United captain, had a reserved parking spot but it was empty – I didn't know it at the time but it was because he was off the road. In the first-team dressing-room, each cupboard had a player's name on it and there was a jacuzzi in the middle of the floor, a step up from what we had in Páirc Uí Chaoimh!

Paddy brought me to meet the physio, a Scotsman named Jim McGregor, up in the treatment area on the first floor. Norman Whiteside and Clayton Blackmore were being treated and Alex Ferguson popped in.

'I heard you were coming,' Fergie said. 'You're one of us now... anything you want, just ask, but you're to be here at quarter to nine in the morning like any other player.'

Jim McGregor took a look at me and he was shocked.

He said it was the worst hamstring tear he'd ever seen in his life, that I had a lump the size of his fist.

'How the hell did you play on?' he wanted to know.

That sounded ominous, but there was a positive, of sorts.

'If you're willing to suffer, we have a chance,' he said. 'I'll have to sign a form declaring that you're able to play and I'll have to be truthful.'

Treatment started straight away. I lay down and he handed me a strap, and said, 'Bite on that!' I noticed a bucket on the ground under my head.

I learned later that it was there to mop up the sweat and the sick because of the severity of the treatment. He went at it hard, and my screams were loud.

Norman Whiteside was lying beside me, getting treatment, and he was laughing at me. 'You GAA lads must be made of paper,' he told me. I didn't try to hide the pain from him, or anybody else. The pain was brutal.

I was taken back to the hotel in a taxi and, even after two treatments, it was beginning to feel better.

The following morning, I was collected by Paul McGrath, who had given Bryan Robson a lift. Robson was asking me about Kevin Moran, who had recently left United to move to Sporting Gijon in Spain. Robson said he still couldn't believe how we'd be playing in front of 90,000 people and not get paid a penny for it.

It was back up to Jim McGregor for more of the same.

He had a big window looking out on to one of the pitches, allowing him to tell lads to go down for a run so he could see how they were going. Whiteside was beside me again, being treated for an Achilles tendon problem.

McGregor told him to go out and do a few laps but he was back in within 10 minutes. 'I'll get the same money lying here on the table!' he laughed.

For me, it was a case of being treated three times a day. Back at the hotel, with little else to do, I started doing a bit of stretching. There was a lovely leisure centre but I had been strictly told to stay away from hot water.

By the end of that first week, the lump had gone and I felt like running but I couldn't. On the Saturday, I had one round of treatment in the morning and then Alex Ferguson gave me a player's pass – United were playing West Ham and I got to sit with the squad members behind the dugout.

The players all showed up beforehand in their suits, they didn't even have to bring a pair of socks with them, all the gear and everything else was laid out. A far cry from home.

The boots were shining as if they were going to Sunday Mass.

On the way there, I asked the driver how he thought United would do that season and he said that, if nothing else, they'd win the drinking league!

The following week I was still getting three treatments each day, with stretching and gym time thrown in. But I got out in the evenings. My driver brought me to the Old Nag's Head, where I got to chat with Mark Hughes and Brian McClair for a few hours. I left early; they were in for the long haul.

I WAS NAMED to start the replay and I was planning to go home on the Thursday, flying from Manchester to Dublin and then on to Cork in time for a team meeting in Jurys Hotel.

Jim put me through 50 minutes of a fitness test at Old Trafford in the morning and I came through that fine; I was sprinting and the hamstring felt great. He signed the letter clearing me to play and told me I'd worked really hard. I boarded the flight for Dublin but as we came in to land, the weather was beginning to get worse.

I didn't think too much of it and I checked in for the flight to Cork – it was due to land at 7pm and the meeting was 8pm. I went to get a bite to eat but then I met the Dublin player, Paul Clarke, who worked as an airport policeman. He said that the forecast was for a storm and that the flight to Cork was cancelled.

People were being sent back on a late train but that wouldn't be in until midnight.

I didn't know what to do but who did I bump into only Con Foley, who had flown me over – he was due to fly the plane from Dublin to Cork!

I told him my situation and he said to hang on, that he might be able to clear it to go back as the plane had to be in Cork for the morning. When he came back and gave the thumbs-up, I assumed that the scheduled flight was back on.

But I was the only passenger; me with three air hostesses!

It was rough coming into Cork. It took about three-quarters of an hour to land. There was talk that we'd have to be diverted to Shannon but eventually we got down. The plane was nearly landing on one wheel.

I felt like the President coming off the plane on my own but I had to rush to Jurys. I was telling the other lads what had happened but they wouldn't believe me at all; they said it was too far-fetched!

TOMMY SUGRUE WAS the referee again.

Nowadays, it's always a different ref for a final replay. In the second game Sugrue was a busy man. Meath had felt that they let us away with too much in the drawn game and they made sure that they wouldn't be caught again.

The weekend before the replay, they had gone to Dundalk and Seán Boylan had abandoned a training match after a quarter of an hour because they were killing each other. They were definitely more geed up and it felt like there was a fight every 10 minutes; they wanted to make it a physical battle.

Gerry McEntee was sent off early on for a kick on Niall, but we couldn't make use of the extra man. We led at half-time, 0-6 to 0-5, but we weren't patient enough.

We went 0-8 to 0-6 ahead in the second-half but they got four points in-a-row and led from there. Liam Hayes was brilliant at midfield for Meath; PJ Gillic slotted in alongside him, and we couldn't reproduce our dominance of the drawn game.

It was 0-13 to 0-9 for them with seven minutes of normal time left and we ate into that lead with points from Dinny Allen, myself and Barry Coffey, but the referee blew up when it felt like we might have been given more time.

It was fairly sickening to lose another final but the injury was fine at least and I felt I played well.

There was one sour note at the final whistle, when Gerry McEntee, with whom I was friendly, ran across the field.

'Ye'll never beat us!' he shouted at me.

I ran after him to clock him but, as I was running, the crowd was coming in and I got hit by the end of a flag on top of my head.

IN THE DRESSING-ROOM, Niall Cahalane was crying, and Dr Con was telling him that the reason he himself had been crying after the draw was because he felt our chance was gone.

We went to the function that night, organised by the Dublin Corkmen's Association, as people had paid their money for that. At the time, there used to be a luncheon organised on the Monday for the two teams in the Royal Hospital in Kilmainham and you can imagine how little appetite there was for that.

I didn't bother going; instead, a few of us congregated at Paddy Cullen's pub in Ballsbridge. As it happened, we missed the GAA president, John Dowling lamenting the manner in which the game had been played and, later in the year, when he would go to Meath to present their medals, Liam Harnan and Gerry McEntee would refuse to accept theirs.

On the Monday after the final, McEntee was feeling guilty about what happened between us. He hoped to apologise to me at the luncheon but when I wasn't there, he asked Dr Con where I might be and so he rang Paddy Cullen's.

We were drowning our sorrows, and I didn't come on the phone to him.

To be fair to him, he got in touch again a few days later. He apologised and I said that I should have taken the call. In life, you meet sincere and honest guys; you realise how much these things mean to them, and it was easy for me to forgive him.

It's an All-Ireland final, you'll do anything you can and the emotions are high. I'm not the kind of person to hold grudges for the rest of my life.

It was something he felt bad about and I would have preferred if it hadn't happened but these things occur in the heat of battle. Gerry McEntee is a hell of a guy and I wouldn't let that incident lower his colours.

We had known each other going a way back. He looked after me when I got the blow to the head in 1983 and we won our first All Stars together in '87 – on that occasion, we each turned to the other and said that it was well overdue!

We parted on a good note and we've always got on well since.

COMING BACK DOWN to Cork after the final, we were low but I don't think there were any doubts about Billy's future. Looking back, 1988 was a very defining year for Cork, as the team grew up as men.

There were savage leaders in there.

We had measured up to the challenge of Meath and a bit of luck just went against us. Meath came out of the drawn game saying they had let us play too much so they had to make it a bloodbath the second day, whereas we came out saying not to get involved and to play football.

No Cork fella backed down, fights and scuffles broke out and each fella fought his battle, but they were willing to go that bit further. Still, I'd never take away from Meath's victories against us, because I know how good they were.

I went back to America within three or four days of the final and resumed with Donegal, who were at the quarter-final stage of the championship.

We made it to the final again, beating Cork in the semi to set up another clash with Connemara Gaels. Niall Cahalane and Jack O'Shea came out again and we won – a four in-a-row of sorts, taking into account 1985 and '86 and the cancelled '87 final replay.

It was something positive at the end of a disappointing year, as was winning another All Star, and it made me more determined to put things right in 1989.

Losing two All-Ireland finals to Meath in 1987 and '88 really hurt, but it also made us in Cork the great team we soon became. The man behind that Meath team, Sean Boylan (right) was the equal of Billy Morgan in total passion, and our tussles with Meath boiled over in a big way in the 1987 (below, where Teddy McCarthy is surrounded by one too many Meathmen) and in the '88 All-Ireland final replay.

PART 3

BELIEVE

CHAPTER 11

I FELT THAT Castlehaven were in a good place in training in the lead up to the 1989 county final against St Finbarr's.

Ten years previously, all of the Collins brothers had featured in the final, though this time only Francis was still left on the team. Christy was part of the management team under Pádraig Burke and, of course, Anthony and Vincie – along with Martin Connolly – had opted not to come back for 1989 after the disappointment of the previous two years.

They were all home as supporters for the final and it did feel a little bit strange for me to be captaining the team, given they had put so much effort into getting me to transfer.

John Cleary and Jim Nolan were survivors from the 1979 final too, but even though we had five of the Cork panel, we were still major outsiders. I think the Barrs were 1/5 favourites, hardly surprising given that they had beaten the All-Ireland club champions, Nemo and they had more experience of finals than us.

When they beat the Haven in 1979, that was the first of three wins in four years and they had been to three finals in-a-row in the middle of the 80s, beating Clonakilty in 1985. All you had to do was look through the Barrs' team; there wasn't a weak link. At the same time, while we would have had five or six well-known players, the others were just as important. That's what made the Haven so special, nobody was treated like a god; I was hammered in training as much as anyone else.

I really felt good before that final, everything was triggering in my mind just right.

There's an old saying that matches aren't won on the day but they're won that week. A lot depends on how you go about things and how you shape yourself up. There was a great vibe in the squad and massive determination.

The game was set for the October Bank Holiday Sunday.

I had received an invitation to go down to the showgrounds, next to Páirc Uí Chaoimh, to speak at the Cork Modern Homes Exhibition and Motor Show on the night before the final. It was a bit dull but dry and I decided to walk down as it was nearby.

I spent an hour there and when I came out, it was starting to rain.

I walked around by the stadium and it began to pelt down. I got down on my knees and I didn't care if there was anyone looking.

I prayed to Almighty God that he'd give me the strength to have the game of my life the following day.

SOMETIMES, NIALL CAHALANE might go down to Castlehaven the night before a game but he didn't for the 1989 final. He was living out in Wilton and he said he'd pick me up on the Sunday morning.

When he collected me, the first thing he asked was how I felt?

'I'll beat these fellas on my own... I'm feeling so good,' I told him.

We were to meet the rest of the team out at Blackrock – the clubs had a good relationship as both Niall and Francis Collins played hurling for the Rockies. It was a wet morning and there was a slight threat that the game might be called off, but it was beginning to lighten.

There was a good atmosphere in Blackrock; they let us out on the field for a bit of a kickaround. By the time we got to Páirc Uí Chaoimh, the rain had eased off and, by the time of the match itself, it was fairly dry.

There was a massive determination within us.

We were ultra-competitive, going for every ball like our lives depended on it. We were against the wind in the first-half but I got off to a good start; I scored the first point, rallying from way beyond midfield and linking up with Francis Collins. The Barrs had four wides in the first five minutes and they had something like 14 for the first-half.

We had led 0-4 to 0-1 at one stage and while they were 0-5 to 0-4 ahead at half-time, we weren't panicking.

There was a lot of scuffling and fighting before half-time but we were focused for the second-half. Michael O'Brien had us level straight after the restart and he had a huge game overall. Loads of fellas did.

For me, it was a day when anything I kicked seemed to go over – the best one was probably a sideline kick from the 21-yard line. We were 0-8 to 0-7 ahead with six minutes left, when Christy Ryan was sent off for the Barrs, but even with the extra man we had to defend for our lives.

Dave Barry had a chance to equalise – he hit the top part of the post and the ball fell into my hands and we cleared it. It was nearly dark when Dave O'Regan got the point to clinch it for us. I always said that Dave would have made it at inter-county if he had had the discipline; he was a mini-Brian Mullins, a hell of a footballer.

It was fitting he got the last one.

Thanks be to God my prayers were answered and I played one of the best games of my life. I got Man of the Match but if you were to give it to anyone else, MC was the man. Here was a guy people were questioning at centre-forward but he was immense – he'd go through the wall for you and then go through the next wall.

Mick Burns was outstanding at centre-back, Niall was brilliant and Tim Joe O'Regan put in a big shift at full-forward. Everything went right for me. I was hoping it was going to happen in 1987, but it didn't and '88 never got going for the Haven. The trauma with both was huge and then in '89, when the other lads didn't commit to coming back, people might have felt we were weaker.

I felt sorry for those guys, only for them I wouldn't have been there. In fairness to them, they were as happy as if they had been playing.

Everyone came back to my pub afterwards and it was so busy I had to go in behind the counter. The bus had to leave at a certain time to get back to Castlehaven for the real celebrations but I ended up not going because it was all hands on deck. It got to the stage where I just wanted to sit down and have a drink without any hassle.

It might be unusual, the captain not being there, but I was delighted for John Cleary and Niall that they were able to bring the cup down. I told them I'd be a bit fresher for the Man of the Match function at Jurys Hotel on the Monday at noon.

The organisers were taken aback when a whole bus-load came up from Castlehaven for that! They had to bring in extra seats but everyone was fed. In fairness to the Barrs, they were very gracious. There was a great respect there between the clubs. I suppose for a long time the Haven would have looked at the Barrs as a club to try to emulate. The whole occasion was one of those really special days that you dream of.

The likes of the older brigade were going to matches all their lives hoping they'd see that day and they were saying that nothing would ever equal it. A lot of those men have passed away now. When you win your first ever senior title, it can never be repeated.

Niall Cahalane's father, John and John Cleary's father, Ned – a Mayo native – were just some of the massive people in the club, along with Dan Collins. Nora Maguire, after her husband died very young, raised a family of great Haven people. She was like my own mother, she saved me from heading back to America. They were all so passionate and they lived for Castlehaven.

You don't always have the best 15 players, but you don't have to have them. A strong spirit will take you a long way and that's one of the reasons that we had support from all of the smaller clubs out around west Cork.

It was easy for me to grow into it. I would be deemed to be a lunatic and a fanatic for football, and I wanted to get myself to a level where I would have no regrets. I always wanted to play with lads who were similar and it was a match made in heaven.

I got that vibe from the Haven lads over in America and I was so lucky to have captained the team to their first county title.

WE CARRIED OUR momentum into the Munster club championship.

We played Laune Rangers of Kerry in the semi-final in Killarney and we won that by 1-11 to 0-8 – not the last time we would clash with the men from Killorglin – and then it was back to Fitzgerald Stadium in December for the final, against the Clare champions, St Senan's from Kilkee. We were the better team for most of the game but they stuck with us and it was like the county final – they missed a chance to equalise and we clinched it with a late point from Francis Collins as we won by 0-13 to 1-8.

I had won a third straight All Star and we had a good Christmas, looking forward to the All-Ireland semi-final against Baltinglass of Wicklow. My business was doing well from the success of winning the All-Ireland and the county. The place always seemed to be busy and we were working hard at it.

I'd have known a lot of the Baltinglass players from being involved with Wicklow vocational schools teams. Kevin O'Brien, Hugh Kenny and Seán O'Brien were just some of the top players they had. They had won their sixth county title of the 80s and were after the third of what would be seven straight championships. Back then, it was still the case that one team had home advantage for All-Ireland semi-finals and Baltinglass preferred to play in Aughrim as they had never been beaten there.

It was a horrible day.

Paddy Russell was the referee and he had to inspect the pitch to make sure the game would go ahead. You had every kind of storm – snow, sleet, rain, wind. There was no cover on the terraces, the people got drowned but even still, the place was packed. There was a crowd of around 12,000. I would have had a lot of contact with Wicklow and I knew it was a massive footballing area. They'd have died for the game.

They won the toss and played with the wind, and had three points in the first five minutes before getting a goal. Another point followed in the 11th minute and another in the 20th but, incredibly, they didn't score again. By half-time, it was 1-5 to 0-2. John Cleary got a great score early in the second-half, but I missed a good few chances. We lost Mike Maguire to a sending-off and went 17 minutes without a score but Baltinglass couldn't score either and I got a free to bring it back to a point late on.

We couldn't find an equaliser, though, and they won by 1-5 to 0-6.

It was obviously a missed opportunity – Baltinglass went on to beat Clann na nGael by six points in the final. Maybe if the semi-final had been at a neutral venue – as is the case now – and on a better pitch, we might have beaten Baltinglass, but you have to give them credit, they were a great side. To have won the club All-Ireland would have been the crowning glory after such a great 1989, but it wasn't to be.

THERE WAS A fairly big consolation for me though as Castlehaven nominated me as Cork captain for 1990. The system in Cork back then was that the county champions got to choose the captain and there was a vote at a club meeting, with me, John Cleary and Niall Cahalane all proposed.

Christy Collins had proposed me as I had been the Haven captain in 1989 and he felt that it shouldn't matter that I wasn't a native. He pointed out that John Joe Kelly, originally a Glen Rovers/St Nick's man and living down in Castlehaven, always said that, once you were a Glen man, that was it. Christy Ring was originally from Cloyne but he had transferred to the Glen and captained Cork as a Glen man.

Still and all, Niall and John were born and bred down there.

John had played for Cork since 1983. You had Mike Maguire and Mick Burns on the Cork panel too. Did I expect to be captain of Cork over these fellas?

No, but they accepted me from day one – you can live in a place 50 years and still be called a blow-in but I was never considered a blow-in and that was to do with the people, the players, the whole setting. I went down there and I was treated the same as anybody else – I wasn't Larry Tompkins from Kildare, I was a Castehaven player.

The best way to pay them back was to try to lift some silverware as Cork captain.

The real reason I came back to Ireland in 1987 was to play with Castlehaven. My debut was held up, and the Haven had to have spirit and courage in building the team capable of being No.1 in Cork. But in 1989 we did it, and I had the great honour of leading the team on the day (top). Here I am (left) with Nora Maguire, who was like a second mother to me.

CHAPTER 12

IT WAS EASTER Sunday, 1990 and Billy Morgan was on his knees, praying to Almighty God. However, the resurrection he was seeking was Meath's supremacy in Leinster.

We had just been beaten by Seán Boylan's side in the national league semi-final in Croke Park, 0-14 to 0-10, and it had arguably been an uglier affair than the recent All-Ireland final meetings.

Dave Barry was taken out of it at one stage and there was really bad blood between the two teams. You might think it was odd that Billy wanted them to go far that summer, but he was keen for us to have another cut off them. Some people said that our 1989 All-Ireland win was devalued because we beat Mayo – those people conveniently forgot that we had to beat Kerry and Dublin too – and we needed to beat Meath in a final.

There was a big crowd there, around 30,000 for the double-header. I can remember going into the old dressing-rooms, at the corner of the Canal End and the Hogan Stand, and the fans hanging over the wire to meet you and shower a few insults. Billy went stone mad in the dressing-room.

He was always a feisty character but it reached another level that day. In the middle of the dressing-room, he got down on his knees and prayed to God that Meath would make the final. 'We'll be there but, by God… we want that crowd to be there too!' he roared.

I was half-crippled that day, but not due to any Meath treatment, it must be said. When I was 18 or 19, working on the buildings and serving my time, I got a twinge in my back one day and it was something that I'd had to manage ever since. I used to rub Deep Heat into it before games but afterwards I'd be in a bit of bother.

That day, I was one of the last to leave the dressing-room, with Billy and Conor Counihan, and it was like the Meath crowd waited for me. There was a big crowd outside and they gave it both barrels.

'Go away off back to Cork… you'll never beat us!' was the flavour of it. Billy went to run at them and the security guys had to pull him back.

It was nearly a riot.

IN HINDSIGHT, IT was important that we lost that game.

We were the All-Ireland champions but it still felt like we had something to prove. Anyone that has played the game knows that you're always looking for something that's going to get that bit extra out of you. There would be no fears about complacency when we had Meath in our sights like that.

As it happened, the following day the Cork hurlers would get a similar kick up the rear as they lost by 1-9 to 0-6 against Wexford in their league semi-final in Kilkenny. The starting forwards scored 0-2 from play and yet all six would still be in place for the All-Ireland final against Galway that September, scoring 5-11 of Cork's 5-15.

We also hoped our journey would end in Croke Park in September and we began the Munster championship against Limerick in Páirc Uí Chaoimh at the end of May, though I was a spectator.

My back was still giving me trouble and I had missed what proved to be Castlehaven's only game in defence of the county title as Muskerry beat us two weeks after the Meath game. There were five sent off, including Niall Cahalane, but the one-month suspension he got was backdated to the Haven game, meaning he was eligible to captain Cork against Limerick. Cork won by 4-15 to 1-3, with John O'Driscoll very good in attack.

There was just over a month to prepare for the Munster final against Kerry, who had a new manager in Mickey Ned O'Sullivan after the retirement of Mick O'Dwyer. The word was going out that I wasn't right and I didn't bother doing anything to dispel those rumours. Instead, I trained away quietly – I was going down to the Mardyke in the mornings and hopping in over the wall to do 20 or 25 laps. Dr Con Murphy was looking after me and monitoring me, making sure I took things easy.

On those early mornings, sometimes I met up with Sonia O'Sullivan. We were the only two 'lunatics' who would be up at that early hour running the track. I took a keen interest in her development, but little did I think at the time that I was running with one of the greatest female athletes the world has ever produced.

Cork training sessions were open to everyone and a lot of Cork-based Kerry people used to attend, so I did only a small bit there in case there were any spies reporting back to Killarney. Six of the team from the 1989 final were unavailable.

Dinny Allen went out at the top after captaining us to glory at the age of 37 and we had a litany of injuries. Teddy McCarthy was out and so was John O'Driscoll, which was a pity after his performance against Limerick, and there were big doubts about John Kerins, Niall Cahalane and Tony Davis.

Tony was named in the team but had to withdraw and it was the same with Barry Coffey, who had been selected at wing-forward. I had been picked at midfield with Danny Culloty, with Shea Fahy at full-forward.

On the Saturday, Billy rang me to check I was alright and I told him I was flying. He wasn't sure what to do in attack and I told him to play Colm O'Neill, who was the most natural corner-forward we had.

THAT EVENING, IRELAND were playing Italy in the World Cup quarter-finals and I felt that the pub was the last place to be the night before a Munster final.

It was going to be a madhouse and I had to get out.

The west Cork fellas were staying in Jurys and I went out there. We watched the match up in one of the rooms and afterwards we said we'd take a walk in towards town. Even though Ireland lost to 'Toto' Schillachi's goal, there was absolute bedlam inside in Washington St. There was one poor old fella with a tractor and trailer and he mustn't have had a clue what was happening; there were fellas hanging off every part of the trailer!

When I met Billy the next morning, he said that Colm would be starting. I said that I'd have a word with him and Billy said, 'Do, because he has only two ways of playing… he's either switched on or switched off'.

Colm was one of the most laid-back fellas you'd meet; a bomb could be going off alongside him and he wouldn't move. I used to get on well with him, though. When we trained in Millstreet, he'd travel with me but he'd express doubts as to why he was bothering because he felt he was never going to play.

It was similar on the morning of the Munster final. He didn't expect to be in the matchday 21, not to mind the starting 15, but I put him right.

'You're on the team today,' I told him, '… and I'll tell you one thing, you're one of the best players on this team. But I'll break your two legs if you don't perform today.'

He was going out with Maurice Fitzgerald's sister, Christine – they later got married and their son, Shane is a professional soccer player – and he was one of these fellas who was so placid you couldn't but like him, he'd nearly be apologetic if he knocked down a fella. On this day, though, he was focused.

We were getting ready to go down to the ground when he spoke up.

'Listen, don't worry about me!'

Early on, I got a free – it was for a left-footed kicker but still fairly central. I left the ball down and called Colm out, and he kicked it over and I think it just set the tone. The lads who had had to wait for their chances definitely took them.

Danny Culloty was lording it alongside me, Mick Slocum was brilliant and kicked a great score off his left; Paddy Hayes and Mick McCarthy were on fire too. We had guys that day that stood up to it, and it showed that Cork had a serious panel of players. In the end we won by 2-23 to 1-11, Danny and Mick getting the goals while Niall, who played after being all but ruled out with a shoulder injury, gave a defensive exhibition.

How many teams could be missing that many players and beat Kerry by so much? Colm kicked 11 points and people don't talk too much about it.

MY YOUNG FELLA, Jack is left-footed and nowadays I'd be telling him to kick with his right and he'd say, 'Sure you never kicked with your left'.

My retort is that, 'I did… I scored one from 50 yards against Kerry'. It was that kind of a day, one you wish you could bottle.

Coming towards the end of that game, there was a really memorable moment. John Corcoran was a man from Ballineen in west Cork who became a great friend of mine and he'd often call to the pub. He had two great loves, the GAA and west Cork, and he was sitting next to my brother, Martin in the stand.

With about 15 minutes left, it was getting really bad for Kerry and some of their fans started to leave so as to beat the traffic back over the county bounds. John was a man of quick wit and he had a great big, booming voice, so everyone around heard him say, 'Lock the gates and make them suffer!' He had seen Kerry demolishing Cork so many times that this was sweet revenge.

Everyone was in good spirits coming out of the game, but at the same time there was an appreciation that winning Munster wasn't enough. We were going to be facing Roscommon in the All-Ireland semi-final on August 12 and, on the other side of the draw, Billy Morgan's prayers looked like being answered as Meath won Leinster.

They would be facing Donegal.

Tony Davis and Barry Coffey were back for the semi, with Denis Walsh and Mick McCarthy the unlucky players to miss out. Roscommon, against whom I had made my senior debut for Kildare a decade earlier, were in a semi-final for the first time since back then and were underdogs but they put it up to us. At half-time, we were only a point ahead, 0-7 to 0-6. Niall was outstanding again and Paul McGrath was excellent up front.

In the second-half, we were finding it hard to get away from them and it wasn't until the last 10 minutes that we pulled clear. Mick McCarthy was brought on and he kicked three points; Tony Nation and Steven O'Brien both kicked points after they followed their men out the field when Roscommon began to sit back.

It finished 0-17 to 0-10 and we came out of that match fairly down in the mouth but in a sense, we couldn't have asked for a better semi-final. It was a big come-down from the Munster final but better for that to happen in an All-Ireland semi-final than the final.

A week later, Meath were very impressive against Donegal, which was maybe a bit unusual for them as they hadn't normally been firing in semi-finals. Then, on September 2, the hurlers, with Teddy McCarthy and Denis Walsh playing, beat Galway in the All-Ireland final. In his speech, their captain, Tomás Mulcahy expressed the hope that we would complete the double a fortnight later and the talk began to grow.

Cork had done the double in 1890 but, apart from Tipperary that same decade, it hadn't been done since – and the previous three examples were all from the time when clubs represented counties. I can say with all honesty though that, within our camp, there was little or no talk about the double and it definitely didn't side-track us.

In our minds, Meath was a bigger focus and we weren't going to let this one slip.

We trained on the Saturday the weekend before the final and the team was to be picked on the Sunday before being announced on the Tuesday night. We trained on the Thursday night, had a light session and a meeting. On Friday, I took it easy and then on Saturday we met up at Kent Station at 2pm.

On the train we could sense the atmosphere building. The supporters were travelling in their droves… music was playing, flags were flying… lads were singing. We had a carriage of our own, and it was quieter in there. Every man was filled with his own thoughts. I could sense a massive focus within the squad.

I sat beside Colm on the train and he never spoke a word. My thoughts were also with Denis Walsh, after being on the team all year and missing out on the final. It was an awful pity for him that he didn't get an opportunity to win a second medal in the one year, like Teddy.

Teams get 30 All-Ireland medals nowadays! I'm not sure if that is right, either, but Denis earned a medal that year, big time! But being the man that he is, he got on with it.

WE STAYED IN The Burlington Hotel and we had an access code to go down the back lift because the lobby was jammed. A few of us went out to Shelbourne Park on the Saturday night but everyone had a good sleep.

The focus was just a bit different from the other times playing Meath.

This was one we had to win.

There was enormous pressure on us to make the breakthrough and lift Sam Maguire in 1989 when we met Mayo in the final. Here, I get to work against John Finn and (below) TJ Kilgallon. The brilliant touch of Dave Barry (below) helped steer us home safely.

CHAPTER 13

THERE WAS A lot of tension before the 1990 All-Ireland final, but I think it gave us unreal focus – there was a lot of motivation there.

As a captain, you have extra things to attend to, like introducing the team to the President, but it was a case of embracing that.

It was Dr Patrick Hillery's last All-Ireland final as President and he got to witness history.

FROM THE WORD go, Danny Culloty and Shea Fahy were outstanding at midfield and the full-back line couldn't have done better.

Tony Nation kept Bernard Flynn out of the game and Niall Cahalane got on top of Colm O'Rourke, with Steven O'Brien limiting Brian Stafford's impact from play. It was largely a backs' day, except for Colm O'Neill at the other end.

He was winning every ball and Mick Lyons wasn't able to handle him.

He won a few early frees that I converted and then he came out the field, picked up possession and went on a massive run. He shot from the 21-yard line and the ball hit the underside of the crossbar, came down and was cleared.

Lyons later said, 'The word around was that Colm O'Neill was soft… he didn't seem soft to me!' Unfortunately, he was to prove that shortly before half-time. Meath won a defensive free, Colm picked up the ball and Mick went to grab it, and Colm hit him; it was a spontaneous thing.

Colm was so worked up that, if Mick Lyons acted the maggot, he was going to clock him.

One thing you'd say is that Lyons didn't lie down to win an Oscar. He could give it and take it, and he didn't try to get Colm sent off but Paddy Russell made his decision.

The funny thing is that I think it affected Lyons for the rest of the game.

He was after getting such a roasting and he couldn't operate as the spare man. Maybe if Seán Boylan was to have his time again, he might have done things differently. They just left Lyons behind me all the time, meaning I had him and Kevin Foley. Lyons only touched the ball once after that, though.

He was the type of fella that loved having a man to mark.

We went in at half-time a point ahead, 0-6 to 0-5, and Meath hadn't led at all. Paul McGrath was on fire in the corner, Shea was playing great stuff, the backs were outstanding. Most of the players didn't even sit down inside in the dressing-room; there was a rush to go out there and finish the job.

There was nobody consoling Colm O'Neill – it was hardly even mentioned. Shea and Paul got big points straight after the restart and Barry Coffey was putting in a huge shift at left half-back. Just as important was an outstanding John Kerins save to deny Brian Stafford. If Meath had gone ahead, it's hard to say what would have happened.

WITH ABOUT 20 minutes to go, Mick McCarthy turned to shoot and got half-taken out of it and went down injured. Dr Con went on to take a look at him and made the call that he should be taken off, with John O'Driscoll coming on.

We were a point ahead at that stage and, straightaway, Johnno was fouled for a free that I put over. Then, Barry Coffey came out of defence with a ball and sent it high towards me but it went over my head.

I chased it.

Martin O'Connell was coming one way and I was coming the other; he was getting there first but I put in my foot to make it difficult for him.

Whatever way my knee collided with him, I could sense I had done something majorly wrong, but I hopped up off the ground quickly because I was afraid that Dr Con would bring me off like he had done with Mick.

With a cruciate ligament, there's a sensation and a pain initially. and then the blood gushes towards it and the pain goes.

It was like a sudden shot.

A few minutes later, I was thinking I'd be okay.

I carried on but I felt I couldn't move the way I normally would.

With 10 minutes left, we got a free under the Hogan Stand and I knew I wouldn't have the distance. Shea came short, turned and never looked at the posts as he shot but it flew over the bar.

He was having a great day.

The week before the final, the two Meath midfielders, Liam Hayes and Gerry McEntee had met to formulate a plan and decided that four points from midfield should be enough to secure the All-Ireland – they were right, but all four were scored by Shea!

I got a free after that to make it 0-11 to 0-7, but Meath are Meath and they came at us hard in the last 10 minutes.

Stafford got two frees to bring them to within a score but that was as close as they came. Mick Slocum and Steven O'Brien both made important late interventions and we had two to spare at the end. When the whistle was blown, it was one of those moments of sheer joy and satisfaction.

We had beaten the team that was the best around and, for us, it was important that we set down the fact that Cork were a serious side to beat. Cork and Meath were two great sides, a good bit ahead of the rest; two massive teams with massive players.

If one didn't arrive, the other would have won four or five All-Irelands, but then in another sense, each brought the best out of the other.

I WAS STILL high on adrenaline and wasn't worrying about my injury, especially as I had a pressing engagement in the Hogan Stand, receiving the Sam Maguire Cup from GAA president, John Dowling.

When I lifted the cup, the crowd had covered the whole field; I could not see a blade of grass. It was clear to see what winning the double meant to the people of Cork.

In my speech, I spoke from the heart. I tried to name all of the people who had meant so much to me and Cork GAA over the years.

The 80s had been tough for the city, with Ford, Dunlop and Verolme all closing, so something like this had to be celebrated and it was. I couldn't come back down the normal way so the security men and gardaí brought me down and into the dressing-room from behind. Jack Lynch, who had won All-Irelands in both codes, was in there and there was fierce excitement, though to look at Teddy McCarthy, you'd never know he had created history.

He had done something that nobody else had done by winning two All-Ireland medals in the one year, but he was as cool as a breeze.

Jack came over and we had a bit of a chat.

I was delighted for 'Kid' Cronin and Frank Cogan, who had come on board to help him as masseur and who had coached us earlier in the year when Billy had been suspended. The Kid was a friend to everybody and, like Dr Con, he was an easy man to chat to if you were feeling tension. He was a hell of a boxer in his younger days and he knew the levels of pressure that guys would be under.

When the whole thing settled down, though, I realised I was in a serious situation. I couldn't even go for a shower.

My knee was butchered and Dr Con knew I had a problem.

Two of the ligaments had gone – Dr Con wrapped a heavy bandage around the knee and it was the best thing in the world.

It stabilised it and I felt support.

We were heading back to The Burlington Hotel with a Garda escort but our function was in the Marina Hotel in Dun Laoghaire. We were caught in a deluge of traffic and when we were stopped outside Gill's pub near Croke Park, the county chairman, Denis Conroy hopped out and so did Niall Cahalane and Mick McCarthy – they were going for a few pints and they said they'd see us back in the hotel!

When we did eventually get to The Burlington, I was grateful for Dr Con's handiwork as the place was wedged. With the force of the crowd, my knee could easily have buckled.

I brought the cup into the hotel and, out of the corner of my eye, I saw four friends of mine – Dave and Fred Cowhig, Noel Murphy and John Kelly – sitting up at the bar. I had enough to contend with, going up to my room to put on my suit, without bringing the Sam Maguire with me, so I left it with them.

'Look lads, you probably deserve this more than me,' I told them. 'I'm going upstairs... mind it for a few minutes!'

I felt it was a nice thing to do for the guys who had followed Cork football through some bad days and they still talk about it today. I went up and gave myself a bit of a wash and got into the suit and headed downstairs.

WHEN WE GOT to Dun Laoghaire for the function, the crowds were something else. I was told that some of my uncles were there, trying to get in but we were in a closed-off area and it was like a stampede outside. There must have been more than a thousand people there.

Later on, the window of the function room came in with the heave. It was a great night for the likes of Joan Cooney, a Kilnamartra woman who had worked all her life in Croke Park as the assistant to the Director General and President of the GAA, to have Sam back in Cork.

When I spoke that night, I made reference to the achievements of Teddy McCarthy and also Denis Walsh.

Later in the year, when we were presented with our medals, I think Denis Walsh and Jimmy Kerrigan were given a piece of glass each as a special presentation. It's the kind of thing where you'd love to cut up your own medal and give it to them.

As well, I felt sorry for Colm as he had had a whale of a game up to the sending-off but he wasn't down in the mouth about it.

I'd say it was 4am or 5am when we got back to The Burlington, but I didn't have much chance for sleep as I had to go on the radio with Gay Byrne the next morning, as was the tradition at the time. I had met Gay the previous year, when he used to do the Housewife of the Year and I was one of the judges for the Munster section.

Gay hadn't a clue about sport but he used to put so much research in that you wouldn't know it. On the radio that morning, Gay nearly knew more than me and Jack Lynch, who was on another line.

Usually, the chat with a winning All-Ireland captain took 10 minutes but we were on for a half-hour, it kept flowing.

Dr Con wrapped up the knee again as tightly as he could.

He had made contact with Tralee General Hospital and I was to go there, most likely for an operation, on the Wednesday morning. Fionán O'Carroll was the specialist down there.

We had the lunch in Kilmainham Gaol and it was the first time that the Cork and Meath teams talked a little bit. We had experienced that lunch as a beaten team so we knew what it was like, and they were fairly gracious.

When we got on the train at Heuston, Andrew Roche of Iarnród Éireann, a Corkman, presented me with a massive cake. We stopped in Mallow on the way down and I was hardly able to get off because there was such a crowd. Similarly, when we landed back in Kent Station, my first thought was that I was delighted I wasn't working – the pub was packed!

My brother, Tommy was there, my mother was there, as was my aunt and a cousin of mine, PJ, who had come down the year before and was a massive help to me. Tony Keogh had come down and so too had my uncle-in-law, Tom Kelly from Galway, whose involvement with the county board there had allowed me to see those great players up close.

There was heightened security at the train station and nobody was allowed in but the people at the station made an exception for my father. Just before we got on the bus, I brought the cup across the road to the pub.

I got my father on to the bus, and the wives and girlfriends were there too. Marty Morrissey was covering the homecoming and he did a lovely interview with my father on the trip. My mother and my aunt did not want to come on the bus and walked alongside the bus for a while but they had to stop as there were so many people.

Every building on Mac Curtain St was packed and there were people everywhere, all the way up St Patrick's Hill. You just can't beat it when you get to Paddy Barry's Corner and see the crowds, though I was looking down and fearing the bus would roll over someone.

It was a special moment, the climax of everything.

Mícheál Ó Muircheartaigh was the MC and he said there were close to 100,000 people present. There was a truck on St Patrick's St, opposite the old *Examiner* office and that's where we got off for the speeches before going to the reception at the Imperial Hotel.

The successful hurling team were there waiting for us, which we had had no idea about. It made it all the more special and a memorable moment – one shown on the 1990 edition of *Reeling in The Year*s – was when myself and Tomás Mulcahy exchanged cups.

It happened spontaneously and the crowd erupted even more.

Back then, the double was something that people hoped would happen again – and it almost did in 1999 – but as time has gone on, there's a growing appreciation of just how special it was.

1990 was all about letting the whole country know that Cork were worthy All-Ireland champions and to do that we needed to beat Meath. But first we had to beat Kerry in the Munster final when I had the greatest honour of leading my adopted county (above, with the late John Kerins, Denis Walsh and Tony Nation just behind me). John Kerins and Mick McCarthy (shaking hands below) were tragically taken from their families and all of us much too early in their lives. For me and Shea Fahy (bottom right) there was always a brotherly bond after moving south from Kildare.

CHAPTER 14

I WAS ONE of the last to leave the Imperial on the Monday night after the All-Ireland win. The players' families were there and, while you'd have loved for everybody to get in, it just wasn't possible.

It was nice and relaxed and I got a taxi with the cup at around 1am.

I went in the side door of the pub, trying to avoid the crowd, but there were so many people there that they had spilled on to the stairs. I said I might as well go into the bar and the place erupted.

It looked like there was a thousand people there!

I'd say I broke records that night as regards accommodation – I don't know how many people stayed and I certainly didn't have all of their names. I was supposed to be going to Tralee early in the morning but there was a tradition to bring the cup around to a few schools and there was also a reception for the team at the Beamish & Crawford brewery.

I STILL HAD had no sleep when Billy Morgan knocked on the door at 8.30am and I threw a bit of water on myself and changed my clothes.

The tiredness didn't really hit me; if I had slept for a few hours it might have been worse. I had a coffee and I woke up a bit, and I was flying again. We went to Coláiste Chríost Rí and a good number of the team showed up. From there, it was on to Beamish and a guy from the Kevin O'Leary Nissan garage on the Douglas

Road came up to me.

They were launching the new Nissan Primera at 6pm that evening and they wanted me and Tomás Mulcahy to attend.

I said that I couldn't go, that I was supposed to be in Tralee, but Dr Con said he'd make contact with Fionán O'Carroll, the surgeon. By all accounts, he wasn't too pleased when Dr Con rang him, but the plan was that I'd leave early Wednesday morning.

Tony Keogh drove me to Kevin O'Leary's, where they had one red car and one white one. I said I'd take the white one, being from Kildare, but they wanted the two of us to drive them from the forecourt into the showroom and I couldn't as my leg was still knackered. What ended up happening was a that a few fellas pushed the one I was sitting in.

The Sam Maguire and Liam MacCarthy Cups were put on the roofs for a few photos and myself and Tomás were given a few drinks.

Nowadays, you'd be getting the car as your thanks!

TONY KEOGH WAS the chauffeur for the trip to Kerry on the Wednesday morning. I checked in early but hadn't met Mr O'Carroll. When I asked if I had to stick around, I was told that I could leave for a bit but I had to be back by 6pm and had to fast from 11pm onwards, ahead of the operation on the Thursday morning.

We went down into the town and we went into a pub. I think it was called Barrett's, where we had a lovely meal. We drove around for a bit and said we'd go back into that pub later on. I had water earlier but when we went back, I had a drink or two without going mad.

Tony had a few as well. He was staying in Tralee too because he thought I might be out after the operation and able to go home.

Then, this man came up to us from the other end of the bar.

'I'm Fionán O'Carroll,' he said.

'And I'm doing your operation tomorrow. My advice to you now is to get out that door and go down to the hospital… otherwise there'll be no surgery.'

I got the biggest land of my life!

I left the drink there, high-tailed it out the door and back down to the hospital.

They operated on me on the Thursday morning.

My cruciate and medial ligaments were smashed, and I had a plaster cast all the way up my leg. In total, I ended up staying there for two and a half weeks. There was a notice up on my door saying not to disturb.

I was on a lot of drugs and I was getting violently sick.

Dinny Long, who had won an All-Ireland football medal with Cork in 1973, was living and working in Tralee and he called in to visit. He ignored the sign but Fionán O'Carroll was a tough man. He happened to see Dinny and told him to get out and leave me alone. I felt sorry for Dinny in that instance but, overall, I have to thank Tralee General Hospital. They looked after me brilliantly.

I missed a lot of the big celebrations due to being in hospital but I was out just in time for the team photograph at Páirc Uí Chaoimh. Looking at it now, you'd say I looked drained and I was.

If you look really closely, you'll see I was wearing a pair of black tracksuit pants rather than my Cork shorts and socks, but the Sam Maguire did a good job of covering up my legs!

The prognosis for a return looked like being a year, if not a year and a half.

The two most high-profile players to have done their cruciate were Kerry's Pat Spillane and the great Offaly dual player, Liam Currams. Liam was a hell of a player, he brought flair and excitement. I made contact with him and learned that he had actually had the same injury twice, which contributed to an early retirement.

I knew then that I had a battle on my hands. I was in the plaster for 10 weeks and I was behind the counter on crutches – when you're your own boss, you're reluctant to take time off. The bar game sucks the life out of you and, that winter, I would say that it took a good chunk out of me.

When you go into your own business and you put everything into it, you have to work at it; it doesn't come easy. People are coming in for service and if that's not there, they won't come back, no matter who you are. I'd be a fierce man to get to know people and that takes energy. You're there and you're being tested.

They're seeing if you're genuine or not. It's about good PR.

That was hard, but in fairness to Tommy and PJ, they were great. My mother and father were down a good bit too and it was all hands on deck. The cups were in big demand but when they weren't being used, they were kept in the pub – Sam and Liam!

A friend of mine, Jimmy Linehan from Glenville, made a shelf for them by the fireplace, and people used to come in and they'd be starstruck at seeing both of them.

AT THE BEGINNING of November, there was a big function out at the ESB south-west regional headquarters in Wilton for the double-winning teams. Denis Conroy was to give a speech and he called to me beforehand as he used to live in St Luke's, just up the hill.

I always got on brilliantly with Denis, he was a huge character.

He had run for the chair previously and been beaten, and then when he ran again in late 1987, he was 75. After we won the double, he liked to use the line, 'It took them a hundred years to do the double... but it only took Conroy two weeks!'

I had been ribbing Denis about the big speech but he was unfazed and left the pub around 6pm. Then, out in Wilton, after Frank Murphy had given a great speech about Cork GAA, Denis stood up.

'First of all, I want to thank the CIÉ for this function,' he said.

Frank whispered, 'Denis... it's the ESB'.

'Ah 'tis all the fecking same!' was the reply! The crowd erupted and for a half-hour he had them eating out of his hand. That was Denis in a nutshell.

I was still on crutches at that stage but I was back on my own two feet by the time of the All Star Awards at the start of December. This was still the time when there were three nominees for each of the 15 spots, unlike nowadays, where you're nominated as a back, midfielder or forward. I was nominated again at centre-forward and so was Dave Barry, who had played there when I was in midfield.

Ultimately, my three-year run came to an end and Val Daly of Galway got the No. 11 spot. Interestingly, Paul McGrath was nominated in two positions – left half-forward, where he had played in the Munster final against Kerry, and right corner-forward, his more usual spot, where he was selected on the team for the second year in-a-row.

The following day, I appeared on RTÉ's Saturday show, *Sports Stadium*, to receive my award for winning Goal of the Year. It had come in the league quarter-final against Kildare in Portlaoise, funnily enough scored past my neighbour from Eadestown, Seán Sargent, who was in goal.

Goals were few and far between in my career, so it was nice to win it.

John Fitzgibbon had won the hurling award and the two of us went on television to be presented with the trophies by Mick Dunne – they were Waterford Crystal, one of the nicest I ever received. I was dressed up but John was in casual gear.

He was definitely a one-off, a real kind of a guy who just did his own thing. Mick asked him, 'What was the highlight of your year, John?'

And there was silence.

Just in case you've any doubts, I can confirm that 30 seconds is a long time to have dead air on national TV! Poor Mick couldn't ask the question again, so he just had to wait. Eventually, John said, 'Seeing Elvis's house in Memphis'.

Mick was a calm fella, but he nearly went through the floor that day!

OTHERWISE, REHAB WAS the central focus for me as 1990 turned into '91. The consensus was that it would take a year if not more to properly recover.

I certainly hadn't heard tell of anyone else doing it quicker, but, me being me, I wanted to be back for the Kerry game as we targeted five Munster championships in-a-row and three All-Irelands, but there was a fly in that ointment – Clare had proposed the introduction of an open draw and the motion was passed.

Naturally, when the draws were made, Cork and Kerry were on the same side.

It meant that, if Kerry got over Clare, we were headed to Killarney for a Munster semi-final on June 16 rather than meeting in the final in July as usual. Essentially, I had lost a month of recovery time. To try to build the thing up, I used to go cycling most Sundays, building up the mileage gradually, going out to Glanmire and back, then to Watergrasshill.

There was one particular Sunday morning where I felt I was doing well so I said I'd go as far as Mitchelstown on the old main road to Dublin, the N8. It had been a nice day when I left the pub at around 10.30 am but then the weather started to worsen; it turned windy, wet and cold.

I was so far from home, I had no option but to stick at it but I had no gloves so my hands were frozen. I'd say I got off the bike about 20 times, trying to walk for a bit just to warm myself up.

I couldn't jog as it was such a hard surface and, as anyone who knows what is now the M8 is aware, it's pretty much uphill all the way.

Five or six hours later I got back home but by that stage I could hardly feel my toes.

There had been a few hail showers too and I wasn't far off having frostbite. Back then, pubs used to have to close between 2pm and 4pm on a Sunday, and it was locked up when I got back. My brother, Tommy was gone out and I was so numb I was barely able to get the key out of my pocket but, when I did, I couldn't turn it.

I had to wait until he came back to get in.

I was just walking up and down outside trying not to freeze. I jumped into the shower and stayed there for hours. I was definitely shaken for a couple of days after that, it gave me a bit of a fright.

That aside, things progressed well enough. I had been back to Tralee to see Fionán O'Carroll a few times and I had a programme to work from, so I was in the gym at the Silver Springs Hotel four times a week. Even though I wasn't much of a swimmer, I went to the pool a good bit too, putting a weight on my ankle and trying to lift my leg.

Dr Con was a massive help in terms of getting me information on what to do and I spoke to a few physios. I also paid a trip to Dunboyne in Co. Meath to see Seán Boylan – he's a herbalist by trade and he gave me a few bottles of his 'jungle juice', as the Meath players used to term it.

I did miss a trip to Canada, where the two Cork teams played the respective All Star teams in the indoor Toronto Skydome. Looking back, it's the kind of thing I half-regret missing out on but, at the time, getting back fit was the sole aim.

Mícheál Ó Mhuircheartaigh experienced this at first hand. The team was in high demand fund-raising for different things and Micheal was down south to help with one of these events. He expected to see me, but was told I was on a more important mission. I wanted to be fit for the Kerry game and was spending all of my free time in the gym.

Micheal called up to see me. He could not believe I was in the height of training in December.

I HAD DISCUSSED with Frank Murphy and Dr Con the possibility of going to a specialised facility to try to speed up the recovery.

At the time, there was nowhere like that in Ireland whereas nowadays you could go to the Sports Surgery Clinic in Santry. They were anxious to get me somewhere, and they looked to England.

Through their contacts, they came up with the Lilleshall Rehabilitation Centre in the British midlands, which was used by the soccer players and top stars in other sports for recovery.

From around 1987-2000, I had one annual holiday that couldn't be interfered with. I loved National Hunt racing, like so many people in Kildare – if you weren't carrying the racing paper on a Saturday morning, there was something wrong with you!

And so, when they told me that it was arranged for me to go to Lilleshall in March, I said I had no problem going… once it wasn't Cheltenham week!

Lifting the Sam Maguire Cup (above) was something I had never even dreamed about and I will forever be thankful to Castlehaven and the people of Cork for affording me such a huge honour. What a year 1990 was for Cork. We did the historic double of All-Ireland football and hurling titles, and when we got back home we were welcomed by our joyous supporters who got to see myself and Tomas Mulcahy swap Liam MacCarthy and Sam Maguire Cups to a rapturous applause.

CHAPTER 15

WHEN I WAS in Manchester in 1988, it really brought home to me how brave GAA players are and that view was reinforced when I went to Lilleshall in 1991.

Obviously, soccer players are on television more and they get more money and their profiles are higher, but I think that GAA players deserve huge credit for the effort and pain and dedication that they put in. A GAA player is trying to get himself out in the workforce, and get the best job possible and live his life.

On top of that, he has a commitment to his club, who depend on him for leadership. You step up then to county level, which is vast and huge; you're playing for the pride of your county and the jersey.

You add it all up, and you'd safely say that the professionals are only trotting after the GAA player.

For me, it certainly shrugged off any notions of an inferiority complex. At the end of the day, the pros have two arms and two legs. They have serious ability, I don't doubt that, but equally the GAA player is up there too. It's possible to be physically stronger than them, even if we get nothing for it.

PUBLICLY, THE LINE was that the Munster championship would be too soon for me to be back. Cork were likely to be heading to Killarney to face Kerry on June 16, but the line from the camp was that I wouldn't be back until the All-Ireland semi-final, if we were to get there.

Truthfully, it was what I thought would be the case myself.

Still, I was working hard and my knee was coming on.

I was five or six months into my rehabilitation at this stage and I had done a lot. The trip to England was a bid to see if we could speed things up a little bit more. In effect, it was like an all-inclusive holiday – you paid your money and stayed there for the week and everything was looked after, food and all of that.

The only difference was that there was no time to be lounging around!

I flew over on a Sunday and checked in that night. Lilleshall was about an hour's drive from Birmingham, hidden away in the woods.

There was a tree-lined avenue about two miles long that opened up to a load of pitches and courts for various sports. There were running tracks and big indoor arenas, with pools and a massive gym.

On the Monday morning, I had to be up for 7.30am. There was an array of options for the breakfast, though all healthy. The closest thing to a fry were the bits of cold bacon!

The early part of the day was about examining guys and seeing what they needed for the week. I had reports from Dr Con and they were looked at by the doctors, who wanted to know what I had done over the previous few months.

After that, it was 45 minutes or so with the physios doing stretches to get an idea of how far advanced I was, and what levels of strength and resistance I could cope with.

Following a light meal, guys were split into three different groups, 10 or 12 in each. I was in group A, with other fellas who had had ligament operations and were on the way back – those who had had their operations more recently were in another group as the ligaments were still tender and they wouldn't be able to do much.

The rest of the guys there were from sports like golf, tennis, rugby league, rugby union, basketball, soccer and so on. Apart from rugby union, I was the only amateur.

In my group were Dave Bennett, who had scored for Coventry City when they won the 1987 FA Cup final against Tottenham Hotspur, and Chris Bailey, a British tennis player who had been in the top 150 in the world.

Lunch was from about 12.15-1pm and we came back then to the gym.

All of the weights were in one part and then there was a big area with skipping ropes, belts and different levels of step-up benches. We were put into smaller groups and went from one section to another.

We were working a lot on step-ups and going down on one knee, and stretching the leg out. They were concentrating on the inner parts of our knee joints and working on making sure we had good balance, as opposed to doing weights to build up our thighs. There were a lot of side-to-side exercises and hopping in and out through cones. We had to jump over small hurdles and try to land then on the weaker leg.

At the end of the day, around 4.30pm, we were taken to a volleyball court and hanging up at the side was a yellow jersey with, 'You wally!' written on the back of it.

A few of the lads who had been there previously were telling us that the jersey had never been washed and whoever performed the worst in the game of volleyball had to wear it until breakfast the next morning. An added difficulty for the volleyball was that you couldn't stand up – everybody had to sit on their rear ends because it was all about movement.

Thankfully, I avoided the jersey but the rest of us still had to put up with the stink from it!

The jersey was used as a deterrent for a lot of things – if you were late back from lunch or not putting in what was felt to be enough effort, you got landed with it.

The philosophy was that you worked hard and finished at 5pm, which suited me fine as I never had a problem with work ethic. After dinner, I was wrecked tired because it was a tough day – and the first one was probably the easiest.

THERE WERE DAYS where we were sent off on 40-mile cycles, albeit with a van following us in case there were any problems.

I loved that, naturally, as I was so used to it.

The first seven or eight miles, we went at a reasonable speed, just a warm-up. After that, it was time-trials, where you'd peg it for two miles and be timed. Then, we had to do 10 miles in a certain time before another time-trial and so on.

The last seven miles was effectively a race back to Lilleshall and all of the cycling I had done beforehand definitely stood to me.

I was the first back and I'd say I was a mile ahead of the next fella, even though they were all professionals. The other lads couldn't believe that me and my kind in the GAA weren't getting paid.

They were fascinated that I had played in All-Ireland finals in front of huge crowds but that I had a day job too.

Every day was hard.

I wasn't really a big swimmer and I hadn't learned until later in my life, but in Lilleshall, they'd just throw you in. They wanted me to use my legs in the water, and I used to run in the pool with resistance belts.

That was the first bit of running I had done since September, 1990 and when I got out of the water, I was knackered. Then, the step-ups were cruel hard.

It was like the bleep test, we'd start off nice and grand and think... *This is handy*, but they'd speed it up and then slow it down. They knew when to allow you to recover but the sweat would be pumping out of you.

Through the day, we'd be assessed; the physio would examine the knee, making sure you weren't damaging it. Any swelling and the ice would go on.

The grub was good and healthy, always plenty to eat but they'd measure out the portions so you wouldn't be overdoing things. There was a bar on the campus but none of the athletes would be drinking. In the evenings, there would be games on out on the pitches, various sports, and we'd head down to watch.

At the end of the week, I was assessed.

The head doctor and head physio gave a letter saying that I was okay to go back to contact sport, but the end of June or start of July was the target date for easy work. And full contact then for August.

NATURALLY, THAT DIDN'T fit in with my plan to play Kerry in June but I was fierce determined. When I got back home, I was able to put into practice what they had been teaching me in Lilleshall.

I got bicycle tubes and I was tying them on to radiators at home to do the stretching exercises. Being a chippie, I made boxes I was able to jump up on for the step-ups and, in the pool, I knew the right exercises to do.

It helped me massively in relation to moving the recovery forward, knowing I was doing the right thing.

Cork were training away but I didn't really join up with them.

I never had a problem training on my own or with like-minded fellas. Tony

Leen, a native of Ballymacelligott in Kerry but working with *The Cork Examiner* – and now the sports editor – often went training with me in Ballygarvan. Donal Burke from Castlemartyr was another great buddy of mine and we trained a lot together too.

Cork had been relegated from Division 1 of the National League and, from what I could gather, things were a little bit scattered. That can seep in when you've had success and maybe in 1991 the same levels of work weren't being put in.

Billy Morgan was anxious; he was saying they needed me for the Kerry game, but I felt it was too early. I came back to training around the middle of May, a month before we were due to play.

Billy thought I'd put a bit of fear into Kerry as I hardly ever played a bad game against them. I felt I might have been better coming off the bench, but he was anxious to start me.

At the start of June, there was an A v's B game in Kilmurry and I was picked on the A team for that. Thankfully, I came through it okay, kicking two points late on.

I was picked at centre-forward for the Kerry game, but our great run against them was to come to an end. Kerry had a teenager named John Cronin making his debut and he got the goal that proved to be the difference in the end, 1-10 to 0-11.

Realistically, we took Kerry for granted, amazing as that sounds.

We thought we'd roll over them like the year before, but you don't do that against them in Killarney. It was a game where our team wasn't tuned in to the level needed.

In the second-half we had a lot of possession, but it was one that got away.

No disrespect to Kerry, but we were a better team than them at that time. On the day, though, they performed much better. We took our foot off the pedal and that was the start of letting Kerry back into it.

THE FOLLOWING WEEK, Castlehaven were playing in the county championship against Carbery. We had got a bye to the second round, meaning I didn't miss any games with them, and we looked to have done enough but Carbery got two late points to draw it, and they were a good bit better than us in the replay at the start of July.

I played in midfield in both games and did well enough – funnily enough, I didn't score in either match – I was still a good bit off my peak.

It was the earliest a summer had finished for me since I had arrived back in Ireland but I made sure to keep training away.

If I gave myself two or three days off, that would have been the height of it. In Lilleshall, they kept saying to us that it was important to keep the knee built up, but at the same time not to overcompensate to the extent that I'd weaken the other knee.

Hardly surprisingly, it was the first year since 1987 that I wasn't nominated for an All-Star, or involved as a player on All-Ireland final day. I was at Croke Park for the decider but in a different role, providing co-commentary on the radio with the great Mícheál Ó Muircheartaigh as Down beat Meath.

That was a very good Down team with some great players. Had we got past Kerry and then Limerick, we would definitely have improved, but I don't know if we'd have been good enough to beat Down that year.

IN CORK, SOME people were beginning to wonder if we were going into a transition period after the loss to Kerry. Obviously, the executive of the county board felt the same way as, incredibly, they tried to remove Billy as a selector.

Presumably, there were people who felt that if Billy wasn't a selector he wouldn't stay on as the coach. In fairness to the delegates, they voted overwhelmingly against that proposal and the players felt the same.

We had a meeting in The Munster Arms in Bandon and everyone was firm that we wanted Billy, and that message was relayed to the county board.

We had to show that 1991 was just a blip.

While I was recuperating from my injury in the 1990 All-Ireland final, all I thought about was getting back playing and, as always, Castlehaven was No.1 in my heart. We would have many more outstanding days through the 90s, winning big in '94, and chasing an All-Ireland title through '97 and '98. Here I am in the 1997 championship final against Beara, and (below) with Niall Cahalane and his son, Damien after the Munster final against Fethard.

PART 4

HAVEN AND HELL

CHAPTER 16

I DON'T THINK the Queen of England has ever had much interest in the GAA, but one thing we have in common is that 1992 was forgettable for both of us. She described the year as her *annus horribilis* because of all the bad things that had happened to her, and mine wasn't far behind in terms of misfortune.

It was a case of things being very stop-start and, unfortunately, the stops seemed to be more common than the starts.

The trouble started for me at the end of February, going into March.

One day, I was walking down the stairs and my knee just locked – but not the right knee on which I'd been operated in 1990; the *good* one… my left! It might have been a case of me placing more of a load on that one as I recovered from the injury.

If 1991 was a race against time because Cork had Kerry in a Munster semi-final in June, this time it was even more of a challenge as the counties had been paired together at the quarter-final stage.

May 24 in Páirc Uí Chaoimh was the red-letter day.

ANOTHER VISIT TO Tralee to see Fionán O'Carroll was in store for me, but the diagnosis of cartilage damage meant that things weren't as serious as feared. With treatment, I was still able to target a return in time for the championship.

I played a challenge game against Wicklow and then, at the start of May, Castlehaven played Seandún in the first round of the county.

We hadn't won a championship game since claiming the 1989 title but, thankfully, that statistic was put to bed. It was fairly straightforward as we won by 1-16 to 0-5 in Cloughduv, That was on the Saturday night of the Bank Holiday weekend and on the Sunday I played in another challenge match for Cork, against Kildare in Midleton. After coming through both of those in quick succession, I looked to be back on track, but fate had other ideas and it was to show it in freak fashion.

Aside from all of the accolades, one of the things that I get asked about the most is the time I missed a Cork game because I got burnt sun-bathing.

It's a complete and utter fabrication, but once something appears somewhere, everybody believes it.

What happened was somewhat different, though no less strange.

I ALWAYS TENDED to go to the Mardyke for a run on the Sunday before a big championship game and, this time, it was essential as I was trying to make up for the lost time while I was out.

I was in pretty good shape and I had a run on the track and went for a few stretches.

The gate at the top end of the Dyke was open so I was able to walk away in – unlike the early mornings, when I'd have to hop over the wall!

I had brought runners and I had thought I left socks in them but, for whatever reason, they weren't there.

I didn't give it too much thought and I did my bit on the track.

It was a nice day and there was a match on at the Mardyke. Tyrone were also playing Derry in the Ulster championship and I had a transistor radio, so I listened to that and sat on the bank for a while before I went on home. I had noticed that the instep of my right foot had gone very red, but I didn't give it much thought and worked away in the pub for the evening. Then, the next morning, it was redder and a bit itchy, so I went to the chemist on Mac Curtain St looking for cream.

A blister was developing and, after 20 minutes of training on the Tuesday night, it cracked. I put cream on it again, thinking that it'd be alright, but the whole thing had become infected and, on the Thursday, it blew up like a balloon.

I went to Dr Con and he said he'd have to put me on strong antibiotics.

I didn't train Thursday, but I still thought it would be okay.

On Friday, it swelled even more and Dr Con said I was in trouble, that it looked very angry. I was definitely very angry!

In these situations, you tend to panic, looking for something that might work. I threw cider on it as I had heard somewhere that that would kill the infection. You can imagine the pain of throwing that on cut skin.

I tried goose-grease too, but it made no difference.

I had been named in the team at centre-forward but, on Saturday, it was as bad as ever and things were looking dicey. I rang Billy and told him I hadn't eaten in a day and a half. He said we'd see on Sunday how things were, but I was nowhere near being able to start and Danny Culloty, who had been named as a sub, came into midfield and Teddy McCarthy moved to the '40'.

The hurlers were playing Kerry in the Munster championship too and that game was on first, but it was a straightforward decision for Teddy to opt for football that day. Cork won that match by 0-22 to 0-8 – it was the larger of the two winning margins that day, but not by much.

My foot had swelled so much that I wasn't even able to get it into the boot.

I used to always wear size 10 Puma Phantoms, they were a boot I really liked. My sister Mary, who worked in Cleary's in Dublin, had been able to sort it out that I had a good few pairs of them, but that day I only wore one Puma boot... the left one.

Dr Con wrapped a bandage around my right foot and I borrowed a size 11 and a half Adidas boot.

BILLY HAD CHANGED the training regime that year.

After losing in 1991, he decided to do something different and he brought in more sports psychology but I didn't feel I got much benefit from it.

Some of the guys bought into it, but you had fellas who just needed to get out on the pitch and play and they were listening to this talk every night. Then we got these t-shirts that had 'Simply the Best' written on them; they were designed to motivate us.

When you went to sleep at night and woke up in the morning, this t-shirt was there with you and it was meant to transmit positive energy.

The extended panel against Kerry were wearing the t-shirts on the day of the Kerry game and they had another role too.

The dressing-rooms in the old Páirc Uí Chaoimh were always very tight and the teams were next door to each other. You could nearly hear what was being said, so as to send Kerry a message, we had Tina Turner's *Simply the Best* blaring... and the extended panellists had hurleys, belting the wall.

It was like we were going out to war, but once the match started, we were asleep.

I was brought on after a half-hour but I wasn't fit and Kerry were well on top. We were never in the game, even though we missed two penalties. Mick McCarthy, who I had come on for, had been the designated penalty-taker, and so Niall Cahalane took one and Shea Fahy took the other but neither found the target.

Kerry won easily in the end, 2-14 to 0-10.

It was Cork's earliest championship exit since 1946.

When we came back into the dressing-room afterwards, there wasn't much said but I don't think we heard that song ever again!

THERE WAS A chance for redemption with the Haven, who had St Finbarr's in the second round of the county championship at the beginning of June in Clonakilty.

That 1989 final had been the first of three in-a-row that the Barrs lost, with Duhallow beating them in the other two. They probably felt that they owed us one and, though we started well, they got on top and, near the end, Mick Slocum put them 0-12 to 0-11 ahead with a great point.

We got one last chance, though, when we were awarded a free that the papers said was 72 yards out. I kicked the ball out of my hands and went for it, and thankfully it had enough legs.

A month later, it was back to Clon, and the Barrs had the better start this time.

They were up six points in the first-half when I was moved to full-forward and Niall Cahalane went to midfield and he had a stormer.

We ended up winning by 0-14 to 0-10 but, unfortunately, the journey wasn't to go much further. Next up was Bishopstown, in Bandon three weeks later, but I had picked up an Achilles tendon injury in training and couldn't start – a recurring theme that summer, sadly.

As a result of my absence, Niall was midfield again and his brother, Patsy was full-back, but Patsy suffered a really nasty ankle injury early on and that definitely affected us. Bishopstown went for goals and got them, and they were 2-3 to 0-5 up at half-time.

We got it back to a point early in the second-half but they got two more goals in quick succession – what proved to be their only scores of the second-half. I was brought on and so was Francis Collins, but we couldn't turn it, and I ended up getting sent off, the only time in my career. It was down to frustration more than anything.

It was a disappointing end to a disappointing year.

IN 1992 DONEGAL MADE it to the All-Ireland final and their manager, Brian McEniff asked me to come up and speak to the team before the final. I knew Brian's son, Seanie from my college days in Bolton St. and we are still great friends today.

I don't know if it was of huge benefit to them; I just tried to draw on my own experiences and the importance of not being overawed by the occasion. It's easy to say it now, but leaving there that night I really did get a sense that they were going to do it and so it proved.

I was delighted for them – the link to Donegal mightn't have been in my blood, but it was strong. Donal Gallagher had travelled with me that day and I was delighted for him that his home county won. I can remember the spring of 1990. Cork were supposed to be playing Donegal in the national league in Páirc Uí Chaoimh but it was postponed due to a waterlogged pitch.

When I got back to the pub, it was swarming with Donegal people who had come down for the game and initially I was thinking I'd prefer to be playing in the wet, it was that busy! They were so genuine though and so strong in their love of Donegal football.

I actually ended up in their dressing-room after the 1992 final with Tadhg Lovett, a guy from Boherbue whom I had got to know in New York.

I knew guys like Martin McHugh, Anthony Molloy, Matt Gallagher, Manus Boyle, Barry and John Cunningham; they were great players and I was delighted for them.

Donegal were on the up, whereas more than a few newspapers were writing Cork's obituary after two successive defeats to Kerry.

We thought 1998 would be our year in Castlehaven, and we were good enough to win the All-Ireland but we let it slip against Dublin champions Erin's Isle who had Charlie Redmond sent-off (right). Here I am challenging Keith Barr.

EVERY SO OFTEN, speculation would surface about the possibility of me returning to play with Kildare. And that was never stronger than in the winter of 1992.

The fact that it was a relatively quiet time of year probably played a part and the conspiracy theorists had extra material due to the fact that Cork played Kildare in the league in Newbridge at the end of November that year. It was my first time at St Conleth's Park in seven years, though I wasn't playing as I was still trying to recover from the catalogue of injuries that had hampered me that year.

My back, which had begun to give me problems before the 1990 All-Ireland final, was becoming more of a persistent issue too.

When I left the ground in the company of my good friend, Tony Keogh – who happened to be a Kildare selector – things went into overdrive and for a few days it seemed like there was talk of little else. All of a sudden, there were rumours that my pub was on the market and I was off to Kildare.

I was training away with Cork and trying to work on getting fit, and there was never any kind of approach made by Kildare.

My philosophy with rumours like this would be to ignore them but, eventually, the week before Christmas, I put things to bed by going on RTÉ Radio 1's *Sunday Sport* and telling Des Cahill that I was going to be lining out with Cork in 1993, once I was able to regain my place. I also suggested that the papers printing the transfer talk should explain where the story had come from, but such clarification wasn't forthcoming.

HOWEVER, IN FEBRUARY 1993, it was announced that I would be involved with a team that wore white jerseys – it wouldn't preclude my Cork commitments, though.

Eamonn Martin was a man I had got to know; he was from Caherciveen, but was principal of Dungarvan CBS and involved with Waterford teams and he got me on board for the county's under-21 footballers.

I said I'd go down for a few months and get them going, but I ended up staying there for three years and even becoming a selector. It was a great thing to be doing, especially at a time when I seemed to be constantly battling injury. Coaching players got me out and about, and there's no doubt that working with young fellas keeps you young yourself.

They were starting from a low base but the key thing was that they were keen and they had the dedication to want to improve themselves, which is all I would ask for.

FOR THE THIRD year in-a-row, Cork and Kerry were on the same side of the Munster draw and so we had to go to Killarney for the semi-final on June 20.

I got myself right for that, trying to manage my recovery – when I returned to training first, my hamstrings were tight but, otherwise, I was able to get in shape. Colin stayed on the frees and I think that that helped me.

There was a lot of pressure on us but the newer lads didn't feel any of that. After that game, I felt I was really back.

Things were looking up – two weeks later, Castlehaven had the second round of the county championship against Muskerry, and the Munster football final against Tipperary was set for a fortnight after that, July 18.

The night before the Haven game, I would have more exposure to Tipp football as Waterford played them in the under-21 semi-final in Walsh Park. That match ended in a draw.

For the Haven, it was a return to Clonakilty for the clash with Muskerry, shades of my first championship game for them in 1987, and sadly it was to be another night to forget for me. I was alongside Dave O'Regan in midfield and we did actually start well and were 0-3 to 0-1 up before John O'Driscoll got a goal for Muskerry. They were five points up at half-time but we had the wind to come and I kicked a point early in the second-half.

Then, a ball was kicked out.

I JUMPED ACROSS to catch it and turned in the air.

I came down on my left foot and, whatever way I landed, the ligament snapped.

I had the ball in my hand, and I lay down like I was shot. I was lifted to the sideline as I couldn't walk and, having done it previously, I knew what had happened.

At the same time, once the initial pain subsides, you feel nothing and I was trying to run up and down the sideline to show I was able to come back on. However, once I tried a quick turn, the pain was awful.

We had a French doctor involved with us at the time, Dr Christian Jost.

He had been with the French rugby team and used to come over for summer holidays in Courtmacsherry. He fell in love with the place and got a job in Millbrook Clinic in Bandon.

That night, his main concern was my knee and he confirmed my worst fears.

It was a bad night for the Haven and Niall Cahalane had to be carried off too. The parallels with 1987 were all too real for me – losing to Muskerry in Clon and feeling awful, but this was even worse, knowing in my heart and soul I was gone for the Munster final and the rest of the year.

I HAD AN exploratory operation that week in the Bons Secours Hospital in Dublin, carried out by Ray Moran, brother of Dublin and Ireland legend, Kevin.

There was at least some consolation at the end of that week when Waterford under-21s beat Tipperary in their replay in Clonmel. I made sure to be there – if I had had no legs, I wasn't going to miss it!

Again, they had to battle hard and Fergal Cunningham's late goal sent the game to extra-time before they won by 1-14 to 0-12. They were in the Munster final for the first time in 22 years and the opponents would be Kerry, who had beaten Cork in the other semi-final.

Cork did at least win the senior final without me, beating Tipperary in Thurles. The under-21 decider was a week later, Friday, July 24 in Walsh Park.

Páidí Ó Sé was over Kerry and they had players like Séamus Moynihan, Declan O'Keeffe, Mike Hassett and Billy O'Shea, who would all go on to win All-Ireland senior medals. We were going to be up against it and they never really gave us a chance. We were well beaten in the end, but it was a great achievement for Waterford to get to a Munster final.

It was the middle of August when Cork played Mayo – who had Jack O'Shea in charge – in the All-Ireland semi-final and again I wasn't missed as they won by 20 points.

I had my operation at the end of that month in the Blackrock Clinic in Dublin. Again, I had a big plaster of Paris cast put on; whereas nowadays they apply a crepe bandage and the player is exercising the next morning.

I was looking at a long spell out again.

I was on the sideline on the day of the All-Ireland final, still on crutches.

Coming across the pitch before the game, the crowd gave me a standing ovation and it was the kind of thing that cheered me up and at the same time it made me feel really downcast that I couldn't play that day.

Ever since 1987, the Cork fans had really taken me in as one of their own; guys like Con Hallahan from Timoleague. He'd drive to every league game we played – we'd get off the bus and the first people we'd meet would be Con and the family.

Cyril 'The Bird' Kavanagh from Douglas was another.

People see him dressed up for games and they might think he's doing it for show, but nobody cares more. I've seen the side of Cyril that others don't see, either – he made huge sacrifices to care for his parents but he'd never look for plaudits.

Cork supporters will follow you through and through, if they feel you're earning that right to have the jersey on your back. I respected these people, and their passion never quenched no matter what game it was.

Unfortunately, that day they were to be disappointed, despite a great start. Joe Kavanagh was centre-forward, as he had been against Mayo, and he got a brilliant early goal.

Tony Davis was sent off, completely in the wrong.

The referee was Tommy Howard from Kildare and it was a bad decision, people said that he was making up for an earlier incident where Niall should have been sent off. As well as that, Niall took a big hit from Brian McGilligan and that more or less shattered his shoulder.

It was an unusual experience for me, being in the dugout for a big game.

THE LADS IN there are playing every ball the same way as the players themselves and it was strange to see that.

The 'Kid' used to leave the dugout coming up to half-time in games, he knew down to a 'T' how long it would take to walk around the goal and be in just as the whistle went. From being in the dressing-room at half-time that day, I think the whole team lost its focus.

Niall had an ice-pack on and you sensed the match was over.

There was too much consoling of Tony, in contrast to 1990 when you hardly noticed Colm O'Neill had been sent off.

Tony didn't want that, but it was just a natural reaction.

Cork brought on Conor Counihan late and Steven O'Brien went up front, which made a bit of a difference. I had felt that not starting Conor was a bad decision.

I had played against the Derry centre-forward Damien Barton a good few times over the years – as far back as the 1983 All-Ireland vocational schools final. He was a great ball-winner and hard to handle. I would have felt that Counihan was the man for him and put Steven up centre-forward from the start.

Joe Kavanagh was a young player and maybe they could have used him on the wing or in the corner. Teddy started that day, whereas from training it looked like Danny Culloty was going really well. I just felt if they started Counihan and Culloty, with Steven in the forwards, Cork would have been stronger. Not taking away from Derry, they were a good side, but I think Cork had the winning of that All-Ireland.

We were in the Imperial Hotel after the homecoming on the Monday night and I was one of the last people to see the 'Kid', who died in his sleep that night.

THERE WAS A real shadow cast over everything because he had been such a central part of it for so long.

You went to training and matches, and he was there all the time, carrying the gear and the wintergreen and the poitín – if you didn't want him to rub it in, he'd nearly give you a slug of it… if he felt you needed it!

He had a great sense for the big day and he knew how to talk to people when it really mattered. The 'Kid' was part of that team as much as any player for 20 years.

FOR ME, THAT autumn and winter were again focused on recovery. There was never a question in my mind that I wouldn't be able to come back, but that's not to say it was easy. It's a long road, it's a lonely road and you have to do it yourself.

The second time, it was a challenge because I knew what was ahead of me but that didn't stand in my way. I looked forward to it in a perverse way.

Things went well in the process before Christmas and then, in January, 1994, I went over to Lilleshall again. The England rugby player, Rory Underwood was there as well as the Rangers trio of Ally McCoist, Ian Durrant and Dave McPherson. Alan Shearer was also about the place.

I became friendly with McCoist, even if I could hardly get a word in with him. He couldn't get over the fact that I was doing all this just to get back playing a sport purely for the love of it.

One day, he said he had tickets for a game that night; Manchester United were playing Portsmouth in the Coca-Cola Cup at Old Trafford, so we headed up to that. It finished 2-2 and Paul Walsh scored twice for Portsmouth.

Afterwards, we ended up in the players' lounge and I met Roy Keane and Denis Irwin. I knew Roy well as he used to call into the pub when he was home for the summer. He was the most expensive player in England at the time, but Ryan Giggs, Peter Schmeichel and Eric Cantona were the three who had security people around them.

'The rest of us could walk anywhere,' Keane said, '...and nobody would notice!'

Things had certainly changed from when I was there in 1988.

A few players had a couple of drinks but they were gone home early. McCoist wanted to stay all night. I'd say we didn't get out until around 5.30am, with a good drive to Lilleshall ahead of us.

We were back at about 7.30am and, thankfully, it wasn't one of the tougher days, though I think McPherson got the smelly jersey the next day.

We certainly slept well that night!

Other than that, it was the same procedure as my previous visit, hard going. I was pleased that my performance was better than most of the professionals again.

This time, Alan Shearer was next to me on the bench.

He had a tear that they were trying to manage. The numbers he posted were among the best they'd ever seen but mine were better, which I was happy with! I trained closely with Shearer and we were always competing against one another... cycling, weights, stamina exercises. I was glad at the end of the week to know that I could beat 'The Professionals'.

There was a Cork team holiday to Morocco at the very end of January and I met up with them in Agadir after 10 days at Lilleshall. They had been in Marrakesh prior to that. It was supposed to be a holiday but I was doing a lot of work on the bike, I nearly had to be pulled off it!

With my 31st birthday approaching and the injuries becoming more common, I was aware of the fact that the window for success was narrowing. Thankfully, 1994 would provide one of the greatest victories of them all.

Cork county board could not have done any more for me through all of my injuries and rehabilitation, sending me to England and helping me to get the best of care. In Old Trafford I had the great Alex Ferguson (right) welcoming me and looking after me, while in Lilleshall I also got to go head-to-head in the fight back to full fitness against the brilliant Newcastle United and England centre-forward, Alan Shearer.

CHAPTER 18

I DIDN'T PLAY in any of the National League games in the spring of 1994, and I didn't make it back in time for Castlehaven's championship opener, either – the now seemingly traditional clash with Seandún.

The Haven won that by seven points and the next game would be against Mallow in early June. I was targeting that for a competitive return. Cork were beginning their Munster campaign at the end of that month with a home semi-final against Kerry, who had beaten Limerick.

It was around this time that I was sounded out about playing with Kildare again.

MICHAEL OSBORNE WAS the point of contact.

He was also from Eadestown and had set up the Kildare Supporters Club in 1990. He was instrumental in getting Mick O'Dwyer on board and Micko never made any secret of the fact that he would have loved to have had myself and Shea Fahy available.

Michael ran a few stud farms for Skeikh Mohammed and I met him at Kildangan Stud, but it was just out of courtesy as there was never a likelihood that I'd go there. Still, it was an opportunity for someone like me who was big into racing to see the place!

As well as the cruciate recovery, which had gone as well as it could, the back was giving me more consistent trouble. When I'd feel a pinch, I'd visit Noel O'Connor, the osteopath, in Bishopstown and he'd manipulate it.

I'd feel like a million dollars after that, but two weeks later then it was almost a case of being back to square one.

I couldn't halt time.

Naturally, I had slowed down; there's no point saying otherwise.

I was still able to get around the field but when you do your cruciate ligament, you lose 10 or 15 percent of your pace and here was I with a second one gone, a few more aches and pains, and getting older.

I had started my adult career when I was 16 years-old and the miles on the clock do take their toll. I still felt I had a massive stamina base. That was never a problem and strength wasn't either, but I probably wasn't able to get to breaking balls as quickly as I had done in the past.

One thing I had to keep myself occupied, as well as the rehabilitation, was the role with Waterford.

For 1994, I had been appointed selector as well as coach, though that was more a case of semantics than anything else as I was fully involved on that side of things in '93 as well. We had been training since December and the lads put in a huge effort but we were still outsiders for the Munster quarter-final against Clare in Tipperary town in April.

We won that match with a late goal.

The previous year's championship had shown that there was fierce determination in the team but still, people might look at one good run as a one-off. We had showed that there was something substantial there but we had to prove that again in the semi-final, against Limerick in Askeaton. This time we won easily.

There was a second straight Munster final to look forward to in July, but this time it would be the unusual situation of me going up against Cork.

BEFORE ALL THAT, though, there was my own return to the playing fields.

We played Mallow on the Friday night of the June Bank Holiday weekend and I was named as a sub. The plan was to use me in the second-half, but there was nearly no first-half as the referee never showed up to Ballygarvan!

Eventually, county board officials got hold of Eddie Murphy from Douglas, who was reffing a Kelleher Shield (county league) game in Togher between St

Finbarr's and Clonakilty, and he rushed out.

What was supposed to be a 7.30pm game eventually started at around 8.20pm. We were ahead at half-time but only by a point, 0-5 to 0-4, and Mallow were sticky in the second-half. It was still tight when I was brought on with about a quarter of an hour left but that was probably a good thing – if you're brought on when the game is won, you're minding yourself a bit too much whereas I just had to throw myself into it and help us win the game.

I was delighted to get on, my first game back in nearly 12 months, which made the win all the sweeter.

The key thing was that we were in the quarter-finals, with Duhallow the opponents.

I made my return to the Cork jersey in a challenge game against Galway in the middle of June and came through that with no ill-effects so I was named at centre-forward for the game against Kerry – my eighth straight year to play them in the championship.

After winning in Killarney in 1993, we were looking to ensure that we were still the top dogs and we started well enough. It was a battle all of the way. It was good to get a tight and tough game under my belt and thanks be to God I had no ill effects.

We pushed on to win by two points, 1-13 to 2-8.

It would be Tipperary in the final again, with another Haven game in between. Coachford was the venue for the quarter-final against Duhallow and I was back in from the start. Since we had beaten them in the 1989 semi-final after a replay, Duhallow had won two titles in-a-row, 1990 and '91. They live and die for football and even today, they're still the best divisional team and difficult to beat – when the Haven won the county in 2012, it was Duhallow they beat in the final after a late goal.

On this July evening in 1994, they certainly weren't in the mood for defeat. Even though we got the first three points, they were two ahead by half-time after getting on top. Halfway through the second-half, it was the same, they were 0-10 to 0-8 in front, but Niall Cahalane got a glorious point and then I levelled with five minutes left.

Even so, when Niall O'Connor kicked a free for Duhallow, we were heading for the exit.

Time was pretty much up when we won a free from way out on the left, the far side from the entrance to the old pitch at Coachford.

There are trees at that side, so there was hardly any room by the sideline and the Duhallow bench were right up on top of me, giving me lashings of abuse.

I felt a strain when kicking from the ground by then, so I was kicking it out of my hands, which increased the margin for error, but I had to go for it.

The ball went high, it floated and floated for ages, like the one against Galway in 1987, and it landed on top of the net. I'll never forget the Duhallow crowd, they were down on their knees and they couldn't believe it.

The replay wouldn't be until late August, with two Munster finals to deal with before that.

THE FIRST OF those was the under-21 in Fraher Field, against Cork.

Ultimately, getting to a Munster final for Waterford was like winning the All-Ireland for Cork or Kerry. We were unlucky with a couple of goal chances which might have made it interesting.

Still, despite that result, it was a hugely encouraging year for Waterford. Since the start of 1993, they had beaten Clare, Limerick and Tipperary, so there was no doubting that they were the third-best team in the province at that grade, which has rarely been the case for them.

IN THE SENIOR final, against Tipperary, we got into our stride quickly. In the end, however, it proved to be a real battle and we needed all of our experience to pull through by the finish. We won by 2-19 to 3-9.

We had retained the Munster title for the first time since 1990, but you could kind of sense that we weren't firing on all cylinders. It was a mix of the teams that had won the two All-Irelands and the newer players that were coming on, and when we met Down in the All-Ireland semi-final they were too strong for us.

We were beaten by five, 1-13 to 0-11, and we could have no qualms about it.

I felt I battled well that day; I wasn't the force of old but I had come through a lot and I was still well able to hold my own. I don't think the team did an awful lot wrong but Down had proved themselves when they won the 1991 All-Ireland and they did it again in the '94 final against Dublin.

Tony Keogh died on the weekend of that final. I was at his funeral in

Eadestown and then on to the match. It was appropriate that he died around the All-Ireland final as he was so steeped in the GAA.

He was with me from the word go with the Kildare underage teams. He was a regular visitor to Cork after I moved. He'd come down on a Friday and stay in my guest house and go back on the Sunday evening. He loved going to our training sessions, just as he had done with Kevin Heffernan's Dublin teams or Mick O'Dwyer's Kerry.

He was a football fanatic and was so keen to learn. I always valued his friendship and the guidance he provided.

A week after Cork lost to Down, Castlehaven played Duhallow in the quarter-final replay and, just like 1989, we made the most of the second chance. Duhallow started well this time, but Niall and myself got a handle in midfield and John Cleary was on song up front.

We won by 0-11 to 0-8 – not champagne stuff but enough, and a huge game to get through in terms of preparing us for a semi-final against Nemo Rangers.

There is never any incentive needed to win a semi, but just in case there was, we knew that if we came out on top, we would be playing O'Donovan Rossa of Skibbereen in the final after they had beaten St Finbarr's on the other side at the end of July. There was always a huge rivalry between the Haven and Rossa, all the more so since they had won the county in 1992 and gone all the way to win the club All-Ireland.

Before we could consider that prospect though, we had enough on our plate to deal with Nemo. They were the reigning All-Ireland club champions, with 11 or 12 past, present or future county players – as well as all of their Cork lads, they had Peter Lambert from Tipperary too.

Steven O'Brien and Shea Fahy were midfield for them, up against me and Niall. The game was held on Saturday, September 3 in Bandon and everyone and anyone went to it. The bank by the pavilion was full and so was the far side, which was unusual – they were hanging out of the trees! We were getting ready to go out and we were told to go back in as throw-in was delayed.

Sometimes, you'd hear of a game being doubled up as championship and league – this was trebled up as it was the 1993 Kelleher Shield final and the 1993 Tadhg Crowley Cup final, not that either trophy was foremost in our minds.

I was marking Shea, and myself and Niall had one of our best games together.

Honestly, I would say that every one of our lads had the game of their lives that evening. The Haven never feared Nemo; in fact, we loved playing against them. Some people might say that at times, they feared us.

I don't think anyone would have beaten us on the night.

All of our backs were superb. Mike O'Brien was a fella who didn't get enough credit, always played well in the big games and he was outstanding. To win a match like that against a team like Nemo can't be over-estimated. We came out of there in a good place and straightaway the talk turned to the local derby.

It wasn't just in Cork, either – I knew people in Limerick and Tipperary that were talking about it. My friend, Gerry Chawke from Clonmel rang to say there was a group thinking of coming down. Traditionally, it was the case for the Cork hurling final that people would come from all around to see, but now it was the football decider.

THE PLACE WAS covered in bunting and flags, blue and white for the Haven and red and white for Skibb.

One night, every second broken white line on the main road was painted blue – for a good stretch, not just a mile or two. Bernard Collins' farm is on the main road and his kids put out a big teddy bear painted blue and white… and the next night it was red and white.

There was talk then that Haven lads painted a sheep blue and white and let it off in Skibbereen town centre.

I called down to Nora Maguire one evening before training on the week of the final.

Just before I left, she summed up the importance of it all.

'If we don't beat these feckers, I'll have to shop in Clonakilty,' she said.

Kathleen Cleary used to bring her down to Skibb, which was a far shorter drive than going into Clon, but these were the high stakes. I was thinking that we had to win or I'd never be allowed down again.

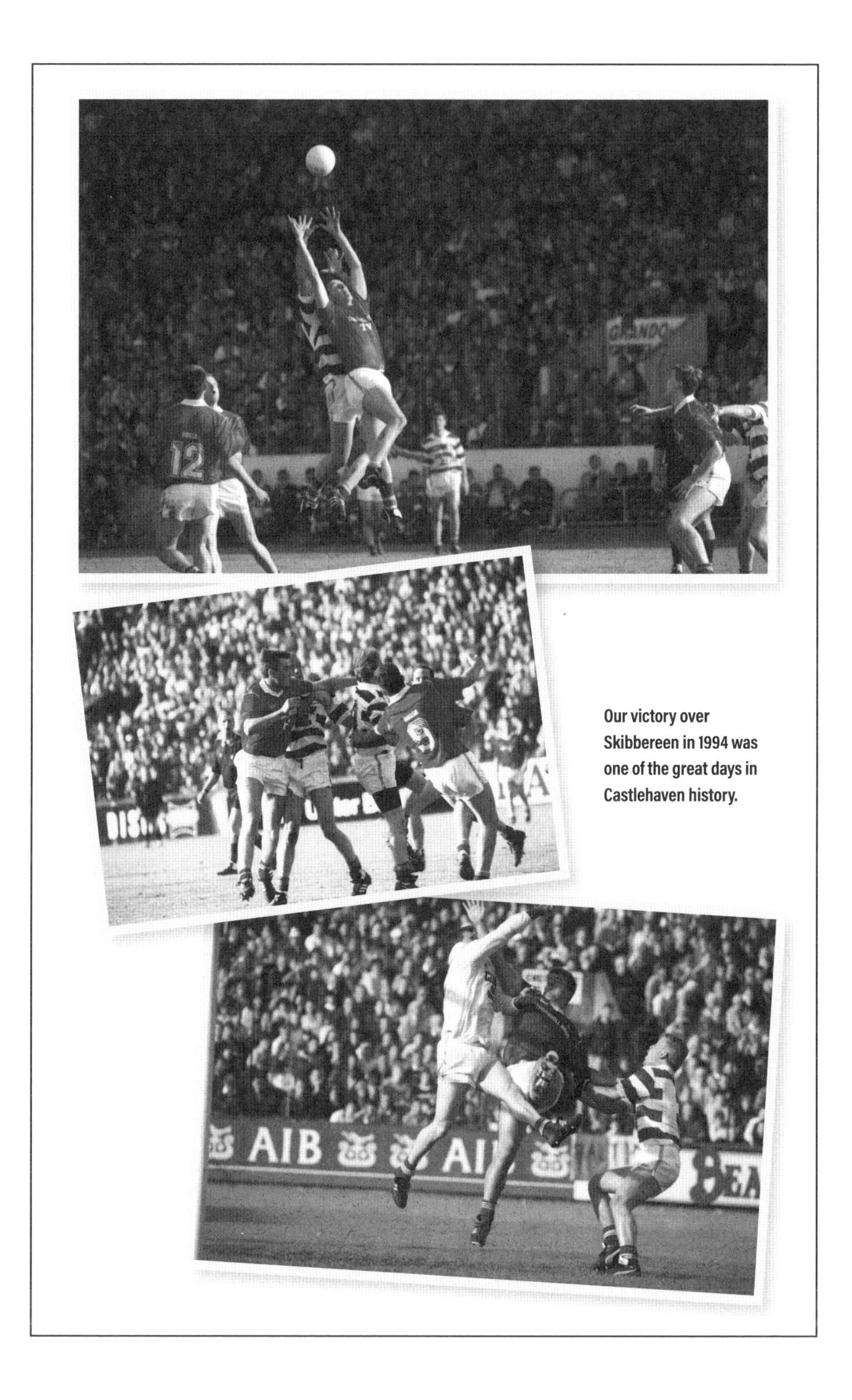

Our victory over Skibbereen in 1994 was one of the great days in Castlehaven history.

CHAPTER 19

I PROBABLY DIDN'T feel the rivalry the same as the native Haven lads, but it was clear that Skibb winning the club All-Ireland had hurt fellas.

That Skibb side was a hell of a team.

They had gone up to Lavey in Derry for the semi-final in 1993 and beaten them in a pulsating game, before getting past Éire Óg of Carlow after a replay in the final. You don't win an All-Ireland by luck.

Even outside of their county players like Mick McCarthy, Tony and Don Davis, Brian O'Donovan, John O'Donovan and the emerging Kevin O'Dwyer in goal, they had solid operators.

There was a crowd of around 26,000 in Páirc Uí Chaoimh on September 25.

The whole of west Cork was trekking to it and plenty more from beyond that. It was a nice day weather-wise and, while it wasn't a classic match – hardly surprising – it was tense and tough. We looked to be the better team for a lot of it, but a point or two was a big lead.

Niall and I were up against Skinner and Brian O'Donovan at midfield, and we started well but when Mick Mac was fouled for a penalty, Ian Breen got a goal for Skibb to make it 1-1 to 0-3.

Pat Davis nearly got another goal just after that but we responded very well.

I wasn't at my best from the frees but we managed to get ahead, 0-7 to 1-3, and then John Cleary got a goal coming up to half-time to open up what was a huge lead. Skibb had also lost Tony Davis to a leg injury he had been carrying beforehand, but just before the break, I was involved in a collision and I came off the worst.

The AC joint in my shoulder was gone.

There was no way I was going to come off, so I told them to get it strapped up as best they could. I survived the second-half, but Skibb got on top at midfield and Gene O'Driscoll was putting in a Man of the Match performance at centre-back.

Mick levelled for them with 10 minutes left and then Brian O'Donovan put them in front. We had lost John Cleary to a torn groin, so it was looking like curtains for us.

We got a break, though.

I kicked a free to level with time nearly up and then Niall scored a massive point. It looked like being a fairytale ending, the captain kicking the winner, but there was time for a Skibb free deep in injury time and Mick put that over.

It finished 1-9 each and the Skibb crowd were elated – why wouldn't they be, as they had come from four down to get a replay.

Myself and John were in ribbons, waiting for an ambulance to take us away. At Cork University Hospital, I asked a doctor how long it would take for my AC joint to recover and he said three months.

'I need to be back in two weeks!' was my response.

I WAS PUT in a sling and we went back down to my pub.

It was doom and gloom, a bit like 1988, when Cork didn't put Meath away the first day. We felt we should have won and it looked like John and I were out.

I wasn't thinking that way, though – I felt I could make it back and I was planning the best way to do that. Noel O'Connor said we'd work at it three times a day and I practically lived out at his clinic in Bishopstown.

Dr Con thought I was mad to even contemplate it.

The shoulder is almost unique in that, no matter what way you go about it, it's the one area you can't strap for support.

I didn't attend a training session for two weeks and I told our manager, Jim Nolan that it wasn't looking good. Noel was generating a lot of friction to try to speed things up but the shoulder was brutal sore from the treatment.

By the Friday before the replay, I was accepting that I had no chance.

I was only able to lift my arm up to my shoulder.

Christy Collins, who was a selector that year, was saying I'd be grand with one arm. Niall was saying the same, but I felt I'd be crazy.

Francis Collins arranged for me to go down to Páirc Uí Chaoimh on the Friday to do a bit of practice with a ball. I had had very little treatment that day and I had to stop after a half-hour because it was so sore. Francis said I'd be wasting my time, that I couldn't carry the weight of the ball.

I rang Jim Nolan and Christy and said that it wasn't looking good.

That night, John McGerety, a good friend of mine got in touch. He would have been a serious punter and he asked me if I felt he should back Skibb. I told him, genuinely, that I was out, and couldn't play.

I rested on the Saturday and called out to Dr Con and we talked about my injury. I told him straight.

'I need to play this game... even if it's the last game I ever play. I HAVE to be out there!' He told me I was mad. But he also told me he would see me in Blackrock the next day.

'We'll see about it then!' Dr Con said.

Christy rang and said they were thinking of starting me full-forward.

I was in the pub, gripping and re-gripping a tennis ball, but I still never thought I'd be able for it. On the Sunday morning, Niall picked me up and the shoulder wasn't as sore. We were congregating at Blackrock again, as we had done in 1989, and Dr Con was there as he had promised.

There was a green area in the estate alongside the club and when I went over there for a kick-around, the shoulder felt better.

DR CON SAID that he could give me an injection that would last 20 or 25 minutes, so he would give it to me just before the start of the game.

John Cleary was out; he needed an operation but he was still togged in case he was called upon. There was another huge crowd in the Páirc again, with the official attendance just under 33,000. Not one but two helicopters landed in the showgrounds with special attendees – the Taoiseach, Albert Reynolds and the president of the GAA, my great friend Jack Boothman.

Even though we were nearly into the middle of October, the sun was shining.

We were more composed when planning for the replay. The first day, maybe we got a bit too emotional about the occasion and it drained fellas. Niall would have been disappointed with his performance in the drawn game, for instance, even though he nearly kicked the winner.

We went into the replay thinking that Skibb felt they had it won.

To be fair, a lot of people felt that – there was huge money on Skibb, they were backed into 1/3 by the time of the throw-in, even though they were unable to start Tony Davis. My brothers told me later that when the teams were announced and my name was called out, it gave the Haven supporters a huge lift.

I had the shoulder strapped, just to give it a bit of cushioning if nothing else. Just before the game was about to start, I ran into the dressing-room with Dr Con. He pressed in where the shoulder was really sore and gave the injection.

I ran in to full-forward and I was able to lift my arms above my head; I was like a new man. The first ball came in high, I went up and caught it and that was important in terms of laying down a marker.

I got on the ball a good bit and we were dominant.

Niall was controlling at midfield and Dan O'Sullivan was doing great alongside him.

We were three ahead by the end of the first quarter but it should have been six as we had had some bad wides. I kicked a couple of good dead balls to put us four in front after around 20 minutes but the injection was wearing off – I was back to where I was beforehand, if not worse.

I was very happy with how it had gone overall, though.

Normally, I hated full-forward as I wasn't a player that could wait for the ball, as you did back then, but we were so dominant at midfield that I was getting a lot of service and laying it off.

Martin Bohane and Mick McCarthy had points for Skibb just before half-time, meaning we were 0-7 to 0-5 in front going in. John Cleary was a rallying force in the dressing-room – in fairness to him, if he couldn't play he made sure he had whatever positive influence he could. I received another injection and it was like I was on a high again.

For the first 10 or 15 minutes of the second-half, I played brilliantly.

Early on, John Maguire – the goalkeeper in 1989 but wing-forward now, with his brother Mike in goal – kicked in a Garryowen and I caught it out of the sky, turned and kicked it over and that set the tone.

I had another point from play and then a free, and we were five in front.

Every time Niall got the ball, he was just looking for me. Paudie Palmer, the commentator on the local radio station, 103FM, said, "To hell or high water, we know where this ball is going".

Skibb were putting different guys on me and they even brought Gene O'Driscoll back in to full-back. I should have even got a goal but Kevin O'Dwyer made a great save.

In fairness to Skibb, they kept battling and that's why they were such a good team. Don Davis had the 'flu but he managed to get a point and Mick got a couple, and the next minute we were only one up, 0-11 to 0-10.

For six or seven minutes, the backs were under fierce pressure but they defended brilliantly, with Denis Cleary and Brian Collins leading the way. At the end of the day, that's probably what won it.

Martin O'Mahony, who had played such a role in me joining Castlehaven, put in a ferocious hour at corner-forward as well before he came off just before the end, the tank emptied. John Cleary, torn groin and all, came on for him, and he went back and won a great ball.

He couldn't kick the ball or hardly run, but he gave a good hand-pass out and we worked it up to Edmond Cleary and he kicked the last score.

WHEN THE WHISTLE blew, it was a great relief as people felt our chance had gone. Definitely, when you win, your pain isn't as severe!

The place was electric. But when the cup was being presented I spotted one fella with his head in his hands. Who was it, only my good friend, John McGerety. He lost a good few bob that day because of me, I'd guess. But he forgave me after a good bit of time!

Having missed the celebrations in 1989, I was determined to enjoy these. Both Tommy and I went down.

'Don't mind the pub,' I told him. 'It can blow up for all I care!'

We stopped in Innishannon and there were bonfires all the way to Union Hall. It was an absolutely massive day. People were so overjoyed that, if you had given them the Lotto numbers, they wouldn't have been as happy.

The first Castlehaven people back west had erected a huge sign on the main road to Skibbereen: at the turn-off for Union Hal… the word 'Party' with an arrow pointing left... and one pointing straight ahead for 'Wake'

It was an unforgettable night in Collins' pub, and from there on to Castletownshend. For me, it exemplified this small club with a massive heart, punching above their weight. To beat their neighbours in such fashion, of course people were on a huge high.

EVERYONE WAS STAYING in Christy Collins' place in Union Hall but when I went to lie down for a bit, I couldn't get any sleep because everybody was snoring like tractors.

I went out on the street at around 5am or 6am and Pat 'The Barber' Crowley was sitting on the wall outside.

All I could see were bottles, strewn everywhere.

We were chatting when Nora Maguire appeared at her front door.

'Come on in... I was so excited I couldn't sleep!' she said.

She cooked us a massive breakfast and the party continued later that day when we got the bus to the Blarney Park Hotel for the lunch. Niall won the Man of the Match award, even though, typically, he said he expected me or Denis Cleary to get it.

He would captain Cork for 1995 and I wanted to be involved too. But that depended less on me than on the ever-more-frequent injuries.

Dr Con Murphy has cared for me since the very first day I arrived in Cork, and his kindness and generosity has always been exceptional. In 1994, between the drawn and replayed finals between Castehaven and Skibbereen he worked wonders as always to help me get back to play. That defeat for Skib was tough on my old teammate, Tony Davis (below and right) who also met with intense disappointment when he was unfairly sent off in the All-Ireland final 12 months earlier.

CHAPTER 20

THE NEXT TWO years were a time of great flux, on and off the field.

After winning the county championship in 1994, we were back training on the Friday night and just over a week later we were in action against The Nire from Waterford, who were making their debut in the competition.

It was an extra-special occasion as the game was played at our home ground at Moneyvollahane, which had opened in 1990 as a replacement for the Black Field in Union Hall.

In order to rest my shoulder, I was named as a substitute and at half-time we were 2-4 to 0-3 ahead with goals from Francis Collins and Edmond Cleary. Ed got another one early in the second-half and we looked to be coasting.

In fairness, The Nire were hardy operators – I was more familiar than most with the talents of Waterford football – and they got three goals to come back to within four. A bit like the Mallow game in the county championship, I was summoned from the bench and I kicked a point as we steadied to win by 3-11 to 3-5.

I was back for the semi-final and we had to go up to west Clare to face Kilrush. They had a great start with a goal inside 30 seconds but they couldn't build on it as our backs got on top, with Denis Cleary outstanding again.

It was 1-0 to 0-1 after 22 minutes when I put us ahead with a goal and by half-time we were 1-2 to 1-1 ahead. In the second-half, our half-back line of Mike O'Brien, Brian Collins and Liam O'Connell were excellent and we kept

Kilrush at bay to win by 1-6 to 1-3.

Having had two tough games, the Munster final against Clonmel Commercials in Páirc Uí Rinn was more straightforward. We played some devastating football in the first-half and Edmond Cleary – who was really coming into his own – and I had goals as we led by 2-6 to 0-2 at half-time.

Realistically, there was no way we were going to throw away a lead like that and we won by 2-14 to 1-4 in the end. It meant that we would have another All-Ireland semi-final to look forward to over Christmas.

THE SEMI-FINAL AGAINST Dublin's Kilmacud Crokes, was scheduled for the end of February and a few weeks before that I had a rare opportunity to line out for Munster in the Railway Cup.

While the competition had been something I was involved in in my early years with Kildare, I hadn't had much of a chance to play for Munster due to all my other commitments. I captained the team against Leinster in Newbridge but we were well beaten.

The competition had gone back a lot in the space of a decade and there was hardly anybody at it.

I had a bit of an insight into Kilmacud as my sister, Jean lived in Stillorgan. The team was more or less backboned by outsiders but they had a really strong side and they beat us by 1-11 to 1-7 in Thurles. Of the three All-Ireland club semi-finals that I have lost with Castlehaven, it was the one where you'd come away and say that we were beaten by a much better team.

They had the better of us in a good few areas and we were doing well to be within four at the end. It had been 1-10 to 0-6 with five minutes left and we made it a bit more respectable. They went on to win the final against Bellaghy of Derry.

CORK FINISHED IN mid-table in Division 2 of the league.

The only game after the Kilmacud match was against Armagh and I missed that because my back problems, which had always bubbled away below the surface, were becoming a lot more serious. For so long, Deep Heat had quelled it but it's only looking back now that I realise that, if you keep battling an injury, something has to give. I was nursing a few injuries, my two reconstructed knees and my back.

There were electric shocks going down my leg when I was running full out and I wasn't able to do what I had been doing before.

A disc was squeezing a nerve and whenever I pushed it, it was like electricity going into the hamstring. For a while, I was getting treated on the hamstring but eventually I had a series of x-rays and they diagnosed that it was being caused by the back.

It meant an operation and yet more time on the sideline.

Rehabilitation is never fun, but I was almost used to it by that stage and I always had a belief that, no matter what needed to be done, I'd be back for the big games. To keep myself occupied, I still had the Waterford under-21s.

We had nine of the 1994 team still available, but even so, six players is a big turnover and performances can vary wildly at underage from year to year. We had a bye to the semi-final for the first time since I had been involved but we were up against Tipperary, who had shocked Cork in the quarter-final.

Maybe they took us for granted but we had built up something durable and we won by 0-10 to 0-5 at Fraher Field. Kerry were waiting for us in the final.

Páidí Ó Sé was still in charge and they had Diarmuid Murphy in goal, Darragh Ó Sé at midfield alongside Donal Daly and a full-forward line of John Crowley, Liam Hassett and Dara Ó Cinnéide, who got 1-9 as they won by 1-21 to 2-5 in Killarney at the start of May.

Kerry went on to win the All-Ireland.

That was my last involvement with Waterford under-21s and it couldn't be seen as anything other than a success. While we didn't win a Munster title, we had reached three straight finals and only lost to Cork and Kerry. Before 1993, Waterford had only ever been in two provincial finals.

THAT POST LED on to new employment, as I helped to set up a coaching scheme in Waterford through Fás with Eamonn Martin, who had got me involved there.

There were 15 coaches working in the county, going into schools and clubs, and we were in charge of it all. It was around this time I also gave a hand to St Vincent's, on the northside of Cork city. Stevie McCarthy got me involved and I said I'd do it because I could see how much it meant to him.

I've always identified with fanatical people.

When JC Daly came out to America, he pushed me in a lot of ways and became a great friend. Conor O'Callaghan from Cloughduv is another good friend, always at matches through thick and thin. I'd call out there on a Sunday morning and kick balls to his daughters, Joanne and Orla. Conor was afraid the ball would hit them and I'd kill them. Joanne would go on to captain Cork to win a camogie All-Ireland.

Stevie had the same kind of fanaticism when it came to Vincent's. The club is in Knocknaheeny, an area with a lot of challenges, but there are people involved there who do absolutely trojan work. Stevie asked me if I'd give a hand with Vincent's under-16 and minor teams, but I could never just give a hand!

It was like a burning ambition inside of me – I'd see guys that are good but could be even better, if they could just be given a bit of guidance. Training is important, obviously, but dedication, desire and commitment are just as vital and some guys need a push.

I had seen players that could have been stars but didn't always apply themselves, and then on the opposite side of the spectrum was someone like Dave Kavanagh, whose will to improve was absolutely infectious.

The Haven lads were like that too and that's why I ended up there.

UNFORTUNATELY, THE BACK injury meant that I missed Castlehaven's defence of the county title, against Beara in Bantry on May 20.

Just like 1990, we exited at the first stage, losing by 0-11 to 0-6. At the end of the month, I also sat out Cork's straightforward win over Waterford at Páirc Uí Chaoimh.

Tommy was an electrician by trade and he was looking to get back into that so we put the pub on the market. I had four weeks between the Clare and Kerry games to try to get ready, and I managed to keep up my record of never missing a game against the Kingdom.

I was named at centre-forward and started at full-forward but I couldn't really get going after the long lay-off – it was my first competitive game since Kilmacud at the end of February, five months previous. The rest of the attack struggled too and we couldn't make more use of the dominance of Danny Culloty and Liam Honohan at midfield.

Eamonn Breen had an early goal for Kerry and they were in front for a lot of the first-half but we were level by half-time, 1-4 to 0-7.

Kerry did go two ahead in the second-half but Niall Cahalane and Steven O'Brien were immense for us and we repeated the 1994 trick with a strong finish to win by 0-15 to 1-9. I felt I got better as the game went on, even though I didn't score.

Teddy McCarthy came on for me near the end and it was a last Munster medal for each of us. That was Cork's fourth win in five trips to Killarney since 1987, but amazingly it remains the last one.

The following morning, I could hardly bend over to tie my shoelaces, but the bottom line was that we had an All-Ireland semi-final against Dublin to look forward to. By the time that came around, the pub was sold.

The day before the Dublin game, the *Irish Independent* published an interview with me by Vincent Hogan and the headline was, *"The hard man who will pay a big price in years to come for his love of the game".*

The opening paragraph summed it up... *"He is a surgeon's pin-cushion. A physio's punch-bag. Held together by twine."* My own words finished off the article... *"Believe me, I still feel I can win another All-Ireland and this is as good a chance as any we'll get. If we do it, the pain, the knock-backs will all have been worthwhile."*

Those were the stakes – the same as what I told the lads at Lilleshall, everything was geared towards winning an All-Ireland.

For the first 20 minutes in Croke Park, things were on track as we led by 0-5 to 0-2 but then Jason Sherlock turned Mark O'Connor and slotted past Kevin O'Dwyer, who was in his first season in goal after John Kerins. Straight after that, Charlie Redmond kicked a free to put them ahead for the first time.

It was 1-5 to 0-6 at half-time and the goal gave them a cushion all the way through. With eight minutes left, they were 1-12 to 0-10 ahead, though we did cut the lead slightly. I was fouled for a free that Colin Corkery converted and then Mark O'Connor charged forward and passed to me and I kicked what was to be the last point of the game – and my last in Croke Park.

I thought I did okay in terms of how the game went, but there was a doubt in my head as regards to the future. I said to Dr Con that I couldn't keep going.

He said I'd have to have a break – to me, a break was a week!

IT WAS THE first time I felt that I was starting to go backwards. I couldn't do what I had before – I couldn't get a ball and race through or take people on.

I was battered and bruised, and I had gone through an awful lot. I'd had a multitude of injuries since 1990 and it was a constant battle to get fit, and stay fit.

For the first time, I was questioning if I could continue.

After selling the pub, I was back on the tools, doing a bit of carpentry work. Liam Cashman, the bookmaker, was doing up a lot of his shops and I used to go in at night-time and do my six or seven hours while the places were closed. Being out of the pub industry was a breath of fresh air in a way.

I had put everything into the pub and, while we didn't lose anything out of it, we didn't gain a huge amount either. I moved into an apartment above the Bord Gáis shop on Lavitt's Quay; my landlord and housemate was a man named Vincent Osborne, who worked for Bord Gáis.

Funnily enough, it was right next to the pub that I would end up owning.

The place was called Baxter's at the time, but I never went there.

Late in 1995, it got to the stage where I was hardly able to run. The back was giving me trouble again, so it looked like another operation was needed.

Dr Con arranged for me to meet a surgeon by the name of Charles Marks. He asked about my everyday life and I said that it wasn't good, I was struggling even though I was still going to Noel O'Connor, the osteopath.

Mr Marks said to give it a break for a while and see how it was in 1996 and we'd take it from there.

I was named to start for Cork against Cavan in the opening league game in October, but I wasn't up to playing and I didn't feature at all before Christmas.

It was at the stage where I could hardly get into the car to go to work.

AFTER CHRISTMAS, I went back to Charles Marks. He said that the problem was after getting a lot worse and that there was no alternative only to do the operation. My bottom disc was cracked and pinching off the nerve; he said it was like a rock down on it.

It was the first time I got a bit worried that I had something major to sort.

I asked him about coming back to play sport?

He looked at me.

'Sport?' he said.

'There's no sport after this!'

With two All-Ireland losses and two All-Ireland wins behind us we were a more confident team during the mid-90s. Here myself and Niall Cahalane and Conor Counihan relax before the 1993 Munster final against Kerry (above) though there was still plenty of business to attend to (below, I look to break through the tackle of Dublin's Paddy Moran in the 1995 All-Ireland semi-final). Everyone was enjoying 'the journey' including my great friend, Cyril 'Bird' Kavanagh.

PART 5

BAINISTEOIR

CHAPTER 21

CHARLES MARKS DID the operation on my back in early April of 1996 and removed the part of the disc that was causing me so much trouble.

When you have a back operation, you have to sign something acknowledging that you're aware of the complications, like having a limp or being on medication afterwards. They were the risks but it was a case of having to go ahead with it.

The best-case scenario was around 10 weeks out.

But the worst was that the show was over.

I'D HAVE BEEN targeting the Munster final against Kerry – as always seemed to be the case – but there was no doubting that it was a tougher challenge than any of the previous injury recoveries.

I went home to Kildare and spent a month there recuperating, as I needed assistance.

At night, I was lying on a board that my brother, Martin had made up. There were so many exercises to do and I was walking the roads and then having to lie down every few hours – I couldn't just slouch in the chair.

I did a lot of work in the gym, and in a hotel in Naas too.

Thankfully, at the end of the month, I had no pain and I went back down to Cork. I felt like a kid again as the nerve had found freedom. Castlehaven had beaten Imokilly in the first round of the county championship in May and the draw for the second round paired us against O'Donovan Rossa in Dunmanway in early June.

This was right on the edge of the 10 weeks since my operation but it would have been impossible not to be involved for such a big game against the local rivals, especially after the 1994 final. Charles Marks was surprised that I was considering it but I felt good after a few sessions and I togged out.

Even so, I was only brought on for around 10 minutes at the end at full-forward. We had led at half-time by a point but were too reliant on John Cleary for scores and Skibb got on top in the second-half.

Gene O'Driscoll was moved back in to mark me and I wasn't really able to influence things, and they won by 0-9 to 0-7. After 1994, they had a huge motivation to beat us and that's probably what swung it their way.

Cork had beaten Limerick and were up against Clare in a Munster semi-final in Cusack Park on June 23, but that was too soon for me. Clare had John O'Keeffe over them and they were no easy touches in Ennis. If their shooting had been better, they might even have won but even though Cork were three ahead with five minutes left, Clare got a draw with Aidan O'Keeffe levelling it. A week later in Páirc Uí Chaoimh, it was just as close and the match went to extra-time but eventually Cork prevailed.

It meant another Munster final against Kerry, but even though I played the full match when Castlehaven played Clonakilty in the Kelleher Shield in early July, I wasn't up to the rigours of inter-county. Cork selector Paddy Sheehan, who would become a trusted confidante over the coming years, could always be relied on to say it straight.

He summed up my chances of making the Kerry match.

"I don't think it would be humanly possible for Larry," he said in an *Evening Echo* article. *"He has been out of top-class football for a long time."*

I WAS ON the line doing water in Páirc Uí Chaoimh for the game on July 21, which proved to be the end of an era as Kerry won by 0-14 to 0-11.

Billy had decided to call it a day after a decade in the job and, as we were walking off the field together, he said something like… 'I'm finished… you can take it over now!'

Whatever about that, realistically I felt I was finished as a player.

If Cork had won the Munster championship, I might have been able to make some appearance in the All-Ireland series, but I was 33 now and had a seemingly endless list of injuries. I had tried to push the boundaries for so long that they were really catching up with me.

I never made an announcement but I felt I wouldn't play with Cork again.

My thinking was that if I eased up in 1996, I'd have a chance to give it another few years with the club.

One day in mid-August, Christy Cooney, the Cork county board chairman, rang asking to meet me and I met him out in Bishopstown, where he was based at the time with FÁS. He confirmed that Billy had decided to step down and he asked if I'd take over the Cork team.

I didn't even tell Christy I'd think about it… I said it would be an absolute honour to manage Cork.

As far as I was concerned, my county days were over because of my back.

Everybody seemed to expect it; I suppose I was seen as a natural successor but it was still a nice surprise to be asked.

THERE WAS TENSION at times between me and Billy but I gave him the same respect I'd give to anyone over a team.

At the same time, if I felt something needed to be upped, I wasn't afraid to say it.

I wanted to win and to be the best I could and for the team to be the best it could be. It wasn't arrogance. Did I win the games on my own?

Of course I didn't.

But I did feel that after 1990, the standards had dropped.

Training was easy. There was very little intensity.

And, most important of all, that driven madness to succeed was gone from the dressing-room.

The day after the appointment, I wrote a column in *The Examiner* and I started it off with a vow.

"I'm not promising All-Irelands," I wrote, *"I'm not even promising Munster titles, but the one thing I will promise the people of Cork is this – I'll be giving it my all."*

Straightaway, I started putting a plan together for training, ready to get going for the start of the National League. In tandem with that was yet another attempt to sort my back out.

Donegal invited me out to New York to play for them in a county quarter-final against Cork. Niall Cahalane, Moggy and I – and Mick McCarthy, who was playing for Cork – were due to leave on the Saturday, the day before the game, but the flight from Shannon had to be delayed because of strong winds.

We spent the night in Limerick, at the Two Mile Inn, but we didn't know if we'd make it. The flight left at 8am Irish time and when we got to New York we had to run off the plane with our gear, leaving the luggage behind us. There was a guy waiting to collect us in New York and we were togging out in the car.

The lads were running out on to the field as we arrived – we were jeered a bit for playing against Cork! We won by a few points but I broke down again with a back injury and so I couldn't go back out for the semi-final, though the lads did.

Donal Gallagher had a friend who knew the physio with the Philadelphia Eagles football team, and Donal drove me down there on the Monday after the game. His name was Mike Wolf, and he treated my back in Veterans Stadium. I felt some relief, but Mike told me things were still dicey.

I TOLD DR CON I wanted to see Charles Marks, but Charles didn't really want to see me.

He said I was a lunatic.

Funnily enough, I met Mr Marks again in 2018. He was the head of the Parents Council for Mount Mercy College in Bishopstown, where my daughter was attending. They were running a fundraiser and he wanted me to promote it and go to the launch. When I met him that day, I asked him if he remembered what he had told me.

'You were a headcase!' he laughed.

Gerry McEntee was the next call, and he said that Colm O'Rourke's brother, Kieran was a back specialist and he was just back from America. I got an appointment with him in Blackrock in Dublin and he couldn't believe I had let my back get to that stage.

It was never really given a chance to recover with all of the hauling and pulling over the years, though I reminded Kieran that, 'Playing against your fellas didn't help!'

He was going to take out the remainder of the disc that was partially removed. If I waited and gave it time, the bones would fuse. The other option was that it wouldn't be a success and I'd end up maybe not being able to work again, or I'd have to wear a brace or have a limp or have no feeling in my legs.

I said I had to have the operation.

That operation took place shortly before Christmas and I felt great again.

BY THAT STAGE, I had got up and running with Cork, with the first league match a draw against Donegal before we beat the new All-Ireland champions, Meath.

There wasn't any huge problem in managing guys who had previously been my teammates. They knew I'd be straight with them, as a player or a manager. Paddy Sheehan was still in situ as a selector and that was obviously part of my remit too.

Terry O'Neill had been the representative of the 1995 champions, Bantry Blues and he remained for the first few rounds of the league before the new county champions,

Clonakilty, nominated Micheál 'Haulie' O'Neill.

Terry would be involved again in 1999 after Bantry won a second county title and he remained a sounding-board for me, while his son, Damien was one of the guys I spoke with about coming on to the panel. He was a real dominant midfielder and he had been exceptional in 1995, and I felt he could bring a lot to the team.

We were training in Inchydoney and at Macroom, up and down the hills, as the first thing I wanted to do was to make sure everybody had the requisite levels of fitness. The lads put in a huge effort, to be fair. Of course, there were times when I couldn't help myself from joining in with a bit of running in order to help my own rehabilitation. I wasn't up to their levels but I felt I was benefiting.

Overall, we were going well as we tried out various guys. I would have been honest and fair with players but I was also trying to juggle the pack. I had played Martin Cronin a few times at centre-forward, for instance – I felt I needed a worker who could bring more variation to the game.

Likewise, Steven O'Brien was tried at full-forward.

We ended up finishing in fourth place in Division 1, which got us through to the quarter-finals. We beat Louth there and that set us up for a semi-final against Kildare in Croke Park. We won 2-10 to 1-9, and it was great to get a win at Croke Park. We had the added bonus of a home final as Kerry had beaten Laois in the other semi and the counties had a home-and-away arrangement for knockout league games.

To win a national title in my first campaign would have been a massive boost, but we couldn't make it work for ourselves.

It's worth bearing in mind that Kerry weren't a powerhouse.

Páidí Ó Sé had taken over and they had All-Ireland under-21 winners in the team, but none of their team had a national medal, so it was a huge hurdle for them. Unfortunately for us, they got over that hurdle as three first-half goals gave them a 3-2 to 1-6 half-time lead.

To be behind after having more scores was a bit dispiriting and they kept us at arm's length in the second half to win by 3-7 to 1-8. A bad day was made worse by the news that Terry Radley had died that day.

Terry was a supporter who had become a great friend and was present at nearly every training session.

PEOPLE WOULD HAVE been expecting us to meet Kerry again in the Munster final but things didn't transpire that way as we were condemned to a very short summer.

As with 1996, Cork had to go to Ennis to face Clare and there shouldn't have been any complacency after needing that replay to win the year before. Confidence had been high but I think the league final brought a few doubts into the team.

Then, there were other external issues.

Damien O'Neill had been flying but suffered a cruciate injury against Nemo in the first round of the county championship, so he was out. Clonakilty had nominated Brian Murphy as captain but he was on the fringes of the team and had missed the league final, with Niall Cahalane skippering the team.

Having the county champions choose the captain was something I benefited from in 1990 but at times it could be troublesome.

Brian was in for the Clare game, while Niall had had a poor game against Kerry and ultimately didn't make the 15 for Clare, with Ronan McCarthy a victim of the league final as well. Niall and Ronan were two guys giving me one hundred percent and if I had my time back, I'd have pushed harder for them to start.

I'll take the blame, I should have been tough enough and forceful enough. They had given me everything and weren't going to let me down, whereas I felt others on the day didn't give enough.

Against Clare, we kicked 17 wides.

It was hard to watch.

It was just one of those afternoons where you knew something was going to happen. We had kicked the game away a million times and it stayed in the balance.

Then came the moment everybody remembers.

Clare won a free and, rather than taking a point as time was nearly gone, Ger Keane took it short to Martin Daly. He still had loads to do but he managed to get past two backs to make space and then slotted a low shot across Kevin O'Dwyer and in, pretty much the only place he could have put the ball.

It was like something you're watching in slow-motion, powerless to stop it all.

THE DRESSING-ROOM WAS not a pleasant place to be.

All the effort we had put in over the winter had come to nothing. There was nothing to say – what can you say?

I came out of the ground and I was devastated.

By this stage, I was living in Summerhill South in Cork city. I'd say I didn't come out of the place for about two weeks; I couldn't believe what was after happening.

I had a squad in serious shape and we had done an awful lot of work.

If we had picked the same team for the Clare game as we had for the league final – the one that got us to that stage – we'd have won. If we had done that, I think we would have been very competitive against Kerry, who went on to win the All-Ireland; their first in 11 years.

We were probably their biggest challengers, but small margins made the difference. I'd hold my hands up, I made mistakes but I learned my lesson.

I would have to wait until 1998 to put things right but, in the meantime, and not for the first time, Castlehaven were there to pick me up.

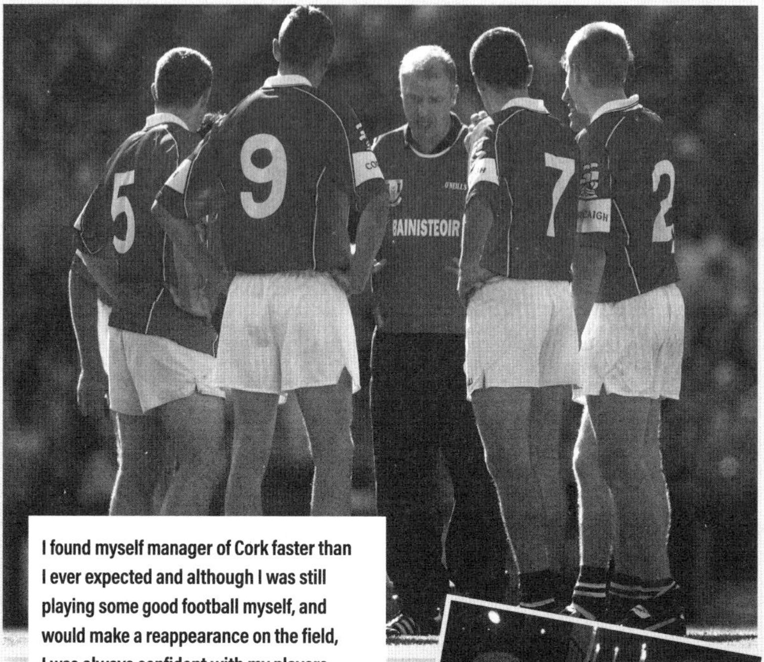

I found myself manager of Cork faster than I ever expected and although I was still playing some good football myself, and would make a reappearance on the field, I was always confident with my players (above) and also talking to the media (below, with Mick O'Dwyer and Dublin's Tommy Lyons). JC Daly, Micko and myself on a night out.

CHAPTER 22

MANAGING A COUNTY team can become all-consuming, as I had quickly learned. Instead of dealing with just one person, as you are when you're playing, suddenly, you have 30 or more people to look after in terms of players and backroom personnel – and this was before the explosion in the numbers of ancillary staff, as you have nowadays.

You were a psychologist as much as a coach.

To that end, it was a nice distraction to still be able to play with Castlehaven.

When he carried out the operation on my back before Christmas in 1996, Kieran O'Rourke had said to give it 12 months before attempting to return playing again, but I felt good in terms of the recovery. I was back in six. To be fair to Kieran, he understood the way that GAA players are always trying to get back fit quicker than medically advisable and I was probably one of the worst in that regard.

I wasn't as quick as I used to be, and the back had to be minded, so I was focused on making sure my positioning was right as much as anything, but, ahead of the first round of the county championship, I felt that I was beginning to play good football again without any discomfort. I was happy enough that I could still be influential at this level.

Our first game was against Avondhu in Macroom in the middle of May and it was standard fare for that time of year, a case of getting the job done with a win.

I was a bit rusty, which was to be expected, but I got the goal to put us eight points clear early in the second-half and was pleased overall that there had been no after-effects.

There was only a turnaround of a week before the second round, a meeting with St Nick's in Newcestown. The thing about Nick's was that we'd generally go in as favourites against them and everybody would expect a win, but they'd make damn sure that we earned it from them. But we were able to dog it out in the end, and win.

That moved us into the quarter-finals against UCC, with the championship paused so as to allow Cork to prepare for the ill-fated Clare game.

While all I wanted to do after that defeat was forget about football, the fact I had that match to look forward to was what eventually got me out of the house and back on the training field. UCC had a star-studded team and we were going to be up against it.

I was centre-forward, being marked by Séamus Moynihan, with Eamonn Fitzmaurice at wing-back, Anthony Lynch in the full-back line and Alan Quirke in goal. In attack, they had Mick O'Dwyer's son, Karl, Johnny Crowley and Mark O'Sullivan.

ONE THING ABOUT the Haven though was that we relished games like that – the better the opposition, the more we tended to rise to the occasion. Dr Con was involved with UCC, as he so often is, and he told me later that, prior to the game, they could hardly talk or hear each other in the UCC dressing-room because we were so wound up on the other side of the wall!

I heard later that Dr Con had a word with them in their dressing-room before the game. 'These lads are easily beat... they're only old men!' he told the players.

Dr Con and myself had a good laugh afterwards about that statement!

Apart from a couple of goal chances for the college in the first 10 minutes, we were by far the better team and we didn't give them a sniff.

By half-time, it was 0-9 to 0-1 and for the first time since my return I really felt like I was at a good level again. It finished 0-14 to 0-8 with the victory never really in doubt and we were through to a semi-final against Imokilly.

I had scored three points against UCC, two frees, and I had shown that I was able to put it up to a good, up-and-coming footballer like Moynihan. I was finding a bit of form and I had people asking me why I was managing Cork when I was good enough to still be playing.

That talk grew a bit louder after the semi-final on August 31.

We were the only club side in the last four as we were up against Imokilly, the east Cork divisional team, while Beara from the west and our old rivals Duhallow were on the other side. Divisions were not allowed to compete in the Munster club championship, so it meant we were automatically through to that, whatever else happened.

The other semi-final was a week before ours, with Beara coming out on top, and we made sure of our progress with a 1-14 to 0-4 win.

There was quite a gap between the semi and the final, meaning that, when the decider came around on October 12, the conditions were savage. It was a horrendous day, more winter than autumn, and the pitch was like a bog.

There were certain places where, if you ran, you mightn't be seen again!

On days like that, things can hinge on one mistake so you try to keep things simple but it's tough going.

Divisional teams can be funny in that if you play them in the first round, you've a good chance of beating them as they won't have had an opportunity to do much together but, the further they go in the championship, the better they become. Beara were flying in the first half, even though we had the wind, and only an excellent point from Martin O'Mahony just before half-time had us within two.

In injury time, we had a chance to win it when we got a free about 50 yards out.

Into the wind. I had the distance but not the accuracy, but nobody could really complain with a draw at the end of a another dog of a game. It was played in savage conditions.

The replay would be delayed until November 9 as the National League was starting up and Garnish, one of the teams making up the Beara side, had the county junior championship.

CORK GOT OFF to a winning start in the league as we beat Tipperary in Clonmel, with a teenage Nicholas Murphy impressing on his debut.

Our first Munster club championship game was a week after the Tipp game and we were too strong for The Nire of Waterford. Cork made it two from two by beating Waterford in Páirc Uí Rinn at the start of November and then it was time to go again against Beara for the replay.

The weather was a bit better but unfortunately the outcome was not.

Beara had no shortage of fine footballers and strong competitors but they hadn't won the county since 1967 and I think, on the day, that that desire to bridge the gap was probably what edged it for them.

You had to give Beara credit but, coming off, we probably felt that the referee wasn't that fair to us on either day and when Niall Cahalane was running past him, he gave him a shove into the back. It was out of frustration but he would eventually face a sanction for it in the form of a 48-week suspension.

It ruled Niall out of playing for Castlehaven and Cork in 1998.

It was tough to face back into training after losing a county final, but one thing you'd say about the Haven is that they always gave full commitment to the challenge. Obviously, we'd have liked to have been in there as champions but we were still the top club in the county and the Haven could never be accused of going through the motions.

We trained well for a few weeks ahead of our home semi-final against Laune Rangers, which was scheduled for November 23 and then, after all that, the match was postponed due to a waterlogged pitch, meaning it was put back to December 7 – Cork had Down in the league on November 30 and our good start came to an abrupt end, as we lost heavily.

Funnily enough, Laune Rangers had lost their county final to a divisional side after a replay as well, East Kerry denying them a three in-a-row. They were still looking for three on the trot in Munster though, aiming to repeat their All-Ireland glory of 1996.

The final score was 2-10 to 1-3 and Laune's goal came right at the end. Coming from where we had been after losing the county final, it was a real statement.

It was still only a semi-final, and there was no complacency in the final against Fethard in Fermoy, which was one of my great games. Niall was out, as was his brother Dinny, who had been sent off late on against Laune, and Dave O'Regan was suspended as well, but still we were able to produce the performance we needed.

We had a lot of young players, like Alan Crowley and Liam Collins, who played exceptionally well that day.

We won by 1-14 to 1-8 and, from where I had been in 1996, with the possibility of having to retire, it was a great way to end the year.

We had an All-Ireland semi-final against Erin's Isle to look forward to, seeking to make it third time lucky after our defeats in 1990 and '95.

We had no idea of the drama that lay in store.

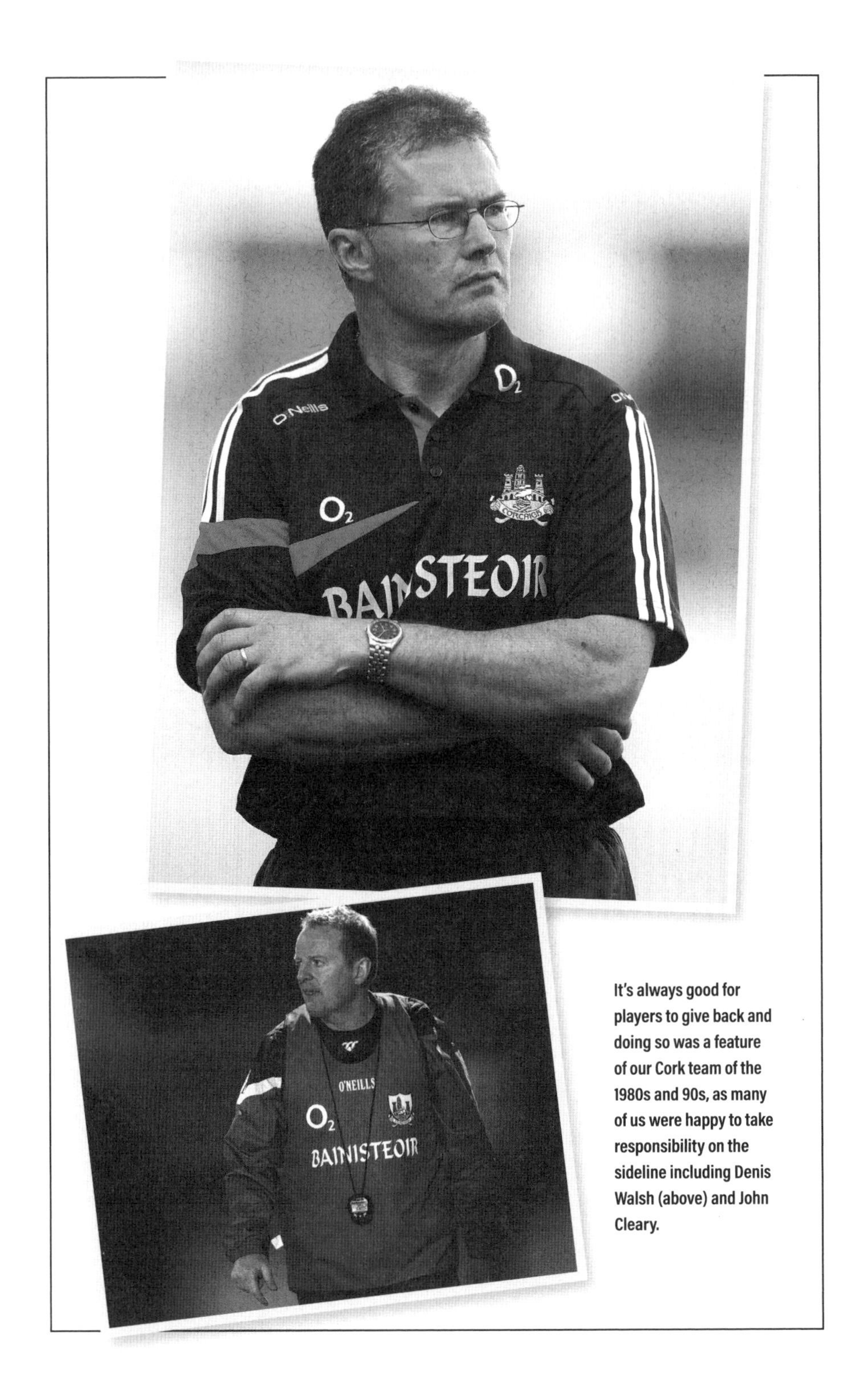

It's always good for players to give back and doing so was a feature of our Cork team of the 1980s and 90s, as many of us were happy to take responsibility on the sideline including Denis Walsh (above) and John Cleary.

CHAPTER 23

AFTER SUCH A strong performance in the Munster club final, there were even stronger suggestions that I should still be playing for Cork.

A piece in the local west Cork paper, *The Southern Star*, a week after the game, said that *"There was general agreement among the large attendance after the match that the man who captained Cork to their last All-Ireland senior triumph in 1990 has still a lot to offer at inter-county level... if he can be persuaded to don the red jersey again, one feels that Cork's bid to lower the colours of All-Ireland champions Kerry at Killarney next summer would be greatly enhanced"*.

I tried to put the matter to bed when Jim O'Sullivan interviewed me for *The Examiner* in January of 1998.

Jim's article began, *"If there's one thing Larry Tompkins can predict with some certainty for 1998, it's that he won't be playing inter-county football!"*

It was what I genuinely felt at the time.

And I had enough on my plate with coaching the team and getting ready for the club semi-final with Castlehaven in February. As well as that, I was belatedly embracing life away from football.

WORK-WISE, I WAS doing bits of carpentry and I was regularly down to Waterford with the coaching. I was doing a bit of promotional work for Flor Griffin, who had an electrical store.

Mainly it involved standing in for photographs – though nothing like the scantily-clad Kerry team with the Bendix washing machines in the 1980s. I had done a bit with Saville menswear on Oliver Plunkett St in the past too, but I was never going to take up modelling full-time!

Castlehaven were sponsored by a furniture company called Protea Pine and they were looking to break into the Cork market. In August, 1997 I started working for them as a director with responsibility for Cork, liaising with pubs, hotels, guest houses and other commercial customers.

It was a good match, given my carpentry background. They were opening a huge store at the Kinsale Road roundabout and they headhunted Orla Fegan from Crosshaven, who was a manager in Blarney Woollen Mills.

Orla and I hit it off from the start and, with a bit of help from her friend, Serina, we started going out.

Previously, I would have felt that if I was getting involved with someone it would interfere with my football. Orla is a hell of a person and it was great to have her there, just to be able to talk to. She might have gone to a few GAA games but there wasn't a huge interest and that suited me fine.

Her work ethic was something that I also identified with and I still don't know how she does so many things. Her dedication and commitment to everything she does is second to none.

THERE WAS ROOM for life outside of football, but that didn't mean that the focus on the chance to win that All-Ireland club medal was dulled. Just like the previous two semi-finals, we had the Leinster champions, this time Erin's Isle of Dublin, with Semple Stadium in Thurles the venue. We were still without Niall Cahalane but Dinny was back, and so was Dave O'Regan and we produced one of the most complete performances in all my time with the club.

We scored 17 points in total and just two of them were from the dead ball.

It was a near-complete performance in front of a big crowd, which was beginning to thin out with a few minutes to go. We were five points up and Erin's Isle were down to 14 men after Charlie Redmond had been sent off. Croke Park was beckoning, even after Erin's Isle got a point and then a goal to come back to within two points.

We went up the field and Colin Crowley was straight through to put us three ahead again but he went for goal and it hit the post, as hard as anything, and came back out.

A ball broke in midfield and went out over the sideline. The kick came in and the ball was trickling out wide but Michael Maguire came out of goal and Denis Cleary, the full-back, went for it too. There was a mix-up between them.

The corner-forward put his toe in between them and poked it back across. The ball went across the square and Niall Crossan shot blindly.

The ball hit the post, went across the line, hit the other post and popped out into my hands and I cleared it down the field.

The umpires looked at one another and put up the flag for a goal.

There was mayhem for a few minutes, but the goal stood. Moggy kicked the ball out, I caught it at midfield but when I came down the referee, Pat McEnaney blew the final whistle. He didn't even give us a chance of an equaliser.

Another All-Ireland semi-final loss and the worst of the three – no disrespect to Erin's Isle, but we were the better team on the day. We went into the dressing-room and, bar a bit of shouting between Moggy and John Cleary, there were no other words spoken.

I've lost All-Ireland finals and major matches, but as a team, I'd never seen a loss have such an impact. It would be very hard to measure how down everyone was. To lose a game like that, where we had clearly been the best team, was horrible.

To lose it to a highly questionable goal was just unimaginable.

We had a few cans on the bus on the way back but still nobody was talking. We were going back to the Garda Club on Penrose Wharf in Cork city for grub – Billy Mangan from Boherbue ran the place and he was a good supporter of the Haven. We were 20 miles from Cork and a few lads wanted a pit-stop and that was the first time there was a word said.

It took us a long time to get over it, but in fairness to the Haven supporters, the crowds that showed up in the Garda Club – just to be there for us – were incredible.

There was talk of appeals and the video of the game was sent to Sky to see if it could be proven that the ball hadn't crossed the line but it was winter, a heavy pitch, and there was no white line visible in the goalmouth.

The umpire just made a decision in that split-second; he put up the flag and there was no going back. In the summer of 2018, there was a 'replay' between the club's modern-day teams as part of an AIB promotion, with Harry Redknapp and Gianluca Vialli picking the teams.

The Haven won handy, but I didn't get to it as I was on holidays.

I'll be honest – that win didn't ease the 20 year-old disappointment.

NOT LONG AFTER the Erin's Isle game came some terrible news as my former Cork teammate, Mick McCarthy died in a car crash coming home from the national coursing meeting in Clonmel. He was only just about to turn 33.

Mick was a lovely footballer and a great character. Even though himself and John Cleary were going for the same spot on the Cork team, they were thick as thieves and always up to some mischief.

I TRIED TO face back into the league with Cork.

One thing I had learned in 1997 was not to take so much on myself and I was trying to off-load more things. Conor Counihan, who was part of the set-up the previous year but not a selector, had that title now and Beara had nominated Barry Murphy as their selector. Paddy Sheehan was part of the set-up too and he did a huge amount of organising.

I used to ask him if he ever slept as he was always on duty!

We had an away draw against Kerry in the Munster semi-final and that was scheduled for the start of July, so we had a good lead-in time to it.

We went well enough in the league and finished second to Down, winning six of the eight games. Training was going well, on the 'Hill of Death' in Macroom, as Brian Corcoran called it, and on the beach at Inchydoney. I always believed in this type of training.

We'd often be searching for pitches to use and clubs like Ballygarvan always looked after us. Crosshaven was a pitch that was always available too, because it was up on a hill so the water ran down and away from it – though I'm not sure Orla had ever visited it. And then, in the midst of trying to run the Cork team, I re-entered the licensed trade.

I had been over in Cheltenham for my annual break, with the likes of Haulie O'Neill from Clonakilty and his namesake, Michael O'Neill from Fernhill House Hotel.

Over there, we used to link up with my friend, Gerry Chawke from Clonmel and his crew and I would soon be calling on Gerry's expertise again. At that time I was thinking of going back into the pub trade, so I asked Niall to have a look at what was available.

When I got out of the pub game, I thought I'd never get back into it, but customers become part of your life and you miss that.

I'd meet my old regulars on the street or when I was working on the tools and they'd say that they were lost without the pub. Niall called me back with a few suggestions, so I rang Gerry and he came down.

He had a great eye for a pub and he always used to tell me that the location of the first pub was wrong – it was too far from town.

We went around to a few places and Gerry would make nearly a split-second decision – we could go into the nicest place in the world and he'd walk out of it. We came into what was then Sallys - Baxter's on Lavitt's Quay on a Friday evening - where we met Orla.

After five minutes, Gerry spoke up.

'Buy this place!'

I said that he hadn't seen upstairs or anything?

'I would drink in here on my own,' he replied. 'That's the difference.'

I respected Gerry's opinion. Niall organised a meeting down in Silver Springs and within 10 minutes I had shaken hands on a deal.

It was done quickly, like the one for the first pub.

In business, you go with an instinct. If you ask too many questions, then doubts come into your mind.

Within a few weeks we got the keys. The pub had loads of character and I didn't want to lose that. But I needed to do some renovations too.

We were aiming for an opening at the end of April and I had nine or 10 days to get it all right. There was a bit of work to it, but I got great help. Men like Donal Burke, Peter Skuse and others were not afraid to roll up their sleeves and help out. My brothers came down, and as always they fell in where they were needed. We were all hands on deck, working around the clock.

I ordered old pitch pine for the floors, which needed a few days to dry out before delivery. Mick Mulcahy in 96FM radio got wind of this. He used to do a 'wind-up' show in the mornings. It was a great hit all around the county.

I used to listen to it all of the time, but I never thought I would be caught out myself.

I GOT A CALL.

It was Mick, pretending to be the pine floor supplier.

'I'm sorry Larry... there's a problem with your flooring,' the voice said.

'We had it drying out... but there was a break-in and a fire, all the timber is burnt.' This was four or five days before opening and I annihilated him on the phone.

'Can't we delay it for a while and put down pallets?' he asked.

I was getting angrier and angrier, but eventually he revealed himself. I had been properly caught and there were more beeps than words in the broadcast!

Otherwise, we battled through, the proper flooring arrived and was put down. The last three or four days before the opening, I had no sleep but when work had to be done, it had to be done. Orla did all of the ordering and hiring of staff, and I did all of the 'heavy' stuff. We enlisted the help of an old friend of mine, Mickey Joe Corbett, the legendary bar man, to help us get on our feet through the opening stages.

We opened at 6pm on Thursday, April 30 and the first man in the door to have a pint was Mick Malone, the great Cork hurler.

That was a major hurdle overcome and the next one to deal with that summer would be Kerry in Killarney. After such a good record in Fitzgerald Stadium as a player, it would be my first time to patrol the sideline there in the championship.

Or so I thought.

Roy Keane and I (above) have been good friends since I started in the pub business in Cork, but while celebrities like him, and Christy Moore (whom I have known since my Kildare days) and Nathan Carter are very welcome, I have always received great support from GAA people and sports people from all over Cork. Here (below) I am in the great company of the Cork ladies football team and their manager, Eamon Ryan outside my place on Lavitt's Quay which I opened in the late 90s as I also started into my management career in Cork.

CASTLEHAVEN HAD RECEIVED a bye to the second round of the 1998 Cork senior football championship; a local derby against Clonakilty in Dunmanway.

Clon had won the championship in 1996, coming from nowhere, whereas we were obviously still hurting after going so close in the 1997 final, not to mention the All-Ireland semi-final loss to Erin's Isle. There was a huge crowd there, about 4,000, expecting a close game.

Clon were probably looking to take advantage of any trauma we still had, but we crushed them, winning by 1-17 to 0-10. The report in *The Examiner* said that, *"Tompkins was irrepressible and must seriously consider making himself available to play with the county against Kerry in the forthcoming Munster semi-final"*.

Later that week, *The Examiner* ran another piece on the subject, with both Niall Cahalane and Dinny Allen saying that I was one of the best six forwards in the county and I should start against Kerry.

OUTSIDE THE CAMP, the debate raged.

And, inside the camp, the selectors asked me if it was a possibility?

I would never put myself in a position where I thought I could not do a good job, and I genuinely felt that I was back playing well.

Maybe I could do something for the team, I thought.

Deep down, I was mad to play. Wearing the Cork jersey was always a massive honour. It was probably going to be my last opportunity to do so.

One last time to pull that magnificent red jersey over my head.

I decided to give it a shot. It was a big decision, especially with the pub only just after opening, but I had Orla behind me all of the way.

I was named at centre-forward.

Conor would be the manager on the sideline and, on the day, effectively I was just another player. If I wasn't performing, I expected to be taken off, the same as anybody else.

We had two championship debutants, Alan O'Regan and Damien O'Neill, who had been such a loss the year before after doing his cruciate. In goal was my Haven clubmate, Michael Maguire, who was far off a debutant. I felt that his kickouts could be of huge benefit to us.

The last time Kerry had played Cork as All-Ireland champions was in my first year, 1987. There were nearly 44,000 in Killarney for this game and I was playing on Liam O'Flaherty, who had really come into his own in the previous year's campaign.

I kicked one good point in the first-half and we were level at 0-6 each, but I couldn't get on the ball as much as I'd have liked.

Still, the game was there for the taking, even though we lost Damien O'Neill to injury again after the restart. Nicholas Murphy came in and Steven O'Brien was moved to midfield, and they got the better of Darragh Ó Sé and Donal Daly for the most part.

We were a point behind when Alan O'Regan got a brilliant solo goal with a quarter of an hour left and if we had just been able to add a point we might have got stronger with the end in sight.

Instead, Kerry hit back as O'Flaherty launched a high ball in and Mark O'Connor got caught under it. Maurice Fitzgerald got possession and lashed home a great finish.

They won by three in the end, 1-14 to 1-11. Had we won, we would have been playing Kildare. It would have been amazing to meet Kildare in the All-Ireland championship.

I DID OKAY.

I didn't pull up any trees nor was I the losing of the game, but I realised coming off that day that I looked a tired and shattered old man.

I knew I wasn't going to get back to the old levels. That's wear and tear, that's time; you're getting slower and it's frustrating because I knew I couldn't give the Cork people the level of performance that I was used to.

I went back to the pub that night expecting to see a big crowd but it was very subdued and quiet. Thankfully, one of the old, great characters and a massive supporter of Cork was there to greet me. Frankie Carey had waited for me, even though he was probably as heartbroken as I was, because he hated Kerry. The hardest thing to deal with, he said, is that we would have to wait another 12 months to beat the feckers!

The disappointment did not stop him from entertaining me, and the rest of the pub, with a sing-song for the night.

On the management side, it was two losses from two championship games but I didn't harbour too many doubts about my ability or the team's. As a personality, I'd be a shy individual but I'd always be a massive believer that anything could be achieved.

There was some consolation two weeks after the Kerry match as Castlehaven beat O'Donovan Rossa by four points in the quarter-finals of the county championship and that set us up for a semi-final against Bantry Blues. This was a golden period for west Cork football.

The face-off with Bantry would be a chance for us to show that we were still the kingpins in the region.

Unfortunately, it wasn't to be, for the Haven or myself. I had a recurring problem with my back and was strongly advised not to play, and that ruled me out. On the night, Bantry were like a well-oiled machine.

They won by 1-13 to 0-6 with a superb performance. Damien O'Neill, alongside Michael Moran, who sadly died in recent years, showed the kind of form that illustrated what a star he could become for Cork, and their teenage corner-forward, Philip Clifford scored 1-3. They went on to win the county.

I THREW CLIFFORD in for the league opener against Offaly in Tullamore and he scored a last-minute goal to give us a draw. We had a good win over

Leitrim at home before we went to Ballybofey to take on Donegal and came away from that with another victory.

It left us top of the table going into Christmas and it showed that we could edge things against a strong side. Liam Honohan made his comeback that day in midfield. I hoped he would be a huge asset if we were to make an impact in the latter stages of the championship.

If you're going to win the major trophies, you need everybody who is available. There's a perception out there that Cork didn't win the 1999 All-Ireland because I got rid of the Nemo Rangers pair, Colin Corkery and Steven O'Brien, but that's not the case.

Steven had been a massive player for Cork for a decade but he felt he needed a break. I met him and I told him I was willing to give him that break for the league, but he was either on or off after that, I warned him.

He was delighted and we agreed to meet again towards the end of the league. Colin had his own business and there was a lot of travel around Europe. He hadn't played in 1998 but I was willing to meet him halfway, once he showed some commitment. I met him in Jurys and, like Steven, he wanted to take a break.

He had too much going on with work and family life, and there just wasn't enough room for county football. I had to leave it.

We picked up our good league form again after Christmas. The first game back was against Galway in Páirc Uí Rinn and, just prior to that, Steven contacted me out of the blue. He was anxious to come back in and do a bit of training.

He was very keen so he came back in.

We named him as a sub against Galway and brought him in with 10 minutes or so left. He picked up possession and took a tumble but was hit – he sustained a broken collarbone and had to be carted off.

That was a setback but we won and there were signs that we were building something good. Michael O'Donovan from Dohenys was one of the players given a chance and he was superb at corner-back. He was first to every ball and would tear out from defence. Owen Sexton was another player who was taking his chance, and Philip Clifford and Aidan Dorgan were showing up well in attack, where Mark O'Sullivan had made a strong return and Brendan 'Jer' O'Sullivan was putting himself in the mix.

We were knocked back a bit when we lost two in-a-row, away to Armagh and

Tyrone, meaning that we had to win our last match, against Dublin in Páirc Uí Rinn.

In a way, that was a good thing as it was a chance to see what a relatively young team could do when the pressure was on. In wet and slippery conditions, it wasn't a great game but we won by 0-10 to 0-7. It meant we finished second and went forward to the quarter-finals – Dublin squeezed into third as Tyrone lost to Armagh.

Derry were our opponents in the last eight at Croke Park and we blitzed them, winning by 3-14 to 1-6. That meant a semi-final against a familiar foe of mine, Meath, who still had Seán Boylan working his magic. If the forwards won us the quarter-final, this was a backs' game on a really wet day. We only scored six points but we controlled the game and Meath managed just three points. When they went for goals, they couldn't get past Kevin O'Dwyer, who had reclaimed the No. 1 jersey.

AFTER TWO WINS from two in Croke Park, it was back to Páirc Uí Chaoimh for the league final, though this time Dublin were to be the opponents after they had beaten Armagh. Beating them in Páirc Uí Chaoimh was a brilliant result, and it gave the team a lot of confidence, particularly as we were re-shaping the team and a lot of the younger lads were playing their first big match.

In 1989, winning the league had been huge for our team in terms of gaining the confidence to go on and win the All-Ireland. A decade on, we were hopeful of pulling off something similar.

My last day in the famous red jersey came in Fitzgerald Stadium in 1998 when I swapped my role on the sideline for a job on the field (here I am getting through Liam Flaherty). We lost and while I did okay, I also realized that the future of the team lay with men like Philip Clfford (below, who captained Cork to the 1999 All-Ireland final the following year).

ONE OF THE great GAA sayings is that league is league… and championship is championship.

It's self-explanatory on the surface level. But ultimately it means that you can shoot the lights out in the spring and it'll count for nothing unless you back it up in the summer and on into the autumn.

It was the challenge facing us after winning the league at the start of May.

People might have thought that there was more pressure as we hadn't managed a championship win in 1997 or '98, but within the camp there was a lot of positivity. Of all the years I was in charge, it was probably the most enjoyable and everybody was working really hard.

Terry O'Neill was back as a selector after Bantry had nominated him and the mood was really good. Being picky, I'd probably have liked to have had a bit more squad depth. As mentioned, Colin Corkery and Steven O'Brien were out and Brian Corcoran had chosen to focus fully on hurling.

On top of that, we had some awful luck with injuries.

After going well following his return, Liam Honohan damaged ankle ligaments in the league quarter-final win over Derry and he wouldn't make it back for the rest of the year. Damien O'Neill, the captain, had a fairly persistent groin injury. At the start of the campaign, those two were probably seen as the first-choice midfield pairing – Nicholas Murphy and Haulie O'Sullivan came in and did brilliantly, but there was a lot being asked of them.

We did what we had to do in the first round against Waterford in Dungarvan, winning by 3-23 to 0-4.

Anthony Lynch and Philip Clifford were debutants after they both had a good league, and Seán Óg Ó hAilpín was making his first championship start too, having been on the panel for a couple of years. Next up were Limerick and, about a week before that, the Sligo manager, Mickey Moran rang me because they were coming down to Cork for a training weekend and they were looking for a challenge match. We played them in Páirc Uí Rinn and Mick O'Donovan broke his collarbone.

It was a disaster because he had been going so well. I was talking to Martin Breheny of the *Irish Independent* after the league final and he said that his performance had been an exhibition. It isn't something you'd often hear about a corner-back, but he was automatic All Star material. I valued Martin's opinion as we went back a long way. I always found him a shrewd and knowledgeable reporter, and his insight into players and teams was incredible.

Aidan Dorgan was another fella who had been going well. He had filled that wing-forward spot that had been troubling us, but then he pulled up with a groin injury. In fairness to the county board, they let me send him to Lilleshall, where I had been twice.

He came back from Lilleshall and I told him to take things easy, but, without me knowing it, he felt so good that he went out and played a game for his club, Grenagh. He hurt the groin again and it was too soon. I felt a bit let down as he hadn't told me. Everybody had been going in the direction we wanted them to go and they were being straight-up if there was a problem with the club or anything like that.

There was still a chance of him coming back later in the year, but Steven was definitely gone. He tried coming back but pulled his groin in an A v's B game so he couldn't run or move.

DESPITE THESE BLOWS, there was great resilience within the team and everybody was looking forward to a proper crack off Kerry in the Munster final at Páirc Uí Chaoimh on July 18. It proved to be one of those days that you wished you could bottle.

We were to meet at Douglas GAA Club in the morning. I was there an hour before anyone else and I went for a run around the pitch, even though it was wet.

When you do a bit of exercise, your energy increases and I was really looking forward to it. We were in a situation where we hadn't beaten Kerry since 1995 and a drought like that wasn't something that I had really experienced as a player.

I felt it was the last throw of the dice for me but it was exhilarating.

If we got the result, it was going to be massive.

We had a good team meeting before we left; everybody knew where I stood on the thing. We had brought Don Davis in for Damien and the plan was that he'd rove around the place and give us plenty of running because he was full of energy. Brendan 'Jer' O'Sullivan was in for Aidan Dorgan, and Philip Clifford was back in as captain.

Aodhán Mac Gearailt got two goals for Kerry in the first-half but we were just so pumped up in our belief that it didn't knock us out of our stride. The team had a real hunger and a desire that carried through from the league. I think the biggest factor was that we stuck with the players in form, guys who were there all the time and put in the work and were in good shape.

They were ready to die for each other.

It was 2-2 to 0-5 at half-time but we felt that there was a lot more in us, even if it took time to materialise on the scoreboard. In the second-half, our backs shut them down completely and they managed just two points. Ronan McCarthy was on Maurice Fitzgerald and he kept him scoreless for the whole match. Seán Óg really came to the fore, and Haulie lorded it over Darragh Ó Sé at midfield.

We had drawn level through Clifford with around 20 minutes gone and then came the crucial score, a goal from Fachtna Collins, who had come on as a sub.

Kerry tried to come back but Fionán Murray, also on as a sub, got another goal with 10 minutes left and that broke them. It finished 2-10 to 2-4 and it was one of the great days. We had built a solid foundation from the get-go that year and that Munster final was the result of all that togetherness.

This was one of the massive occasions in my life.

To see players perform to their best, lads who had worked so hard for me and the county over the previous few years. It needed guts and determination to reach the heights of winning a Munster title. The long hours of running the hills in Macroom and the sand dunes in Inchydoney had paid off.

The rain was pouring down, and the field was filled with red and white, and to have the Bird sing 'the banks' topped off a special occasion.

THERE WAS A great chance in front of us. We had Mayo in our semi-final.

No disrespect meant, but at the time we'd probably always have felt that we had a good chance against the Connacht sides. On the other side, Armagh had won Ulster and they would be meeting – who else? – Meath.

We made one change for the semi-final with Micheál Ó Cróinín replacing Brendan 'Jer'. After putting in such an effort to beat Kerry, it was important not to be complacent but there had been more than a month to recover. Even so, we started a bit shakily and Mayo had six of the first seven points, but then Nicholas Murphy really came to the fore at midfield.

Clifford was outstanding that day too and it was his goal in the 26th minute which levelled the game. It was 1-4 to 0-7 at half-time and, slowly, we got on top in the second-half. Murray came on to get another goal, set up by Clifford, and we won by 2-12 to 0-12.

I was still lining out for Castlehaven and, like 1998, we started off with a win over Clonakilty, which sent us through to the quarter-finals against Ballincollig, a week after the Mayo game. Ballincollig had Podsie and John Miskella, who was also on our panel, but in the championship the Haven never feared anyone.

I was still out of action with my back and Ballincollig went on to win by a few points. It meant the focus was fully on Cork and the All-Ireland final on September 26.

WE WENT INTO that game definitely believing we could win it.

The hurlers had won their All-Ireland two weeks previously, so there was talk of another double. In 1990, the pressure we put on ourselves was to beat Meath rather than win the double.

This team had no hang-ups about Meath. We hadn't played them in any gruelling matches – you couldn't place much store in the league semi-final that finished 0-6 to 0-3 – so it was a different scene. At the same time, that didn't mean there wasn't extra pressure regarding the double.

When the hurlers won, I felt it was a boost for us.

Frank Murphy had said to me before the two finals that he was giving the footballers a better chance than the hurlers.

We travelled up on the Saturday as usual and the mood was good.

This was the last men's game to be played in front of the old Hogan Stand. En route, we went to Fairview Park which was nearby, and had a bit of a kickaround.

Everybody was at ease and in good form. The preparations couldn't have gone any better in relation to where I thought the team was at.

We went with the same starting 15 as the semi-final. Aidan Dorgan had tried to come back but he had broken down again just before the semi-final, which was a shame. He was a massive loss. We had been deprived of another attacking option when Alan O'Regan was injured in a car accident.

We had a lot of the ball in the first-half but didn't do enough with it and they were 0-3 to 0-2 ahead when they got a goal. A ball came in high and Seán Óg went to bat it down but unfortunately Anthony Lynch was the wrong side of Ollie Murphy and he finished low, across Kevin O'Dwyer. It was a critical goal when we were well on top but had missed some easy chances.

Don did very well against Darren Fay but missed a couple of chances, and so did Podsie. In contrast, everything Meath's wing-forward, Evan Kelly kicked went over the bar – he had three points in the first-half.

One fear beforehand was that we wouldn't win midfield because they had John McDermott and Nigel Crawford, two big strong fellas against our greenhorns, but Haulie and Nicholas were very good the same day. Our downfall was kicking the ball over the bar – or, rather, not doing it.

I think we kicked 19 wides in total; it was like the trauma of Ennis all over again. I've often looked back at the video and Colm O'Rourke – no great Cork supporter – was saying at half-time that we should have been six points up. We owned the ball.

Philip Clifford was one of the leading lights again, but we went in three points down, 1-5 to 0-5, after having nearly all of the play. We tried to tell the lads that the game was still there for them if they just calmed down and kicked those balls over the bar. Ten minutes into the second-half, the game had turned around.

Meath won a penalty but Kevin O'Dwyer made a good save from Trevor Giles and the ball went down the field, and Clifford kicked one of the best scores I'd ever seen in Croke Park, a magnificent point from over on the Cusack Stand side.

From being in a position where we could have been six points down, the margin was only two. Then Joe Kavanagh got another super goal, just as he had in 1993, and we were ahead. Joe was an excellent player – he scored two of the best goals ever seen in All-Ireland finals – but we couldn't build on that goal.

We had a chance to go two ahead but Joe kicked wide when he had Clifford inside him. It was probably the right decision to go for the point but Meath were in a vulnerable state and we couldn't punish them.

THEY HUNG IN there and it was nip and tuck.

We brought on Mick O'Donovan at wing-forward and it was something for which we were criticised afterwards – bringing on a back rather than any of the natural forwards on the bench – but I don't think it was the reason we lost the game.

I took a gamble. I felt he might have given us something in that role. He had battled so hard to come back and I felt he deserved that chance. You can be as close to getting a clap on the back as a kick up the backside.

These are the thin lines.

The sides were level with eight or nine minutes to go but Meath kicked a few wonder-points. Seán Óg had a great game on Graham Geraghty, but Geraghty got two points late on where he hardly even looked at the posts, just swung them over. When scores like that go over, it gives the scoring team a huge boost and it's deflating for the team conceding them.

Fionán came on again but couldn't make it three goals in three games. He could have had a penalty near the end; he was hauled back as he was shooting and the ball trickled wide. Martin McHugh was commentating on BBC and he said it had to be a penalty but it was just another one of those things on the day where we didn't get the rub of the green at a critical stage.

It finished 1-11 to 1-8. What did it come down to in the end?

I'd have loved to have had Steven O'Brien out there in the vital stages. He'd have slowed it down when we were a point ahead. Dorgan was an awful loss. Those two could have made a big difference and we were a bit thin on the ground in terms of squad depth.

SEAN BOYLAN SAID to me afterwards that it was one they robbed. When you lose major matches, whether you're a player or a manager, it's massively disappointing.

There's no other way of describing it. It sickens you with disappointment to your core.

Croke Park is the greatest place in the world when you win, but when you lose you want to get out of there. I lost my first final in 1987 and I remember thinking back then that I wished we had lost in the semi-final. Ultimately, though, you have to immerse yourself in that experience.

If you don't get to the final, you never have a chance to win it.

Getting to manage Cork on All-Ireland final day (above) was an amazing experience, even if we were disappointed in losing to Meath. I was also proud to have men like Sean Og O hAilpin (here tussling with Meath's Graham Geraghty) representing me and the people of Cork on the field.

PART 6

STANDING TALL

AFTER THE ALL-IRELAND it was back to work in the pub. We were now in business two years, and we had a good regular trade.

An old friend of mine from Kildare would pop in now and then when he was passing by on his way to his house in Durrus. No matter what time of the day it was, he loved one of our breakfast rolls! We always finished our breakfast service at 12 o'clock but any time Christy came in I made sure that everyone gave him the royal treatment. Breakfast was all-day long for Christy!

He would sit up at the counter, in the middle, with his Lucozade and we would have our chats. It's amazing. Not once was he recognised by anybody else.

Nobody knew they were in the presence of the great Christy Moore.

I had gotten to know Christy when he would turn up at the Kildare matches when I was playing. He would stand behind the goal. Hail, rain or snow. Afterwards, he would meet up with us in Coffey's pub for the post-mortem about the match.

Christy is one of the great GAA supporters.

And a great supporter of mine, and not just a friend. I'd often go to see him in concert, and if he was in the Opera House, just down the road from our pub, he would always give a shout out for the pub… and tell his audience to go visit his 'buddy' there.

IN 2000 WE had a new set-up in Cork which we hoped would bring a freshness to the scene. Terry O'Neill stayed on, and Paddy Sheehan and Tony Nation officially became selectors. Eamon Ryan was also a new addition, and he brought in so many new ideas.

It certainly wasn't a surprise to me when he went on to such incredible success with the Cork ladies football team.

After the league resumed in early 2000, we beat Galway in Tuam and then drew up in Armagh, but we were beaten by Tyrone and Dublin in our last two games, so we finished bottom of the table and were relegated to Division 2.

FIRST UP IN the championship was Limerick in Kilmallock in May. It was a struggle, but we got by them. I had to watch that game from the stand, as I had been banned from the sideline due to encroachments onto the field during the All-Ireland final.

With the passage of time and my other commitments, I hadn't been able to give enough to the Haven and I called time on my playing career. John Cleary retired as well so it was the end of an era in a way, though Niall Cahalane was still going strong.

I would be back in the dugout for the Munster semi-final, against Kerry in Killarney. But that game was to earn me another suspension. To this day, however, I stand over my complaints that afternoon.

After the way the league had gone, with us relegated and Kerry reaching the semi-finals, we were underdogs and we lost by five, 2-15 to 1-13, but that was after we had trailed by 10 at half-time and we had managed to get the deficit down to two in the closing stages.

In fairness to the lads, they came out with all guns blazing after such a dismal first-half. Colin Corkery had started slowly but he really found his form again in the second-half. He got the goal to kickstart the revival and then we got eight of the next 10 points to leave it 2-12 to 1-13 with four minutes left.

We had them on the rack – they went on to win the All-Ireland again whereas we were done in June and left to wonder about what might have been as the back door wouldn't be introduced until 2001. It was just one of those years.

I said afterwards that the refereeing had been a disgrace and these quotes were carried in the national newspapers. This was deemed to be bringing the game into disrepute, so I was called before the GAA's games administration committee (GAC) and I ended up with a 16-week ban but, with Cork out and my playing career over, I didn't actually miss any games.

I FELT THAT 2001 would be my last year.

By that stage, I would have put in five years, which was a big commitment. Unfortunately, Tony Nation had to opt out as a selector. Eamonn Ryan stayed on and

Tony was replaced by fellow Nemo man, Mickey Niblock.

The most crucial game in Division 2 was the first one, against Armagh in Páirc Uí Chaoimh, and once we got over that we were a good bet for promotion. The only game we lost was the last one, away to Westmeath, but, after beating Kildare in the semi-final, we had a chance to atone for that when we met them in the final at Croke Park at the end of April.

We had started really well against Kildare before having to hang on to win by a point and the final was similar, except that we couldn't withstand the Westmeath onslaught. We were 1-9 to 1-5 ahead at half-time but Westmeath were transformed in the second-half and we couldn't live with it.

It finished 3-11 to 2-13 and, while we were back in Division 1, we had something to chew on ahead of the championship.

WATERFORD WERE FIRST up for us and we won well. The game proved to be Seán Óg Ó hAilpín's last competitive football match for Cork. A week later he was involved in an horrific car crash that ruled him out for the remainder of the year. He was a fella who never let me down and was a joy to work with – if we had a team of guys like him, we'd never have a problem. He was a huge loss.

MY MOTHER WAS in hospital at this time.

I was up and down to Tallaght Hospital every few days to see her, knowing things were bad but praying she would get better. But that was not to be.

I got a phone call from my sister, Jean one of those calls that you always dread. I hopped into the car straight away, and phoned Dr Con on the way up to Dublin. He rang the hospital and spoke with the doctors on my behalf, as we had a decision to make. Con quickly rang back.

'Larry, look, if she was my mother I would not put her through this operation because she would not survive... let her go in peace.'

I called Jean back, and told her what Dr Con had said to me. The decision was made while I was still driving up to Dublin. I knew then there was not long to go for my mother. I arrived at 1am.

My mother died peacefully two hours later. She was 71 years of age. She had rheumatoid arthritis from an early age. She was a tough, strong woman and you could only wonder how she had kept going with it for so long. We had been told four years previously that she did not have long to live, but she was not going to give up that easily.

My mother's death was devastating for me and my family. Though small in stature, she was the heart and soul of our house. She ruled the roost too.

We waked her at home, and the number of people who came from far and wide amazed us all. My dear mother is buried in Eadestown cemetery. May she rest in peace.

I've lots of great memories of her. She was a fantastic woman and always gave great support to the family. We were never in need of anything. My parents were honest-to-God people who worked hard in life, and that is something that they embedded in all of us.

They set us great examples.

THE DAY OF my mother's funeral, Cork were playing Clare in the championship in Páirc Ui Chaoimh. Paddy Sheehan was the man in charge for the match and we won by four points. Next up was Kerry in the Munster final.

After a good start, things went from bad to worse and we ended up losing by eight points. But, this time around, it was not all over for us as; for the first time ever, a back door was introduced to the championship.

We were back in Croke Park just a week later, playing Galway. We were asleep for the first-half and we found ourselves a whopping 10 points down at half-time. I lost my head in the dressing-room, as I tried to focus everyone for the second-half. And, if only we had played the whole game like we played in that second-half!

If we had, I feel we would have been in with a great shout of the All-Ireland.

In the first 10 minutes of the second-half, we had five points to Galway's one and they were on the rack. Then, we had a great chance when Brendan 'Jer' came in from the Hogan Stand side at the Canal End and went for a miracle point instead of putting Aidan Dorgan in for what would have been a near-certain goal.

Just like in Killarney the previous year, it was a turning point and Galway steadied before winning by four points, 1-14 to 1-10. To increase the parallels with Kerry in 2000, they went on to beat Roscommon in the quarter-finals, then Armagh, and Meath in the final. We were left looking at it and thinking that we had gone close again but we had nothing to show for it.

I'm the kind of fellow that always thinks you can wring the extra few percent out of yourself and our performances and results had shown that we weren't that far away. Since losing to Meath in the 1999 final, our two eliminations had come against the teams that would go on to win the Sam Maguire and each game had been there for the taking for us.

IN AUGUST, THE devastating news came that John Kerins had died at the age of 39, only a few months after being diagnosed with cancer.

I liked John. He was a great character. His passing was a huge blow to his family, and it was a big shock to all of us. He was greatly missed.

If there was one good story to come from his funeral, it was that the Cork and Meath teams of the late 1980s and early 90s finally buried the hatchet. A lot of their team from the late-80s came down and it was hugely appreciated by our guys.

I never had any problem with the Meath lads but something like this helped everyone to realise that it was just a game and that there were more important things but, at the same time, it was a game you wanted to win at.

County management is a tough, demanding business and you need good people around you all the time. I refreshed my management team midway through my years as Cork manager, bringing in Eamonn Ryan and Paddy Sheehan (above, Mickey Niblock, Paddy Sheehan, Terry O'Neill, myself and Eamonn Ryan). It's also high profile and a manager is hardly allowed to put a foot wrong (below, I arrive at a disciplinary hearing in Croke Park in 2001 in the always expert company of Cork county board secretary, Frank Murphy).

CHAPTER 27

WITH A SUMMER still to enjoy, myself and Orla were able to take a trip to the Galway Races. I love Galway, and it was always a big part of my life.

My aunt and uncle, Sid and Tom Kelly, always had an open door for us in Loughrea. I loved going down to see them and all of my cousins; and the slagging was always great as they refused to forgive me for kicking the equaliser against Galway in 1987. They are great GAA people.

Another great friend of mine from Galway was Sean Purcell, who wore the No.11 jersey as well on one of the game's greatest teams through the 60s. It was a great tribute to my mother that Sean came to her funeral.

There is always a great buzz at the Galway Races. I love meeting up with the Connollys – gentlemen, every single one of them in that amazing family.

Orla and I were at the races when we heard the shocking news of the terrorist attack on New York. We were not sure what was going on, but we ran to the nearest television screens to watch the Twin Towers on fire, and the disaster unfolding. I found it very upsetting, standing there, watching. I had so many great friends in the city.

One of those friends had been a maintenance contractor working on the Towers. We spent the next 24 hours contacting people, and trying to make sure that everyone was okay.

But, I found out that I lost a few friends that day.

IN SEPTEMBER 2001, I was re-appointed Cork manager for another year after deciding to let my name go forward again.

Ordinarily, we'd have been gearing up for the first few autumn league games but from 2002 onwards a calendar-year season was in place. That meant more time to get lads ready for the new year and I decided to bring Colm Crowley in as the physical trainer, which took some work off my hands.

He worked wonders with the lads and that allowed me to focus on the coaching side.

WE HAD AN up-and-down campaign back in Division 1 of the league, beating Galway, Dublin and Tyrone but losing to Roscommon, Westmeath, Offaly and Donegal. Six points wasn't enough to make the play-offs but that allowed us to focus on the championship opener, a Munster semi-final against Kerry in mid-June.

The game was the same day as the Republic of Ireland played Spain in the last 16 of the World Cup. We watched most of the soccer upstairs in the Castle Heights Hotel, where we were based but, unfortunately, just as the match went to penalties, it was time to head to Fitzgerald Stadium and we had to listen to the rest of it on the radio.

It was pouring rain all day, so it wasn't a bad time for me to be starting my three-game touchline ban!

I found it quite interesting to be sitting in the stand. I definitely felt a bit calmer than I normally would on the line and I found that I got a better sense of what was going on with an elevated view.

Kerry were 0-4 to 0-2 ahead at half-time and they still had a two-point lead with about 15 minutes to go before Colin Corkery, the captain that year, drove us on and he put us 0-8 to 0-7 ahead. Mike Frank Russell levelled five minutes from the end but nobody could find a winner and both sides were satisfied to have another go at it.

The replay was originally set for the following Saturday as there was an event in the showgrounds in Cork on the Sunday, which ruled out a replay that afternoon.

Sadly, Micheál Ó Sé, Páidí's brother and the father of Darragh, Tomás and Marc, died on the Tuesday. I went down to the funeral with some of the selectors and the players. I was very supportive of the Ó Sés, I thought they were a really nice family and I always got on well with Páidí.

We had our battles on the field and the sideline, but they were left there.

One thing I really admired about the family was that they were very down-to-earth and very understanding. Micheál was buried on the Friday and it was totally against my principles that the game should have gone ahead the following day.

Ideally, it would have gone back a week, but the Cork hurlers were playing Limerick then and Diarmuid O'Sullivan was on the two panels. There was talk of the replay being played on the Tuesday evening but instead it went ahead on the Sunday night – it was completely out of my hands.

It was played on a Sunday evening and the three Ó Sé brothers lined out, something I'd have massive respect for, but we won by 0-15 to 1-9.

We were through to a Munster final against Tipperary in Thurles on July 14. Whereas a hurling/football clash was avoided because of Sully in the previous game, this time there was no way around it and we were on the same bill as the Cork hurlers qualifier game with Galway, which was on after ours.

Hurling was always going to be Sully's first priority, which we accepted, and the compromise was that we would name him as a sub. Ideally, he wouldn't have had to be used, but it was a game where Tipp nearly beat us.

We got the rub of the green, alright. For most of the game they were the better team, but luckily enough we had a strong finish and snatched a draw.

We had got out of jail and made sure of it in Cork the following week, winning by 1-23 to 0-7 with me back on the sideline, but there was more drama.

THIS WAS THE first year of blood substitutes and when Ronan McCarthy had to go off for treatment we put Noel O'Donovan on.

We used five 'normal' subs and just before we sent Sully on for Colin I questioned if everything was in order. Frank Murphy was always an expert on these things and he said that everything was okay, that we were entitled to bring on another sub and we cleared it with the sideline official.

We were winning handy and there was no need to bring on a sub – we wouldn't have done it if we thought it wasn't allowed. Then, after the match was over and we had collected the cup, it was highlighted to me going into the dressing-room that there might be trouble.

Frank was kind of laughing it off.

'There's no problem,' he said, '... go away and have a drink for yourself.'

The team were back at my pub in the function room upstairs but the talk began to gather momentum and we had supporters coming up to the door telling us we were going to lose the match.

I rang Frank, telling him I had reporters calling me, but again he told me to relax and not to talk to anyone. It wasn't sorted immediately and I had to go missing for a day or two because there were so many media requests.

It went on for a few days before the thing was clarified by the Munster Council and we were in the clear.

We had Mayo in the All-Ireland quarter-finals in Croke Park. We didn't start very well that day and Colm McManamon was causing us trouble. But we had got a grip by half-time and won by six points.

It felt like the ideal game to have behind us going into the semi-final, but this was a rematch with Kerry and they were gunning for us. They were a wounded warrior, coming through the qualifiers after picking up a head of steam. Everybody looks for some little thing that will rally the troops and, under the circumstances, they probably had it as a motivation that they hadn't been at their strongest when we had beaten them in Munster, due to Micheál Ó Sé's funeral.

I DON'T THINK there was any team in the country that would have beaten them that day. They were like savages against us; they would have beaten the great Dublin team of today.

Séamus Moynihan roasted Colin that day and he was complaining about a lot of handbags stuff on the train down but I said to him, 'You're twice his size, deal with it... you don't want to be going down that route'.

You have to deal with things on the field.

Moynihan was a great player, really explosive, but I felt he was vulnerable as a full-back. Corkery did destroy him in games but that day in Croke Park, when it really mattered, it was the reverse.

We tried every switch in the book to try to contain them, but it was an uphill battle. It seemed like nobody was getting to grips with the game and when you're in a situation like that, watching from the sideline, you are powerless. You're just waiting for the ground to open up. You feel like no matter what kind of move you're going to make, it won't work.

Equally though, looking at how Kerry did in the final against Armagh, I think they played their All-Ireland against us. They couldn't get up to the same level and Armagh beat them. It's not one I dwell on because Kerry were so much better on the day. It's hard to think that this or that could have been done to change things. We were beaten by a team that was on fire but I think, ultimately, it cost them the title.

IT WASN'T ALL bad. We had won a Munster championship and had gathered a good bit of momentum. We were still going into 2003 with a bit of optimism.

I was trying to bring lads in but it was tough as Cork hadn't had a lot of underage success in the mid-to-late-90s. Unlike the 80s when there was so much under-21 success, with six All-Irelands in total master-minded by Bob Honohan.

I actually tried to make a bit of a playing comeback with Castlehaven at the start of 2003. For whatever reason, I just had a feeling that they might have a big year. I went down to Inchydoney a few times for physical sessions but my back seized up after one of them. I came home and I knew that that was the end of it.

Still, my gut instinct was proved right that autumn as they won a third county title – I mightn't have been able to play but a 40 year-old Niall Cahalane was still as influential as ever in midfield. By that stage, my time with Cork would have come to an end.

THAT YEAR, I had actually stepped back on the training as I had pushed them a good bit over the previous few years. I felt that, by easing things, it would help to regenerate that hunger and freshness.

We got off to a great start as we beat Kerry in the first league game on a Saturday night in February as the Páirc Uí Rinn floodlights were turned on. Graham Canty was really strong that night at centre-back and scored a goal in a Man of the Match performance. Crazy as it may seem, though, that was the high point of the year.

We were unlucky in that we finished in third place in Division 1A, just behind Armagh on scoring difference, and there were only four teams advancing, two from Division 1A and two from 1B. Limerick at home were the opposition in the Munster first round in May and I knew that it would be a sticky game.

They had got to the final of Division 2 of the league and they had a solid side. After the experience with Tipperary the previous year, there shouldn't have been anyone taking them lightly but I sensed that something bad was going to happen.

I felt it coming into the game, I felt it in the dressing-room.

We lost by 0-16 to 0-6 and it was just horrific.

Nearly everything that could have gone wrong did go wrong. I felt that my days were done after that.

There was just no go in them.

Limerick weren't bad – they went on and nearly beat Kerry in 2004 and '05. Even when I played, there was nothing easy against them.

I'D BLAME MYSELF for everything and ask myself what I did wrong? I actually brought Conor Counihan back to give a bit of freshness and we tried to rejuvenate it a bit. We had good, hard meetings in Jurys Hotel about where we were.

Every player spoke and I listened.

A lot of hard things came out.

Leaders have to drive it on the field or in training.

Unfortunately, that year, they were dead. What made it even more difficult was that Donal O'Grady, who had come in as hurling manager, gave the dual players an ultimatum. Tom Kenny had played against Limerick but he was gone now and so was Seán Óg. Donal knew they were going to choose hurling, so it was an easy thing to say.

They were gutted because they had to make a decision and I thought it was unfair. The players themselves felt that they could do it and I was happy to facilitate it. Fair enough, he wanted them to be fresher for hurling and focused on that, but it was a big downer for us. It was a pity that we didn't have another year with Sully, say.

Seán Óg came in to meet me to tell me his decision.

He's so passionate and so honest, he found it hard to get the words out. He was a guy like myself, he was going to get the best out of himself. It's hard to replace these fellas. It left a bit of a void.

The draw for the qualifiers sent us up to Roscommon at the start of June and my county managerial career came to an end at Dr Hyde Park, where it had all begun for me as a 17 year-old in the league in 1980.

The place was always a graveyard for me – I think the best result I ever got there was a draw – and we lost by seven points, 1-14 to 0-10. We were never able to get going and Colin Corkery and Brendan 'Jer' were sent off near the end.

MY TERM WAS up and it was a natural end to things. I'd lived with these guys and did everything I could to get over the line with them to win an All-Ireland.

Would I change anything that I did?

Some lads might have felt they found it hard to make the team but these were judgement calls. I'd have the same respect for them as anyone else.

The sessions were long but they made the lads fit – they were the kind of sessions I'd have loved. Fellas gave it everything.

I would have done anything to see them win the All-Ireland.

In Cork, I think they come together too many times for collective training. People probably hear me say that and find it strange as I trained like a savage, but you lose your appetite and freshness. Guys are pulled in every direction and it's a trek to get to training after a day's work in a county the size of Cork.

Then multiply that by three or four times a week.

I would love to have been able to change that and bring them in half the amount of times. Equally though, I'd nearly have to go and live with them to see what they were doing, if that makes sense!

The show was over, however!

I loved the challenge of county management, even having every single movement watched (above) and analysed, sometimes fairly and occasionally unfairly. And going head-to-head with the likes of Sean Boylan and Paidi O Se (below) was a great thrill for me, but I knew that it was soon time for me to move on in my life.

CHAPTER 28

THERE WAS NEVER any pressure put on me to step down, but I knew myself that the time had come and it was my own decision.

In New York, my social contact with home was always writing letters and I sat down and wrote a sincere letter to the county board, just thanking them for the opportunity to manage their great county.

For me, the way I'm built, I felt I had failed in that I didn't take them to win an All-Ireland and the last few lines of the letter reflected that. From that point of view, it was hard to walk away because the fact that we didn't get over the finishing line was, and is still, a source of regret.

At the same time, I knew I couldn't do any more for that squad and it would have been unfair to be hanging in there.

People would criticise the county board for lots of things, but I was never left wanting for anything when I was there. Barry's Tea had been good sponsors and when they left, Esat Digifone had come on board. I acted as a go-between for that deal; Catherine Tiernan came to meet me at my pub and that led to negotiations with the board.

Esat were very supportive and they later became O2 and their presence ensured that we got great backing. When I started off, there was nothing like that. My son would be looking at old pictures and he couldn't believe that there was nothing on the front of the jersey.

We were glad to just get a pair of socks on the day of a big game.

IT'S A PITY that sometimes players find themselves in a position where they have to fight for things that should be provided as a matter of course. There's a lot to do to get yourself right and focused to play, rather than getting bogged down in a lot of these other unnecessary distractions. Sometimes, people get too bogged down and lose sight of the real thing, which is to get the best out of yourself and the team.

An All-Ireland medal goes a long way in a place like Cork.

I was just short of my 40th birthday when my time with Cork ended, which was still fairly young in managerial terms. Over the years that followed, a number of counties made indirect approaches – Clare, Waterford, Limerick, Wexford and, of course, there were always rumours that I'd be going to Kildare – but nothing concrete ever materialised. I needed a break from county football.

I had a long, hard run – when you look back at it, I had no break from football for nearly two and a half decades. On top of that, when you go into business, that takes over your life as well because you have to put the work into it. I was in a situation where I was just glad to take a back seat in GAA terms, having been on the merry-go-round for so long.

Castlehaven were going well and I went down a few times to watch them training ahead of the county final against Clonakilty; I used to enjoy that.

On the Tuesday before the final, I bought the *Evening Echo* on the way and the headline on the back page was, *"It's Conor's job"*. There was a county board meeting that night and it seemed that Conor Counihan was a certainty to take over the role I had vacated. Then, when I was going through Ballinascarthy on the way back up, I had the radio on and it said that Billy Morgan had been reappointed.

I jammed on the brakes and pulled in the car.

My first thought was that Conor had withdrawn, so I rang him.

'What did you pull out for?'

He said he had got a call telling him that he hadn't got the job. I spent a half-hour on the phone to him. Conor's a guy I'm really fond of – the same as Niall Cahalane or Teddy McCarthy, he got the best out of himself and he's genuine with it. If I was stuck at 3am, he'd be one of the fellas I'd be calling for help.

I was delighted for him when he got the job in 2008 and led Cork to the All-Ireland in 2010. Fate is a fierce thing – maybe the man above was saying, 'It's not going to happen in these years'.

I don't think Cork were going to win an All-Ireland in that period in the mid-2000s and Conor needed strong, up-and-coming players like Ciarán Sheehan and Aidan Walsh. I was very pleased too that Terry O'Neill and my Haven clubmate, Jim Nolan were there as selectors, along with Ger O'Sullivan and Peadar Healy.

Sadly, Terry died in late 2019. He was a great buddy of mine, a very passionate guy.

AFTER MY RETIREMENT, I dived into my work. I renovated the pub, upstairs and down.

We did a lot of planning and decided to gut the place and bring it back to its former glory. On the night we were starting, a couple of regulars pitched in to help us with the clear-out. Joe Fitz, a fanatical GAA man, would not trust anyone else to take down the photographs of the major historical moments in Cork GAA history.

Joe has been a great friend for years and I know he got a great kick out of doing that. We had a lot of tradesmen who were customers and we used as many of them as we could. One that did more than his fair share was Connie Fitz, the tiler. He kept us all going with his stories during the long days and nights.

It was a hard couple of months, but it helped to keep my mind busy and left me with no time to think of football.

ON JANUARY 23, 2004, Orla gave birth to Kate and that put football further down the list of priorities.

It was a game-changer but at the same time it's amazing. I used to be flying around the place and, to a degree, I didn't have a care in the world. I used to work on buildings in New York, a hundred storeys up, without a fear.

We used to go up to Hunter Mountain in the Catskills to do a bit of skiing for the craic and when we were asked if we were junior, intermediate or senior, we'd say that we were senior and then fall all the way down. With the help of a drop of brandy from Martin Connolly!

All of a sudden, a child comes along and I'm nervous getting up on a step-ladder or flying on a plane. Would I go up on a scaffold on a skyscraper nowadays?

I'd have to think about it for a while.

You can't describe what the change is like to anyone who isn't a parent, but every parent understands it. It's all about this new arrival and that's not overlooking your spouse. It just becomes an all-encompassing responsibility.

Kate was someone I had to look after; I had to make sure everything was right for her. We had been living in an apartment up above the pub and then Kate came along.

Access to schools was a big thing and Model Farm Road ticked the boxes as St Catherine's NS and Mount Mercy College were within walking distance. We found a house in Cherry Grove and moved in in March, 2005, just over a month after we had got married.

JANUARY 28 WAS THE date and it was the last function at the old Jurys Hotel on Western Road. It was a place with which I had a great affinity, going all the way back to when I first arrived in Cork.

It was a massive GAA place – no matter what time of day you went in, you'd bump into somebody in that big long corridor or in the foyer. After Munster finals, we used to go down there with Dr Con and I enjoyed meeting with the Kerry lads. The hotel used to sponsor a monthly sports star award and when I was going through my injury ordeals, they made the pool and gym available to me.

Gestures like that meant a lot and I always felt that, if I ever got married, it was the place I'd go.

It was to be knocked and redeveloped in the spring, so the timing was just right for us. Fergal Somers, the manager, was a Kildare man and I always got on well with him. We invited over 400 people, from New York and San Francisco, from Spain and from all over Ireland. We were in shock; there were no refusals.

A limousine company was getting a business going in the city and they contacted us and said they'd love to provide two limos, one to go to Crosshaven to collect Orla and the other to come to the pub. The wedding was in St Peter & Paul's, a five-minute walk, but I said we'd have a drive around the block anyway!

The limo pulled up outside the door and myself and my father and my brother, Martin, who was the best man, got in. We were ready to go but the limousine wasn't budging. It was conked outside the door with the flashers on and we had to get out and walk over.

The next minute, Orla's brother, James rang Martin to say that the limousine that was in Crosshaven couldn't get out of the driveway! It had to be towed by a tractor to get them on the road, but she got there... she wasn't that late afterwards.

It was a lovely day. Ann Marie, Orla's sister, had a catering business and she organised her staff to come in and cater for the guests as all of our staff were going to the wedding. It was the first time that dickie bows were worn behind the counter!

Jimmy Magee was there, the former GAA president Seán Kelly too, Ogie Moran, Tommy Doyle, the Bomber Liston and obviously a lot of Cork players.

Everyone came back to the pub for a few hours after the church but we had to ring the bell and stop serving because everyone was getting comfortable! It was a great social occasion.

Orla and I stopped for photos at the Mardyke. We always loved the place and it was a home from home for me because I had done so much training there. I didn't have to hop over the fence and nor did I get sun-burnt – there was no fear of that on January 28! It was an ideal day, a bit chilly, but the sun did come out.

It was just brilliant to meet so many great friends. For a honeymoon, we stayed fairly local as Kate was small.

I was great friends with John Glynn in the Citywest Hotel and he looked after us well. It was something different, but do you know what, it was great to just relax.

Just before Jurys was to be demolished, all of the effects were taken out of it and auctioned off. I went along to the auction with one particular item in mind. There was a beautiful old framed painting of Punchestown racecourse, with horses and jockeys jumping over a stone-wall fence in the Cunningham Cup. It used to be a in a prominent place, just by the entrance to the main corridor and I wanted it.

I WON THE auction and I still have it at home in the hallway, and it's a nice link to the past. My father died in 2013 when he was 89 and, from the time he was six, he went to Punchestown Festival every year. When we played underage with St Oliver Plunkett's, some of the matches were in a field alongside the race course.

Obviously, I'd have spent a lot of time in there doing my individual training, running up and down that hill to build endurance.

There's a part of my soul in that place!

After settling down to married life in 2005, I did a few training sessions for

Castlehaven, which I enjoyed, but the main focus was on developing the pub. We had put a lot of money into it and we had to work very hard on it.

But then we were blindsided by something we hadn't anticipated at all.

With all of my family on our wedding day in 2005 (above) and Orla and myself below) living it up in a limousine and looking forward to the next exciting chapters in our lives.

AT SOME POINT during 2005, Orla noticed an imbalance with Kate's legs. We went to Dr Con and he referred us to Dr Anthony McGuinness, who in turn sent us to the orthopaedic surgeon in Crumlin Children's Hospital, Mr David Moore.

We drove to Crumlin and when Dr Moore looked at Kate, he could see that her left femur, or thigh bone, was growing more slowly than the right. She would have to undergo a limb-lengthening process. It wasn't in any way hereditary and it was just something that occurred, seemingly at random.

There are around 65,000 children born in Ireland each year and it's thought that one child out of that total is affected with a congenital femoral deficiency. There was nothing we could do until she was over three years of age, when she could have a CT scan to see accurately where they needed to operate.

When Kate learned to walk, she had to compensate for the discrepancy but we were told that her first big operation wouldn't be until she was around four and a half.

The operation was scheduled for the end of March, 2008 and about six months before that we met Mr Moore to go through the procedure. By that stage, there was a couple of inches of a difference and, if she never had an operation, the forecast was that that margin could become around 10 inches by the time she was fully grown.

The likelihood was that this was going to need four or five operations.

It was a tough thing. Jack had been born in August, 2007 and, naturally, we were fearful that he might be vulnerable to the same thing. We brought him to Mr Moore, with whom we became very friendly, and he carried out a lot of tests on Jack. Thankfully, there were no problems with him.

I HAD MY share of injuries and I was no stranger to the operating table but, without a doubt, Kate's operation was the hardest thing I've ever faced.

To put it in stark terms, it involved breaking the bone and putting the leg in a frame, with poles going through and nuts and bolts outside. They would leave a gap between the two parts of the bone, which were then supposed to move further away day by day to lengthen the bone. My sister, Jean looked after Jack while Orla and I stayed in the parents' accommodation at the hospital.

Crumlin is an unnerving place. Every hospital has its stories and heartaches but a children's hospital just brings everything right back down to earth for you. We had to stay there for seven or eight days and, genuinely, I'd say to anyone who reckon they have a problem they should should spend a day or two in there.

You see some tragic cases, but you're left marvelling at the power of the human spirit. Kate had her own issues but I came across so many parents and kids who were in even more trying situations.

When Kate went down for the operation, nothing else meant anything.

This completely innocent little girl had done nothing to anyone and she was having to go through this ordeal. I stayed down in the theatre until she was knocked out and then I went into the little chapel, to pray that things would be okay and just to summon whatever strength I could from the Almighty to help me and Orla help her.

After the operation, it was tough going.

Simple things, like just dressing her or putting her off to sleep became big jobs. When the medication wore off, she was in agony. The bones couldn't just be set a good distance apart and expected to join up – the gap had to be small and then gradually extended.

Every six hours, Orla and I would have to rotate a thread a quarter of a turn, to pull the bones slightly further apart. She'd be asleep and we'd be on an alarm clock to make sure the schedule was adhered to.

One day equalled one full turn of the thread.

Then there were exercises to do, an hour three or four times a day.

Orla had to bathe her every day, to make sure that the little incisions were clean. They were not allowed to scab or heal. The screams that came out of her were piercing; I used to have to go outside the house. And this was just one procedure... and you're looking at maybe another four.

We battled through it.

Every week, the pain was easing a bit and her exercises were getting a bit better, but you have to remember that she was just four and a half. When we were doing the exercises with her, trying to lift the leg to straighten it and get the muscle structure right, she'd nearly bite the hands off us.

Her appetite decreased because her whole system had been turned upside-down. The hardest thing was to go in at night and make the adjustments when she was trying to sleep but we knew what had to be done and we faced it, and that was it.

She was in the frame until the end of July and it was a great day when she had the operation to get it off. We had to go up to Crumlin every week for six weeks and then it went to longer intervals. They had her walking on a treadmill and naturally it was sore. Overall, though, we were delighted with how Kate was progressing.

Crumlin became part of our lives and, in fairness to them, they were outstanding there. It was full-on; we were kept going with running the pub and everything else in our lives.

CASTLEHAVEN HAD GOT me involved in 2009, helping out Christy Collins. It wasn't intended to be anything major but I could never half-do anything so it became a bigger role. I liked to get my teeth into something and become a proper part of it and I did that for a year, operating as an unofficial selector.

Clubs would ask me to give them a session every now and then – I did a good bit with Tracton – and I went to a lot of summer camps. I enjoyed that, dealing with enthusiastic kids.

Mick Lewis was a great Mitchelstown man and I was friendly with him for a long time. He used to go to all the Castlehaven games and was always very supportive. In around 2007 or '08, he had asked me to go down and coach their junior team but I couldn't commit to it with Kate's situation.

As Kate progressed and Jack was getting a bit hardier, there was an opportunity for something again though and late in 2010, two Mitchelstown clubmen, Garry Coleman and Barry Kiely, came to meet me at the pub. They asked me to come down for a few months, but for me there was never such a thing as going to a place for a few months!

In fairness, Orla said it would probably do me good to have a break from the pub and home, and I said I'd get involved with them for 2011.

Mitchelstown is a big town and the club had been senior in the distant past but they were without a county junior title since 1961. We trained hard and there was a good set-up with guys who had a lot of potential. The county junior championship is almost like trying to win the Olympics, there are nearly a hundred teams.

I was looking at various divisional championships and you had Kanturk, Rockchapel and Knocknagree in Duhallow, then Bandon, St Colum's and Tadhg Mac Cárthaighs in Carbery. These teams were better than a lot of the teams in intermediate but they couldn't get out of junior.

Even to reach the county section was immensely hard.

The divisional championship games were such battles and you could get beaten on an off-day by a team that wasn't as good as you. Thankfully, we won North Cork, beating Clyda Rovers in the final, and we made it to the county final after we got a late goal to beat Courcey Rovers in the semi-final. We robbed them and then we were nearly wishing we hadn't when we got to the final against Kanturk inside in Páirc Uí Rinn on a Friday night.

They were nearly like a senior team and they wiped us off the field.

We knew their capabilities and knew we'd be under pressure but we thought we were ready. The game was gone and we were just looking for a bit of redemption and to win the second-half. We picked it up a little bit but we were hammered.

People thought I'd walk away but I had become engrossed in it. In 2012, we were strong favourites to win North Cork again but Ballyclough had come down from intermediate. We ended up playing them in the final in Castletownroche, but we had forwards that night, good-quality players, who just couldn't kick the ball over the bar. We lost by a couple of points. It was probably a harder defeat than the county final, because we should have won.

I walked out of the ground that night with Mick Lewis and Cyril Kiely. The two of them would live and die for Mitchelstown but they were full sure that that was the end of it. I came back to the pub and I drowned my sorrows. We were a better team than them, but it was one of those nights that it just didn't happen.

THE PUB WAS always packed for Cheltenham Week, but in 2013 we had a huge crowd for the festival. However, my Dad, who would be a great racing man, had more pressing things happening.

After coming through an operation, things had gone downhill for him. But we were still keeping the faith. On the Thursday evening, I took the decision to travel up to Naas to see him; I had a feeling in my gut he wasn't going to make it.

Friday was going to be a busy day for us with the racing. It was Gold Cup day, but in fairness to Cyril 'The Bird' he stepped up to the mark as a true friend and helped us out through the day.

When I arrived in the hospital at midnight and saw my Dad, I knew I had made the right decision. He was very happy to see me, and he became calm. It was a long night. My Dad passed away at 8am, Lord have mercy on him. There was a great turn-out for him, but no funeral is easy, especially as both of our parents were now gone from us.

I was a lucky man to have such a dedicated father but I knew he was happy to be with my mother again, as they had been together on this earth for over 50 years.

KATE'S NEXT PROCEDURE was supposed to be in 2013, but we went to Crumlin and they said they'd delay it for a year or so as the shortfall wasn't dramatic – it was only about half the distance that they had been expected it to be.

Instead, she had to get plates inserted into the knee joint to prevent it from growing crookedly. She faced the operation at the start of that year and it was tough again but it wasn't anything as bad as the first one. She was on crutches for a few weeks and I was becoming a master in all of the exercises.

When Kate was only two and a half or three, I had contacted Seán Boylan to see if he could provide anything from his herb garden, as he had done to help me with my injuries. Herbs are good for your bones and muscles, and he had certain drinks that would help. He obviously couldn't correct the situation, but the concoctions couldn't do any harm.

That said, herbs are not easy to take and it was tough on her. We had to mix it with orange juice to soften the taste! I'm still convinced that Kate drinking the herbs made a massive difference to the development of the bones. She drank Sean's herbs every year for 10 years.

After that, I rang Garry Coleman and Barry Kiely and said I wasn't going to walk away from Mitchelstown. I got rid of a few lads and I had a panel of no more than 19 or 20. Fellas were coming and going so I asked them for full commitment or else they could forget about it.

We trained harder than we had done previously and we had lads who would give everything for it. We walked through the divisional championship, easily beating Buttevant in the final.

In the county quarter-finals, we had Kilmichael. They had beaten Kilmurry in the Muskerry final, their first divisional title since 1987, thanks to pure heart.

The match was fixed for the following week, which was very unfortunate for them. I thought we'd have their measure but they went the whole distance and we only beat them by a few points. We met Glenbower Rovers from Killeagh in the semi-finals and they were no easy team to beat, either, but we got back to the final, where we were up against St Colum's, from Kealkill in west Cork.

I had gone down to see Colum's play Tadhg Mac Cárthaighs in the Carbery final below in Dunmanway. They needed a replay but they got over it and I had to admire them because they were so durable. Alan O'Connor was playing outstanding stuff for them.

After our semi-final, I was thinking that we couldn't have asked for a better game as we had slogged it out. Mick Lewis rang me and, even though we had won, he was disgusted.

'We won't do at all,' he said. I told him not to panic.

Mitchelstown play in red jerseys with a black hoop and black shorts, the same as UCC, while St Colum's have orange jerseys and black shorts. I felt that there could be an issue for the final and I sent down both jerseys to the county board for them to make a call. I wanted to know in advance so that we could prepare properly.

It was left up to the referee and he said they were fine, which seemed unbelievable to me, but we got on with it. Duhallow have the same colours as Colum's and we ended up getting a set of their jerseys for training, to get lads used to it, but even then we could see that it was awful. Players couldn't pick out who was who and the wet conditions on the day of the final made it even worse again.

We made a good few mistakes and they got a scrappy goal in the first-half when we were well on top. We were a point ahead at half-time, 0-5 to 1-1, but Alan O'Connor levelled at 0-7 to 2-1 early in the second-half. It was nip and tuck but they missed an easy free with five minutes left when it was level and then we got a difficult one over on the dressing-room side. Jimmy Sheehan was kicking it and I thought that he mightn't get the distance so I was running out to tell him to give it to someone else.

'Larry... I'll put this thing over the bar,' he shouted at me, and I'd admire him to this day for having that kind of conviction. I left him at it and he kicked it as true as a die, straight over. It was a kick to do justice to winning a county final. We got the kick-out and Dave Dineen, the midfielder, kicked the last point.

We won by 0-12 to 2-4.

HERE WAS A club and a team that had gone 52 years without a county title, which is a lot of history to live up to, so I was just delighted for those guys.

Shane Beston, for example, was a player that oozed with class. It was just a pity that he didn't get more of a chance on the county scene, given his capabilities, when a lot of other guys got more chances. There were fellas there that sat in the stand that day and, if they had applied themselves, they would have been part of it, but it showed what can be done when you have a group of guys that are totally committed.

That was a great day and one I'd look back on as a real highlight.

Sadly, Mick Lewis died in June, 2015, a tragic accident while he was on holidays in Tenerife. I'll always be grateful to him for giving me the opportunity to be part of such a special experience.

MYSELF AND TOMAS Mulcahy were chatting one day, not too long before the 25th anniversary of the 1990 All-Ireland double. We felt we could make the celebration a big affair, and raise a good sum for charity into the bargain.

So, we got the ball rolling and set up a committee, comprising of some hurlers, footballers and members of the county board. A date was set (August 28) and we set about selling tickets. Both teams we clashed with in the All-Ireland finals that year, Tipperary and Meath, were also invited. Tickets sold like gold dust. The only problem was that Cork did not have a venue large enough to accommodate all of the people who wanted to attend.

I was delighted one of the charities we chose was Helpful Steps, with Jamie Wall walking in, in an exoskeleton. Colin O'Shaughnessy, who has Elite Gym in Cork, is a founder of the charity and he has helped us with Kate down through the years with her rehabilitation.

It was a great success for the charities, and for us 'old' footballers and hurlers it was a fantastic opportunity to meet everyone again and catch up.

With my beautiful, courageous daughter, Kate and Kate with my aunt and uncle, Sid and Tom Kelly (below) who were also so kind to me as a boy and man. With my son, Jack (above right) who is just as competitive and talented as his sister and who has already received silverware from no less a figure than Colm Cooper.

CHAPTER 30

I WAS IN the room with Orla for the birth of our daughter.

But only just, I suppose. Because I did not think I was going to be present for the birth. That was not my plan.

Orla was asked if she wanted me present, and she said she did. So, I was gowned up, but I was thinking I was only paying a short visit. I actually thought I was going into the room to wish Orla the best of luck.

Orla was having a C-section, and the next thing everyone was gowned up and the room was shut down, and I was still in there. Orla was being opened up. I was given a stool and told I could sit. I just kept watching my wife's brave face.

Before we went to the hospital, Orla had told me several times whom I needed to call after the birth, but I had paid little attention to her. I did not understand what Orla was talking about.

I didn't have a clue... why would I be phoning a whole load of people?

But, once I held my daughter for the first time, I understood. I was back, sitting out in my car once everything had settled with Orla and I had my black book in my hands, and I was phoning every last person I could think of, and I was proudly, emotionally, telling them that our daughter, Kate Tompkins, had arrived into this world.

WE THOUGHT KATE might have to go through an operation like the one in

2008 every few years but, thank God, she didn't need that kind of major surgery again.

There were various procedures she had to have on her patella tendon and things like that when the kneecap was moving and had to be stabilised. Her fifth and final operation was in January, 2018. A girl is fully grown at 16 and when Kate reached 14 years-old, there was still a distance between the two legs so they had to slow the growth down on the 'good' leg.

Mr Moore was playing it down but any operation is major and this one took a lot out of her.

She was at an age where she had to get the same anaesthetic as an adult and that went right through her system.

They had to damage the growth plates in her good leg so that the other one would catch up and it ended up being a very tough operation, and she was on crutches after it. It was harder because she was at the stage where she knew everything that was happening.

She got violently sick for quite a while and it was a hard one to come back from.

She was off school for a few weeks but had to go back when she was still on crutches. It was a difficult five or six months before she really got back walking and got the strength back in her good leg. Orla and I had to do exercises three times a day with her, staggering our shifts in the pub to make sure one of us was around.

Eventually, Kate got through it all.

From four and a half until she was nearly 15, it's only really in the last year that everything has been easier. If I was driven, then she was extra-driven!

She was fantastic, and she just got up and got on with it.

WE SAT DOWN with Dr Moore in Crumlin when Kate had just turned three. He gave us his diagnosis and his plan for Kate. She would have her first procedure when she turned four.

I'll never forget his words.

'Don't panic... she'll just never be a dancer.'

We left very upset but Orla was having none of it. 'No one is going to tell me what my daughter can't do!' she told me.

So, when we got home our first stop was Sinead Murphy's; the best ballet teacher in Cork. We enrolled Kate in her classes. Kate loved it. She wasn't even able to skip but she kept on going, and she still loves it to this day.

Kate had proved them wrong. She has won awards in Feis Maitiu and she has danced and sang her way around all of the theatres in Cork. She was chosen to dance and perform in the panto at the Cork Opera House a good few times.

She still loves the stage, performing and acting.

She's a fantastic swimmer too – she just has that drive about her to get better. She didn't see any obstacle in front of her and she wanted to get there.

I cannot stress enough how great the people in Crumlin are. You win All-Irelands and you walk through Harlem and all of these other things that you feel show toughness but you go in that theatre door with a girl that's not much more than a baby and everything is out of your hands – it's a feeling of powerlessness.

Things are very much put in perspective.

CRUMLIN HAS SUCH strong links with the GAA. Obviously, you have the traditional visits from winning teams on the Monday morning after the All-Irelands and down one corridor is every county jersey.

I used to be quizzing Kate about which one was which.

We still raise money for Crumlin every year because of everything I saw. And one person in Crumlin helped us to keep our sanity and was there with us every step of the way. She still keeps us in line, as we have to attend the hospital every year. But I don't know how we would have got through it all without her.

Marie Noonan was our Mother Theresa. No words of mine can do her justice.

Marie and others are the special kind of people in there; they throw everything in their lives to one side to make sure that those kids are being properly looked after.

There were people crying morning, noon and night, and there was heartache, but it opened my eyes. Thanks be to God, Kate came through it fine and she's on the right side of it now, hopefully.

WHEN ORLA WAS pregnant for the second time, Helga Cleary, John's wife – who's from Kildare too – said, 'I hope it's a girl because if it's a boy you'll probably kill him!'

Jack is 12 now and he's highly involved in lots of sports.

He plays wing-back or centre-back in hurling for Bishopstown under-13s and he's full-forward or corner-forward in the football. He got involved in tennis in Sunday's Well, initially through summer camps, and he was spotted by one of their top coaches, Ger Flynn. She encouraged him to keep at it and he began to do well in a few competitions and was picked on the Munster squad.

Jack attends St Joseph's BNS in the Mardyke. The Sciath na Scol, the competition for primary schools, had been frustrating for them as they had gone close to making the hurling finals in Páirc Uí Rinn on a few occasions only to miss out. In the past, I had often gone down there over the years presenting medals as Paddy Walsh, the man telling me in 1987 to go back to Kildare, is highly involved in it.

I knew how big it was to get to the final and it would have been gut-wrenching for them to miss out on that but thankfully they made it last year in football. They played Ballinora in the final on a really wet day. Jack got the first goal and they beat them well.

One of the lads' fathers is a garda and he provided an escort back to the school so they were delighted.

Last September, St Joseph's were invited down to play in the Colm Cooper Tournament in Dr Croke's, playing teams from all over Munster. They rotate the captaincy for every game to give guys the opportunity and it just so happened that Jack was the captain for this.

Funnily enough, it was one of the few times I didn't go to one of his games and didn't they win the whole thing! They beat Milltown of Kerry in the final and the 'Gooch' presented the cup to Jack.

Jack would be similar to me growing up in that he's a bit shy – which I'd prefer compared to being forceful – but he gave a good speech and thanked everybody. The teachers had texted the parents to say that they would be home at a certain time but nothing about how the tournament had gone.

The lads planned it that they'd all come off the bus and pretend to be gloomy, and then Jack was the last to come off and he had the cup in his hand!

Jack tried a bit of rugby too but he didn't have the time. He is going to Presentation Brothers College after St Joseph's. He might pick it up there again and we'll see how it goes. Jack has good ability and hopefully now he can drive on.

I'll be happy to be a spectator.

I still give the odd session when a team ask me but my days of being heavily involved are gone. It gets to the stage where you can't go to sleep at night because you're thinking about the next thing. It was nice to be doing a bit without having it consuming me.

Orla, Kate, Jack and myself in our premises on Lavitt's Quay with extra special company in the form of the Sam Maguire and Liam MacCarthy Cups (above); and all of the family got to celebrate my career in 2019 when I was inducted into the GAA Hall of Fame.

EPILOGUE

UNFORTUNATELY over time Billy Morgan and myself grew apart.

That is not unusual when it comes to football and hurling teams.

Everyone is so immersed in what they are doing together. Everyone is concentrating on working hard and winning, and there is a shared purpose. A unique bond. And that existed between Billy and myself in a very special way, once upon a time.

But then we took separate roads.

Again, that's how it happens in all team sports. Life, and individual needs appear, and relationships are never quite the same. Though it was unusual how I took over the Cork team immediately after Billy. I did not step into his shoes. We are very different men. We each have a phenomenal passion for the GAA, but we do things our own way.

I loved his passion as manager, and I responded to it. Though, equally, he accepted my frankness when letting him know what I thought of the team training. But, he took it on the chin. And he never showed any hurt or resentment. He knew that I was speaking from the heart, and only had the good of the team in mind.

I'D FIRST MET him in New York. He worked behind the bar in Rosie O'Grady's in Manhattan, the hugely popular GAA pub. Dublin All-Ireland winners, Fran Ryder and Brian Mullins also worked in the joint. This was a couple of years before Billy came back home to manage Cork. He used to play in goals for Leitrim, and when I joined Donegal in 1985 I'm pretty sure I banged a couple of goals past him. He was getting on, but he was still a good keeper. He placed his kick-outs expertly.

When I came home from New York in 1987, he wanted to meet up with me quickly enough. We had our first sit-down in Skibbereen Golf Club, I remember. That first time, I told him I had no interest in joining the Cork team. I explained that I was not back in Ireland to play for *his team*; I was back to play for Castlehaven and, after that, I was getting right back to resume my life in New York.

I imagined myself living in New York for another 10 years.

I was so happy there. My life was just starting, really, and I did not want to live anywhere else. I loved the buzz. I loved the people. I had great friends, like Donal Gallagher, and I felt that New York offered me every opportunity in the world.

But, as I left our meeting, I was struck by Billy Morgan's passion. And his ambition. I was impressed, but equally determined to pass on anything he had to say or promised.

I never had a plan, no grand plan at any rate.

Did I ever think I would be away for years from my family in Kildare? Not a hope in hell.

Did I ever think I was going to end up in New York? Not a hope in hell.

Did I ever think I would end up in a Cork jersey? Not a hope in hell.

It all just happened.

The journey kept going, and going.

Everywhere I went, there was a challenge in front of me. And I like challenges.

No, I love challenges.

BILLY MORGAN DID not offer me the challenge I needed at the beginning. And I told him that straight. I told him I was not going to be travelling up from Castlehaven to do his team training sessions. I told him I would do more in the mornings down in west Cork.

He asked me what I meant?

I told him that he and his team did not have a hope in hell of beating Kerry. As I told him, I did not think that there was a hope in hell that I would end up on his team.

I was telling him man-to-man, not player-to-manager.

Once I became part of his team, I never stopped telling him over the next few years what he needed to hear, in my opinion. We worked well together.

We achieved something unique with a brilliant group of footballers.

IN JANUARY, 2019 IT was an honour to be in City Hall and pay homage to Dr Con for his contribution to so many people all through his life.

On a personal level, I do not know where I begin in thanking him for looking after me since the very first day I arrived in Cork. Between all of my injuries and heartbreak, the despair and agony, Con has guided me every step of the way.

Any time I picked up the phone, he has always been there for me and my family. He is one amazing man.

There's only one Dr Con.

LAST AUTUMN, JOANNE Clarke, a Louth woman who is the curator of the GAA museum, got in touch to say that I was to be inducted into the GAA's Hall of Fame.

That was a huge honour. I'd go back to the days as a child when I used to get the bus into Dublin with my father to watch all those games in Croke Park. I saw all these great players as idols and to be spoken of in the same breath as them means an awful lot.

I didn't necessarily dream about being in the Hall of Fame – I dreamt about getting the best out of myself – but to be up on the wall with these guys shows that I went some way towards realising my potential. There was a sense of pride to be placed in the same category as these other stars.

Colm O'Rourke and Ogie Moran were inducted at the same time as me and I reminded Ogie about his recommendation back in 1981 to find a gym to build up my strength. In fairness, I don't think he expected that I'd end up trying to stop Kerry from winning Munster championships!

IN 2004 I WAS asked by Sean Kelly, who was President of the GAA at the time, to be assistant-manager to Down's Pete McGrath for the International Rules series against Australia. We played them in Ireland in our first year, a series we won quite easily. Then it was off to Oz in 2005.

I was dreading the flight, since becoming a father I developed a fear of flying. I mentioned this to Dr Con, who was the doctor for the tour. He promised me a tablet to calm me, and allow me to sleep. I think he must have given one to Pete too, because the pair of us were the only two members of the Irish party who did not sleep a wink during the 24 hours of flying. We were walking up and down the aisles of the aircraft all during the trip.

Perth was our first stop. Like cities in Ireland, it is a laid-back place but unfortunately we lost the first game of the series there. We had to win in Melbourne the following week. It struck me as a very clean city in which to live; there hardly was any city centre traffic, and everyone appeared to be cycling or walking.

The second match was a real grudge affair, as the first match had been very physical and there was a lot of fighting. Tensions were running high. We prepared well that week, and we were confident going into the game. The Aussies had all of their top players available, which is not always the case in International Rules, and even though they were one-up in the series it was clear they were still hurting from the demolishing they had received in Ireland 12 months before. We were competitive in Melbourne, but it wasn't enough. It was disappointing, but I was 'down under', and there was still opportunity. I got my hands on tickets for the Melbourne Cup.

Growing up close to Punchestown, I have never lost my deep loving of racing, and I was delighted with myself. The Melbourne Cup did not disappoint; the weather was fabulous, and there was champagne for breakfast!

The racing did not disappoint either.

Makybe Diva was running and going for three in-a-row, which had never been done before. History was duly achieved, and I was there to watch from up close.

STEPPING BACK FROM senior football had given me quality time to spend with my family, and I soaked up the opportunity. I love watching all sports, and I have tried to instil this love into my kids too.

We have had great opportunities to travel and see places. In London, much to my wife's dismay, we visited nearly every football ground in the city; from Wembley to the Emirates Stadium, and grounds in between. We brought Kate and Jack to Wimbledon also, as Jack loves his tennis.

I love bringing them to matches, and Croke Park is one of our firm favourites of course. Though thanks to my good friend, Paul Cunningham I was also able to bring Jack to Old Trafford for a game there. That was special, as was our visit to Barcelona and sitting in the Nou Camp, but nothing compares to our experience as a family in New York.

We did Orlando first, as that is a playground for children, and then we did all of the sights in the Big Apple, visiting my old favourite Madison Square Garden where the tour guide happened to mention to us that the New York Rangers were playing in the semi-finals of the ice hockey championship the next day. That got me thinking...

I asked the guide on the way out what were my hopes of getting some tickets? Not a hope, I was duly informed.

He actually said if I was very lucky, I might be able to get one up in the 'Gods' in the Garden, and that it would set me back between $4,000 and $5,000. Once we left, I made a few phone calls.

This is why I love the GAA and its people.

After putting the feelers out to see if I could get two tickets, for myself and my son, I got a call within three hours. I had to be in the Upper East Side by six o'clock, where I would be met. And I met a Kerryman, Andy O'Grady, who has lived in New York for 40 years, and he handed me two tickets.

I did not, however, understood how fortunate I was until Jack and I arrived back at the Garden the next evening. The touts were selling tickets outside for $10,000. We entered, and found that we were sitting in a VIP section, right in the centre of all the action almost. The best tickets in the house! All thanks to my GAA life and the great and generous people I have met along the way.

WE PUT THE pub on the market at the beginning of 2020.

For 31 years, I've been running my own pubs. A time comes when a person thinks they might like to maybe take a step back, but who knows what will happen? We'll just have to wait and see.

The years in the business stood me well. It's hard work, long hours and sometimes you might go for days without any sleep. I started in 1989. I was a green horn, but it didn't take me long to learn the ropes.

The pub is an open door, and you get to meet a lot of characters. Yes, I have also met my share of lunatics that have come through the door through the years, but I have made many more friends and a lot of genuine people in my years behind the counter.

Since I have been such a fitness fanatic, some people have often thought it was an odd choice of career. But I love talking with people and getting to know them. We have had great laughs and, yes, some tears too. But I wouldn't change it.

My job as a publican is to make people welcome. In my first pub we had a guest house and we tried to create a home-from-home for people. In Lavitt's Quay we have a function room and it has been an honour to help people celebrate their milestones… some of the most important days in their lives.

We have done it all in our pub, from karaoke nights to Christmas parties to New Year's Eve celebrations, and there have always been nights filled with music. On this front, I have to thank Ted Dunne for his expertise and help down through the years. Being in the business, you also rely heavily on having the right staff to help set the whole tone, and I have been very lucky with the people we have had working for us.

Yes, we all make mistakes, but we also do our very best every single day.

A lot of people come and go. Some very well-known people have always made a point of popping in when they are about… Ronan O'Gara, Roy Keane, Niall Quinn, Kevin Moran, Anthony Daly… but they have always been treated the same as every other customer that walks in the door.

I HAVE ALWAYS had the deepest respect for Roy Keane.

He is different than most men, and different to nearly all the great sports people we have known in our generation. He was a genius on the field. Off the field, he has travelled his own individual path.

Along the way he stopped drinking alcohol. He showed such strength and conviction in making that decision, and living by it. When I ran my pub across the road from Kent Station, I used to see Roy quite often. He was playing for Nottingham Forest at that time, before moving to the glamorous Manchester United spotlight. I'd see him park his car.

It had 'Roy 1' as his number plate,

A big red car. He'd come into me and urge me to come with him… he wanted us to go down to the old Silver Springs Hotel, though he also sat at my bar on many occasions. He would have so many questions about our games against Kerry and the All-Ireland finals against Meath, and he would wonder about our training and general preparation.

More recently, he was in our pub on Lavitt's Quay, with some of his family and friends. I saw that the group were enjoying themselves, and it was near to closing time. But I sent Tonya, one of our staff down to them, to tell them that they didn't need to worry about last calls or anything like that.

Roy himself was on a bottle of Cidona, and some Pringles crisps, if I remember. He and his group were told that there was no panic on going home, but Roy was immediately on his feet. I could see him from behind the bar.

'Lads, I'm going now!' he announced. 'If ye want to stay, that's fair enough… but I'm out of here!'

I turned to Orla as he was speaking.

'God be with the days,' I told my wife, 'when I couldn't get him out of the place… when I couldn't get him out of the city!'

I'd first met Roy back in the late-80s; he's got a brother who is the spitting image of him, and I didn't know it was Roy for sure to begin with. But I got to know him as a straight punter. And, of course, on the field I deeply admired everything about the man.

I admired his total obsession, and secretly I hoped that he saw the same thing in me. Though, I also recall one significant thing he said to me one evening. I was chatting to him about everything he had won with United, and he stopped me in my tracks.

'Fuck it... I didn't win an All-Ireland hurling medal!' he stated. And I knew what he meant, straight away. Nobody is accepted in Cork as being one of the greats, unless they have won an All-Ireland hurling championship.

MANY CUSTOMERS HAVE said that the only problem with my pub is trying to leave! It has not been nicknamed 'The Glue Pot' by accident.

I love chatting with everyone, and having the banter. I have made good friends from all walks of life and not just sport... because I've been lucky to get to know Dáithí Ó Sé and Nathan Carter, and people from TV and entertainment too.

In the big snow storm a few years ago, the Beast from the East, we certainly got to know one another very well. Nathan had to cancel his concert, and I was just about to close up early because the weather was getting worse, and worse. When in pops Nathan and his crew.

They had nowhere to go, and nothing to do. I had the fire lighting, and how could I turn them away?

We had a night of great craic, and we almost got a full concert from Nathan and his band into the bargain. The next time he was in Cork, he brought his mother in to meet me, which was a pleasure.

Of course, my love of racing is not lost in my pub. I have been lucky to get to know JP McManus, Tony McCoy and Charlie Swan from my trips to Cheltenham. They are all good, sound people and they have all been helpful any time I needed them to aid me with my Festival preview nights. Though, more than anybody, in recent times I would have been lost without the expertise of Joe Seward, who is a mind full of knowledge.

I have to say that the success of the business is down to Orla, more than anyone else. She is the heart and soul of our business, and the work she does is simply incredible. It's all the more inspirational to me, because Orla also runs her own Mediation business as well.

It has been a great journey in my career outside of football, and it has been an honour to have been part of the lives of so many people.

THE COVID-19 PANDEMIC meant that the pub was closed at the time I finished this book but at least it allowed some work to be done around the house.

Ordinarily, you don't get a chance for any of that when you run a pub – I'd find I'm gone early in the morning, maybe home for a couple of hours and then having to take the kids somewhere and often we're caught late at the bar.

Time moved quickly enough during the lockdown – and it was great to spend quality time with my family.

My football career helped me to build the profile of the pub and I'm happy to discuss GAA with anyone who comes in. People are still very interested in meeting me and talking to me and taking a few photos.

Then, there are the regulars.

Every Friday night, for example, Finbar McCarthy and crew come in and we chat about GAA and life. What else could you ask for only that people come to where you work and discuss your passion?

Sometimes, it's easy to take for granted what has gone on in your life and it's only in sitting down for this project and thinking about all that, I've realised how many great people I've met.

The players, the coaches, the managers and, above all, the supporters.

Being in business allowed me to get to know them even more. I wanted to help them as much as help myself.

It's like when I brought the Sam Maguire Cup into The Burlington in 1990 and left it with Noel Murphy, John Kelly and Dave and Fred Cowhig. They felt as much a part of that as I did, even though they never played with the county and would have loved to have done so. They were just so passionate about it and I have thousands of memories like that.

When you go back and relive them, you realise how much has happened.

SADLY, MANY OF those I've encountered have passed on.

John Corcoran, the man who shouted to close the gates in 1990, died in 2016, far too young. John was one of these great characters who you could never get enough of; he was a walking encyclopedia of GAA.

From Donegal New York, there were the likes of Phil Brennan, who sorted out so many of us with work... Mike Meehan, Mike Cassidy and Jimmy McGonigle. It was a social club as much as a GAA club and it brought together all these different characters, but there was a ferocious bond.

Back home in Eadestown, you had Mick Fitzpatrick – my father's travel partner for all of those games – who died in his forties and then, at the other end of the scale, Jim Sargent, who only died recently, having reached his nineties.

Two of my Kildare teammates, John O'Donoghue and Mick Fogarty, were two more men who were taken before their time.

In early 2020, Pádraig Burke, the man who managed Castlehaven to their first county in 1989, died tragically. He was far too young, but his memory and achievements will live on. He was a tough man, the ideal guy for getting us over the line in 1989.

I liked his style, because he'd never give way to anything.

That was the Haven way, personified by Mike Whelton, Mick Burns, Dan Joe O'Mahony and Martin O'Mahony's father, John, who all passed on, too. You have to enjoy it all, because it's so fleeting.

BETWEEN THE GOOD times and the bad, from Wicklow to Kildare, from New York to Cork, I've had great times. Winning the county championships with my brothers with Eadestown, especially the first junior B one with Martin as captain, was magical.

My parents were alive and they took massive pride in that.

People went to Mass on a Sunday morning and congregated afterwards and all that was talked about was the game about to be played that day. To see Dave Kavanagh's journey from a fringe club player to an inter-provincial player was magical.

New York improved me, without a shadow of a doubt.

I was 20 or 21, starting off again, but it toughened me up. Donal Gallagher became a great friend and that experience really helped me. You don't have to win an All-Ireland to be a great player and we had some marvellous guys there. There was a great set-up and we had a ball. It showed me the extent to which people who emigrate tend to look after one another. Then, on to Castlehaven and Cork... I lived the dream.

Every so often, I'm asked to go to a club to present medals (Paddy Corkerey was the first man to ask me to do that) and I'll be asked how much I want? People are so genuine; they'll throw an envelope or a voucher into the car but my reaction would always be that I'm not doing it in order to get something.

They show me respect by asking me to do it and I repay that respect, and I say to my kids that it's the most important thing a person can have. I look at the coaches in Bishopstown now with the teams Jack's on and I admire all of them.

I'd drive back 10 miles if I thought that Jack didn't say thanks after a session. No matter what you do in life, you leave things on good terms.

That's the way I have always been.

I'VE TRIED TO be genuine, fair and positive in my life to date. I think people have taken me that way and I don't think it's a bad way.

I just always wanted to do the best I could and I believed I could achieve it. Jack and Kate will get into that mode, please God, and find their own way in life. If you show respect and appreciation, those things will always come to the fore.

And you'll stand tall in any crowd.

It's been a new chapter in our lives, but we continue to enjoy the company of old and new friends thanks to our pub business. Here we are on one of our bus trips (right, Tom Henehan, Gerry Kiely, Con Healy, myself and Gerry Chawke sitting); and our final bus trip away to Donegal (my late father is on the far left holding the flag). My county GAA career is now long over, but I do get reminded of the good old days, and one such occasion was extra special when I was in the company of the legendary Mick O'Connell in Dunmanway at a special celebration of All-Ireland football captains.

GALLERY

A thank you
to some of my
Teammates
down through the years

Wicklow Vocational School, Leinster Champions 1980

Kildare Minor team, Leinster finalists 1980

Eadestown, Kildare Junior B champions, 1980

Eadestown, Kildare Junior A champions, 1982

Kildare under-21 team

Kildare senior team

All Star football team, New York, 1985

Donegal, New York champions, 1985

Castlehaven, Cork SFC champions, 1989

Cork, All-Ireland SFC champions, 1989

Cork, All-Ireland SFC champions, 1990

Castlehaven, Cork SFC champions, 1994

1989 Cork Jubilee team, Croke Park, 2014